Advance Praise for *Stressed is Desserts*

*"Brian Luke Seaward is a jewel of inspiration.
The wit, therapeutic wisdom and humor of his stories
shine with the presence of God."*

—**Naomi Judd**, Country Singer/Songwriter,
Author, *Love Can Build A Bridge*

*"Stories are the best way to convey the essence of human
spirituality, and Brian Luke Seaward is a master storyteller.*
Desserts *is nutrient dense in spiritual essence."*

—**Deepak Chopra**, Author, *The Path of Love*

*"A true gem. Valuable, practical and full of invaluable wisdom.
Read this today and keep it by your bedside."*

—**Richard Carlson**, Author of *Don't Sweat the Small Stuff*

*"An invaluable resource to my health library.
I wish I had known about it when I was competing,
but now that I am a coach and father of three, I am going to
refer to* Desserts *on a regular basis."*

—**Dave Scott**, Six-time winner of the Hawaiian Iron Man Triathlon
Author, *Dave Scott's Triathlon Training*

Books By Brian Luke Seaward

Quiet Mind, Fearless Heart:
The Taoist Path Through Stress and Spirituality

Achieving The Mind-Body-Spirit Connection

Hot Stones and Funny Bones:
Teens Helping Teens Cope With Anger & Stress

The Art of Calm:
Relaxation Through the Five Senses

Health of the Human Spirit

Stand Like Mountain, Flow Like Water:
Reflections on Stress and Human Spirituality

Table For Two, Please:
Morals of Inspiration and Wisdom Over the Noon Hour

Health and Wellness Journal Workbook

Managing Stress:
Principles and Strategies for Health and Wellbeing

Managing Stress:
A Creative Journal

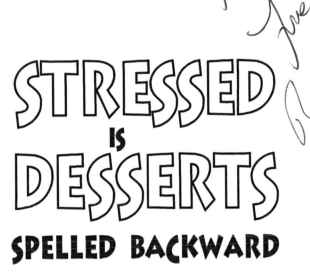

STRESSED
IS
DESSERTS
SPELLED BACKWARD

Rising above life's challenges
with humor, hope, and courage

SECOND EDITION

Brian Luke Seaward, PhD
Author of *Stand Like Mountain, Flow Like Water*

Foreword by
Joan Lunden

Whole Person Associates
Duluth, Minnesota

Whole Person Associates, Inc.
210 West Michigan
Duluth, MN 55802-1908   218-727-0500
E-mail: books@wholeperson.com
Web site: http://www.wholeperson.com

Stressed Is Desserts Spelled Backward

Printed in the United States of America

10   9   8   7   6   5   4   3   2   1

Editorial Director: Robin B. McAllister
Art Director: Joy Dey

Library of Congress Control Number: 2006940828
ISBN-13   978-1-57025-218-1
ISBN   1-57025-218-1

WHOLE PERSON ASSOCIATES
210 West Michigan
Duluth, MN 55802-1908

For my Godparents,
Pat & Caleb O'Connor

Stressed is Desserts Spelled Backward

Foreword

GROWING UP, I ALWAYS THOUGHT that what happened in my life would bring me happiness or cause me stress. One of the most important lessons I've learned is that it's not what happens to us, but our reaction to what happens to us that causes stress. And that means we have the power to control our level of stress. We, in fact, have the power to choose not to react at all to that which happens around us.

It is not what life brings us that determines our level of happiness and self-fulfillment. It is the attitude we bring to life. The most important decision we can make each day is our choice of attitude. It is what will spur us on or stand in our way. Since we are in charge of our attitude, we are the architects of our lives.

In this complex, uncertain, and always changing world, it is easy to lose sight of our power to achieve happiness and fulfillment and let the everyday pressures weigh us down. To best reach fulfillment without giving in to the pressures, we all need encouragement and guidance along the way.

Brian Luke Seaward provides us with much needed hope, faith, strength and direction in his masterful telling of stories that expand our vision and inspire us. Rather than telling us what to do or how we should be, he teaches by example. His stories encourage us to think about life and its stresses with a fresh point of view. They help us approach life's twists and turns with anticipation rather than fear. Luke Seaward shows us that while we cannot escape stress, there are many ways to deal with it effectively. His words have touched my life profoundly and helped me to find the grace and dignity, the patience and compassion, needed to navigate my ever-changing course. They have helped me understand that it is the way I choose to see the world that will create the world I see.

— **Joan Lunden**
Author of *Joan Lunden's Wake-Up Calls*

Introduction to the Second Edition

WELCOME TO A SECOND SERVING OF "DESSERTS." Like a second piece of apple pie, this serving promises to be as good, if not better, than the literary piece first served in the Spring of 1999. Tucked away in nearly each of the sections are several new inspirational stories that I hope will warm your heart and place a smile on your face.

As a motivational speaker, *Stressed Is Desserts Spelled Backward* quickly has become the most popular talk I am asked to give, ever since this book hit the bookstores nearly a decade ago. I think the reason for this, as well as the popularity of this book, is the fact that everyone likes a good story. In the spirit of the renowned mythologist, Joseph Campbell, who gave us the wisdom to decode stories through the template of "The Hero's Journey," these stories not only are here to lift our spirits, but to act like a compass pointing the way home again, should we get lost or distracted along the way.

One thing I have learned over the years in telling these stories is that stories never really end. In fact, they keep on going. Who ever coined the phrase, "Never-ending story," sure got that right. In talking to my new publisher, Carlene, we decided not to make additions to various stories that have more to unfold, but rather give a synopsis here in the introduction. Of the many stories that have kept on going, here is a quick rundown for those who are curious to know, as newscaster Paul Harvey says... the rest of the story:

> Andrew (*Making Andrew Laugh*) caught up with me at a book signing for this very book in the D. C. area and introduced me to his wife, Lauren. Lauren was eight months pregnant with their child Alexis. A week after I saw them, Andrew mailed me a card with a photo of their newborn daughter. We have been in touch ever since. One day I received an email from Lauren telling me that Andrew was back in the hospital, this time with a bone infection. For nearly six months Andrew lay in bed recovering. Remembering how much humor was part of his healing path, I contacted several friends and colleagues to send him jokes and funny cards. He got over 200 emails and get-well cards from around the country.

Dan (*Dan's Divorce*) remarried soon after the first edition of "Desserts" came out. He is happily married to a beautiful woman, Sherry, and they have a new daughter.

In the spring of 2005 I received a phone call from Sandi's husband (Susan in the story, *Curiosity and the Cat Scan*). Holding back tears he told me that Sandi had passed away several days earlier. He remarked that she had outlived her doctor's prediction by about 10 years. "Sandi's last decade of life was in many ways her best," he said. "I know she will always be grateful to you and all you did for her. And by the way she was really touched when she received cards from Joan Lunden and Naomi Judd, which I understand was your doing."

Katy (*A Cosmic Joke*) got married to a wonderful man named Norm in 2003. Katy left her job in marketing and moved to New Hampshire where she works as a teacher in special education. She and Norm are planning to move to Florida in the spring of 2007, and when I spoke to Katy a few weeks ago, she had just returned from a vacation in Barcelona, Spain. To say she is happily married is an understatement and she also never failed to remind me that it was worth the wait.

Matt Phenninger (*The Healing Power of Prayer*) still shows no sign of a brain tumor ten years after he was first diagnosed with this condition. Needless to say Matt, his father Jack, his mother Kay, and everybody in Midland, Michigan are euphoric. Matt is now in graduate school completing a degree in Engineering.

Allison Fisher (*A Fish Called Allison*) passed away right before the first edition came off the press. What you may not know is that her mom, Pat, and her Father, Ron have established a scholarship in Allison's name. They host an annual fundraising event, *Angel on a Jazz Note* every fall in Allison's memory. Please check out the website www.allisonfisherfund.org.

Whenever I meet someone who tells me that they read *Stressed Is Desserts Spelled Backward*, I often ask them, "What was your favorite story?" As one might guess, the answers varied greatly. Many people were touched by the story of the cab driver in Chicago. Nearly everyone commented about the last story of Carolyn, the remarkable story of a nurse whose son died of SIDS. But I have to say that the story, *Breakfast with Uncle Fred*, tops the list of stories that most people said was the most memorable. I would be interested to hear which of these stories is your favorite, so if you have a moment, please email me at blseaward@comcast.net.

Over the years I have received countless letters, cards, emails and phone calls from fans describing their delight with "Desserts." Many tell me they would read a story before going to bed so they would end the day on a good note. My brother-in-law, who confides that he doesn't read that many books, shared with me that "Desserts" was good bathroom reading (I think that was a compliment). Many people, I discovered, gave or bought the book for a friend or a loved one going through a tough time, as a sign that things would get better. The majority of these were cancer patients. I was delighted to hear that "Desserts" had been translated into a few languages, including Chinese (although I am pretty sure the title didn't translate exactly as in the American edition).

What really brought a smile to my face was to learn that "Desserts" was a popular gift item in several gift baskets from the company www. Cancergifts.com.

This edition of "Desserts" contains over fourteen new stories of inspiration, love and humor that have worked their way into my presentations over the years and they just begged to be included in this incarnation. You will find these new stories scattered throughout the book. I hope you enjoy reading them as much as I have enjoyed sharing them. All best wishes,

—**Brian Luke Seaward**
Boulder, Colorado (2007)

STRESSED is DESSERTS Spelled Backward

Dessert and Coffee—Make It Decaf!

From Crumbs to Crêpes

*"I'm an old man and I have known a great many problems
in my life, most of which never happened."*

—Mark Twain

THE RADIO HOST HAS JUST INTRODUCED ME to her listeners. At her
request, I then made a few comments about the nature of stress and
various ways in which to effectively deal with the pressures of life. It
was 2:00 p.m. in Colorado where I was seated in my living room. It
was 4:00 p.m. in Washington D.C at her radio station. This was the
"Voice of America" and this show was being broadcast live all around
the world.

"Sebastian from Paris, go ahead," she said.

"Oui! Merci. Thanks for taking my call. My mother has cancer
and I was wondering how best to deal with this?"

I gave a short bit of advice, which pleased him, and we were
on to the next call. For the next hour, people called in on a toll-free
line from all over the world.

There was Kim from Tokyo. Marion called from Johannesburg,
South Africa. Terif rung his line from Cairo. There was Sarah in
London, Monica in São Paulo, Mohammed from Sri Lanka, and
Chee from Kuala Lumpur. Rajesh was the last call from New Delhi.
For the entire hour, I was connected to the heartbeat of the planet.

The World Health Organization calls stress "a global epidemic,"
and while I have quoted WHO several times over the past few years, it
was not until that afternoon in 1997 that I realized how true this fact
was. Stress may be as American as apple pie, but it is also as worldwide

as bread pudding.

It doesn't matter who you are, where you live, how much money you make, or how dysfunctional your parents were while you were growing up, stress is a stranger to no one. For better or worse, stress is an inevitable fact of life.

A theme common to stress is that of loss, be it loss of a spouse, child, job or life itself. While there is no escaping stress, there are many ways to deal with it effectively as I hope you will discover, as you make your way through this book.

In a world filled with so much stress, surely there must be some good from it. Ageless wisdom tells us as much with metaphors that have become household clichés— from silver linings and lemonade to lessons, blessings, and gifts. In the midst of chaos and catastrophe, at first it may be difficult to see the silver lining or sip the lemonade. Even so, we must remind ourselves that there is a reason for every circumstance, even if we never become aware of it, or perhaps more likely, we don't agree with the reason when we do get a chance to glimpse the bigger picture.

The bigger picture can often be clearly viewed from the vantage point of stories. Since the dawn of humanity, stories have been shared as a teaching tool, to guide souls further along the human path, sometimes as advice, more often than not, as a reminder of what we already know at a deeper level—that there is no separation from our divine source. Psychologists on the vanguard of conscious thought tell us that stories speak to the audience of perceptions housed in the right hemisphere of the brain. Stories penetrate and nurture those cognitive functions, which are receptive to thought, open to ideas, impressionable to stimulus, and sympathetic to emotions. Nowhere is this better understood than through the recounting of fables, folklore, and fairy tales, each built on the foundation of a moral or human truth. Even parables were the preferred method of teaching for Jesus of Nazareth. It seems fitting therefore, in the tradition of fables and fairy tales, for me to structure this book around a series of stories, each of which ends with a "moral," a nugget of truth that can be digested as a spiritual nutrient to feed the soul.

Today, in the age of high technology and rushed lifestyles, stories are proving to be extremely popular means to bring the focus of life back to a soul level rather than operating at the unstable apex of ego. Theories and facts speak to the rational, linear mind, while stories address issues of the heart and matters of the soul. In truth, both allegory and fact are needed to walk in balance along the human journey. So let us begin with a story.

Running up a flight of stairs with a glass milk bottle is not the smartest thing to do, but teenagers do foolish things. At thirteen, I had a habit of teasing the winds of fate, but the winds were particularly strong-willed on this day. Unsure footing prompted a sudden fall, shards of milk-covered glass became airborne like a hundred arrows released simultaneously from an enormous bow, and one became embedded deep in my left hand. Blood soon pooled with milk, and a river of pink fluid cascaded down the wooden steps away from the kitchen.

Sitting anxiously in the post-op recovery room with my mom, my left hand bandaged with several inches of gauze, I learned that as bad as the accident was, it might have been much worse. The nerve that allows the hand muscles to contract was nearly severed. A fraction of a millimeter closer and my hand would have been paralyzed for life. The outcome still uncertain, I prayed with confidence. While my mom left the room to call my dad with the news, I turned to strike up a conversation with the young man who lay on a gurney beside me. Aside from a bandaged head, I noticed that his right hand and arm were atrophied. He had cerebral palsy. Learning of my accident, he assured me I'd be fine. Before the nurse came in to wheel me to my room, he winked at me, made an eloquent reference to "spiritual muscles" (what some call inner resources), as he told me a joke, and then explained that exercising my funny bone would help me heal more quickly. I simply smiled back at him. But the lesson stuck—and sure enough, laughter and optimism not only helped heal my hand, but many other difficult situations looming on the horizon.

A year later, I learned first-hand that spiritual muscles include more than just humor and optimism. Riding home from church early one winter morning, our car was hit head-on by a truck that had skidded on ice and snow into our lane. My father and two sisters lay unconscious, bleeding, perhaps dead. Shaken, but uninjured, I ran for what seemed like miles in knee-deep snow to the nearest house to

3

call the police and ambulance. With each breath of cool air, I found myself drawing upon the inner strength of courage and faith. Later that day, in a tense hospital waiting room, perhaps by coincidence, I spotted a man with cerebral palsy walking toward the emergency room. Once again I reflected on these spiritual muscles, as I prayed for the lives of my family.

Humor, patience, compassion, courage, curiosity, humbleness, forgiveness, faith, creativity, persistence, confidence, and love comprise a short list of the divine inner resources that are our best medicine for tough times. The muscles of the soul are the tools we use to help dismantle and remove the roadblocks of life. I know first-hand that these muscles transcend the obstacles we call stress. Growing up under the roof of two alcoholic parents, I exercised them regularly (particularly faith and humor). I know they work! Like our physical muscles, these spiritual muscles need to be flexed, stretched, and moved against some form of resistance, quite regularly to remain effective when confronting the problems we all encounter on the human journey. Ignored, they will never disappear completely, but will certainly atrophy with disuse.

Experts in the field of stress management don't necessarily concur on what stress is exactly. It's a rather complex subject. One thing they do agree on is that, by and large, stress is a perception, an interpretation of an event or circumstance, which ultimately is understood to be a threat. Perceptions, most likely produced by the ego, sound the stress alarm and we quickly move into the survival model of fight or flight. While the stress response—the dynamics of human physiology that shunt blood to the arms and legs, increase breathing, and increase metabolism to do one thing, move—may be ideal for threats of a physical nature, this response is totally inappropriate for all other kinds of stress. Most of the threats we have today are not physical, they are mental, emotional, or spiritual. I venture to say that about 90 percent are of a spiritual nature (involving relationships, values, and purpose in life), which makes it all the more reason we need to exercise the muscles of the soul to deal with the big and small challenges we encounter as we go through our lives.

As a child, I sought refuge from the dissonance that alcoholic dysfunction can bring to a family. I found solace in two places: the wooded forest behind my house when I felt the need to be alone, and my grandmother's kitchen for those times I needed a trusting smile and hug. My grandmother, small in stature, was mighty in character. Well versed in Washington D.C.'s high society, extremely well educated, and quite savvy with regard to life's complexities, my grandmother was sharp as an owl, and as graceful as a hummingbird. She too, had encountered her share of stressors in life: the Depression, several miscarriages, the premature death of her husband, and immobilization due to two broken hips. Although a private person by nature, she would openly recount her stories to me—with a little prodding. Through it all, she sailed through life quite gracefully. Anytime she saw a hint of distress in my eyes, she was quick to fix some milk and pastries, saying, "Remember, honey, *"Stressed is desserts spelled backwards."*

In her footsteps as a teacher, I have met scores of people—students, workshops participants, and complete strangers—whom I think of as everyday heroes; people, who, by the grace of God, emerge from what can only be described as a trip to hell with dignity and aplomb. Their experiences, many of which are included here, are testimonials to the use of inner resources and the remarkable capacity of human potential to deal with life's challenges in a way that promotes spiritual growth.

Tiramisu, Crème Brulée, and New York Style Cheesecake may be the most popular desserts these days, but it's obvious to me that humor, patience, and faith are the ingredients we need to transform any curse into a blessing. It is my wish that this collection of stories serves as a reminder of what we already know—that indeed, we are always in the presence of the divine. And as we exercise and flex our spiritual muscles, we kiss the face of God.

In an age of victimization where whining about our problems has become the national pastime and calling a lawyer is the automatic reaction to an impending disaster, it is refreshing to note that there is an option: to let go of stress and move on gracefully, rather than play the recurring role of victim. More times than not, we can have our cake and eat it too. And each time, the taste of dessert, after a long hard haul on the road of life, is a sweet one, indeed.

STRESSED is DESSERTS Spelled Backward

On A Wing and A Prayer

"Help!" This word might not sound like a typical prayer, but it most certainly qualifies. No matter what mess we find ourselves in, lifting our eyes and voice to the heavens is the most common response, even among those who don't believe in God. It may stand to reason that the bigger the problem, the more intense the call for divine assistance, but the use of prayer as a coping technique is ubiquitous in every culture for all situations.

Moments of intense stress may lead us to believe that we have been divinely abandoned (if not punished), but those same moments of chaos may eventually bring upon the realization that help is only a prayer away. Prayers, in all their forms, are a call to faith; a belief or an intuitive knowing that we are part of something bigger, bigger than words can ever describe. Faith asserts that this bigger "something," (call it God, Allah, the Great Mystery, the Tao, or the big Kahuna), throws us a metaphorical lifeline—and at some point, we will catch it and be pulled in. A prayer answered is like a big hug.

There is no one way to pray. Faith, in the form of prayer, varies as greatly as those who take the leap. All prayers offered in sincerity, however, are equal to the ears of divine consciousness. Remember, patience is a silent partner in the prayer process as we put forth the clarion call to summon God's attention. All prayers are answered, but in God's time, not ours. That's where the wings come in—when we take the leap.

Faith is quite a personal undertaking. Scientists cannot measure it. Theologians cannot quantify it. Yet to those who employ it, faith is very real indeed. The following stories are examples of faith; the realization that no matter what the situation, we are never alone.

1. A Cab Ride In Chicago

A BUSINESS TRIP TOOK ME TO THE WINDY CITY LAST SUMMER. I had frequented Chicago many times during my graduate school days at the University of Illinois in Champaign-Urbana. I even ran the Chicago Marathon along Lake Shore Drive in what had to be one of the hottest days on record for the month of October. Aside from several layovers at O'Hare International airport, however, this was my first trip back to the Windy City in nearly twenty years.

I suppose I could have walked three miles down Michigan Avenue to meet a friend from college for dinner, but in my tardiness I decided to take a cab. The bellman blew a whistle, and moments later wheels screeched as the yellow checker drove up to the entrance. The bellman opened the car door and I was off.

I find cab drivers are an interesting group of people. While it doesn't take a Ph.D. to drive a taxi, more often than not, I find cab drivers in big cities a very well educated bunch. Most, I discover, land their first job on these shores driving a cab until something better opens up. Some are in between jobs, trying to make ends meet. By and large, they're an honest group of citizens. This cab driver proved to be no different.

"Hi," I said, looking at his taxi license on the visor. Next to his photo was a picture of the Virgin Mary. A good sign, I thought.

"Hello," he replied with a thick European accent. "My name is Andreí."

Not placing his accent, I inquired where he was from.

"Poland. But I have lived here for several years. What brings you to my city?" he said, staring at me through the rear view mirror.

"I'm here at a conference giving a talk on stress," I answered.

"Stress! Boy do I know stress," he said, shaking his head.

Andreí was right! He did know stress. In the distance of three miles, he filled me in on five years of personal history. As I remember, it goes like this: In 1992 he met and fell in love with a woman. They were married and, within two years, had a baby boy named Anderson. Things started to go bad in the marriage and a year later, they divorced. As it turned out, Andreí got custody of the child. His wife was from Rio de Janeiro, and not a U.S. citizen. Moreover, she had defaulted on several court orders.

For this reason, the judge awarded Andreí custody. His ex-wife had visitation rights. For about two years this situation worked out somewhat well. That is until Andreí went to pick up his son at his ex-wife's apartment, only to learn that both had left for Brazil two days earlier. Technically speaking, his son was kidnapped. Andreí hired a lawyer, but soon learned that the chances of getting his son back to the States were nil. Inquiries to the State Department were met with only pessimism. The idea of taking a trip to Rio proved fruitless. His ex-wife had too many ways to cover her tracks, and in fact had already done so.

Andreí looked heartbroken, yet at the same time defiant.

"How on earth do you deal with this?" I asked.

"I have to accept it. It is out of my hands. I pray to God constantly. I pray for my son's return. I pray he is all right and he will remember me when I see him." Then he paused for a moment. "I have exhausted every possible means. I have no choice now but to accept my fate."

As he finished saying this, the car came to a stop. "Here you are," he said. "Have a good evening."

I paid the fare, stepped out into the pouring rain, and waved good-bye.

As Andreí painfully discovered, there are events in life we have no control over. Try as we might, no amount of money, time, or effort will change a thing in our favor. While determination and persistence are admirable traits, against an immovable object they rob the soul of energy and cause the body unnecessary wear and tear from stress hormones. A Chinese proverb says you cannot push water uphill. As hard as accepting a bad circumstance may be, often it is the only way through it. That day's story served as a stark reminder of how arduous yet essential the lesson of acceptance is so we can move on with our lives.

On the morning of my departure, I wheeled my suitcase into the crowded elevator. When the doors opened at ground level, I approached the reception area, checked out, and patiently waited by the hotel entrance. The bell cap signaled a taxi. I opened the door to see Andreí at the wheel again. He greeted me with a reserved smile.

"You looked relaxed," he said, again staring intently through the rear view mirror.

"Hi Andreí," I answered. "Good to see you again. How are you?"

"Every day gets a little bit better," he answered, "Every day gets a little bit better." And with that, he stepped on the gas pedal and we were off.

A speaking engagement brought me back to the windy city recently. Exiting the train station, I flagged a cab. Throwing my suitcase in the back seat, I climbed in and shut the door.

A distinctly familiar accent greeted me. "Where are you going?" said the driver.

I looked up at the visor to read Andreí's name. Next to his license was that same picture of the Virgin Mary.

"Andreí," I said, "how the heck are you? Any news from your son, Anderson?" It took him a moment to remember my face as he stared through the rear view mirror. Then he broke into a smile.

"Hey, you're the stress guy!" he said. "Yes! Things are a little better. I hear from my son about once a month. He calls collect. There is a chance I may go to Rio in January to see him." Andreí tried to hold back the excitement.

"So tell me, what brings you back to my city?" he asked with a smile.

Acceptance of a situation does not occur overnight. It is a process we must work through, daily. As this proverb reminds us: "The winds of grace are blowing perpetually, we only need to raise our sails."

2. Ribbons and Tea Bags

I had not spent more than three hours in my position on the faculty of a well-known private university in the nation's capitol, when a colleague walked into my office and began to strike up a conversation.

"So, how do you like it here so far?" he inquired.

"Not bad, considering I've only been here a few hours," I replied.

"I don't want to burst your bubble, but it will change," he continued.

I was a bit puzzled, wondering of course, if I had made a poor decision in accepting this job. "Why?" I asked.

"Well," he said, and then paused for several moments. "Let's just put it this way, the students here whine. They whine a lot!"

I can recall my first reaction. Freud would have described it as denial. Being kinder to myself, I called it 'unbridled naiveté.'

"Not my students, " I said with a smile on my face, believing my own words. "My students won't whine."

My new colleague smiled, patted me on the back and said as he walked out, "Welcome."

To my dismay, it didn't take long to find out he was right. My students whined—and they whined a lot. After a month's time, I decided to put an end to it. As part of any good stress management class, they needed to learn that whining is counterproductive to effectively dealing with stress. So, unabashedly, I banned this behavior. The word went out over campus, NO whining allowed in Professor Seaward's classes.

To no one's surprise, the class attitude was slow to change, as are most positive health behaviors. So, I set out looking for a potent way to remind my students that by comparison, they actually had a pretty good life. Most students came from wealthy homes, some had more expensive cars than the average faculty member, and it is fair to say, that the majority of students had, for the most part, lived lives on the low end of the stress scale. I set out to make this point clear in the classroom.

The nation's capitol is rich in personalities with colorful backgrounds, and I was very fortunate to have met several of these people during my tenure there. One such person was Bruce Laingen. His may not be a household name, but his experience has made an indelible impression on the nation's psyche. As Chargé d'Affairs of the American Embassy in Iran, and one of sixty-five American hostages, Bruce quickly became the group's spokesperson. Eighteen years after his release, I invited him to my class to share how he coped with the stress of his lost freedom for over a year's time in a foreign land.

To set the stage, I went out during lunch and bought several yards of yellow ribbon. My secretary and I cut up over fifty pieces, taping each ribbon to the wall at eye level around the room. I decided to make the speaker's appearance a surprise to the class. Students, unaware of his visit, sat curious and silent. As Bruce entered the room, he was quite moved by the sight of fifty-three yellow ribbons, and more than one person saw his eyes well up as he tried to hold back the tears.

In an eloquent voice that reminds one of the ageless wisdom shared by sages, Bruce recounted his story. He and his colleagues at the American Embassy in Tehran were rounded up by student terrorists. A handful of workers were released for health reasons over the next few weeks. The final group of captives numbered fifty-three and were held captive for 444 days. As a prisoner, Bruce was often kept in solitary confinement for days. His fate was at the mercy of his captors. Fear, particularly the fear of the unknown, was his prevailing emotion; he never knew when he and his colleagues would be released or even if they would. Initially, the fear of death was very present too. He explained that he missed his wife and family terribly. Perhaps this was his greatest stress. Days and nights grew quite lonely. Although separated for days on end from his fellow captives, they developed various tapping codes to communicate with each other. Bruce also tried to understand the perspective of his captors, which he said made his tribulation a bit easier to cope. The international ordeal ended on the first day President Reagan took office in 1981. Bruce and the fifty-two others were free after nearly fifteen months of captivity.

That day in class, Bruce cited several factors that he felt contributed to his success as a captive prisoner for a year and a half: faith, patience and optimism were at the top of his list. The students sat mesmerized. Moved by his story, I could already see the changes that would begin to take form in their lives as they gained a new perspective on the meaning of stress.

It is easy to complain about the shortcoming in life and at times we all do. But to get stuck in the habit of whining only attracts more whining. In truth, most of us have it pretty darn good. And by comparison to people like Bruce Laingen, we have it very good. My students got the message. As he reiterated, perspective is essential in dealing with stress.

Saying the words, "Thank you," he pulled a yellow ribbon off the wall, placed it on his lapel, and gave the class a wave of his right hand. The room filled with thunderous applause.

He ended his presentation with a quote that became the motto for our class that semester:

"Human beings are like tea bags.
You don't know your strength until you're in hot water."

3. The Search For Proof

WHILE ON A NATIONAL BOOK TOUR, I did a book signing in a large mid-Atlantic city. There were about thirty people gathered around to hear me share some thoughts regarding the relationship between stress and spirituality. As I began to tell a story, I noticed a man, about thirty-five years of age, dressed in a tie-dyed t-shirt standing close enough to hear, but far away enough to leave without distraction. After standing for twenty minutes, he took a seat. I continued with my discussion, every now and then looking in his direction. His face showed an uncomfortable mixture of anger, disbelief and a yearning for the truth. Puzzled by his expression, I concluded with the statement that stress is not divine abandonment; rather stress provides the opportunity for spiritual growth.

When I was done, I asked the audience if they had any questions. The man with the tie-dyed shirt raised his hand, and then began to speak.

"What if I don't believe anything you've just said?" he inquired aggressively.

I tried not to look too shocked, but my facial expression revealed my true feelings. I was stunned. I quickly asked for divine intervention to provide me with a satisfactory answer. It came none too soon.

What I thought to say was that human spirituality isn't a theory, it's a collection of experiences that more often than not cannot be proven or validated scientifically. Intuitively, I felt he wanted proof. It was then I remembered a story I usually tell, that I had forgotten to mention. In a visit to Arizona I had a dream in which I met a man who was the son of the woman who hosted my visit. In the dream, he had asked me to give his mom a message that he was all right and not to worry. Unbeknownst to me, this son had died of SIDS (Sudden Infant Death Syndrome) over thirty years before. I had become a messenger of faith.

As I recounted this story, the man's look of anger dissolved completely, only to be replaced by a look of wonder. He appeared to be experiencing a sense of comfort. Then he spoke to the group.

"My wife was killed, brutally murdered, about a year ago. I have spent months trying to make sense of her death, but I have found no comfort in anything I have come across. But just now, the story of your dream reminded me of a recent dream I had of my wife. I had completely forgotten it till you mentioned yours. In my dream, my wife came to me, looking young and radiant. She gave me a warm embrace, kissed me and told me that she was OK, not to worry about her, she was all right. It's funny, but I hadn't remembered that dream until just now. It wasn't a typical dream, it seemed so real." As he said this, a tear welled up in each eye. Not a person in the audience stirred, yet we all knew we had just experienced a rare divine moment.

When it came time to autograph books, the man waited patiently in line until his turn came. He shook my hand with a firm grip and told me his name was Michael. We exchanged glances that spoke more profoundly than words. He thanked me as I signed his book, and then he slowly walked away with an air of confidence that comes from a divine moment, and a prayer answered. Michael found his proof and everyone there became richer for it.

Prolonged anger becomes a dark veil we hide behind for protection. But that which initially protects, over time has the power to hurt us physically and emotionally as well. The search for proof is one way to deal with anger. Keep looking till you find it.

4. A Bird in the Hand

There has been much attention recently regarding the power of prayer. Prayer, it is said, was one of the first coping techniques for stress. When I was young, the prayers I was taught were like poems that were to be recited, primarily it times of need, always in times of trouble. My style of prayer has changed over the years, but the use of prayer as a coping technique in stressful situations hasn't. I pray all the time. As the ancient saying goes, "All thought is prayer," and there is not a day that goes by where I am not consciously praying about something.

Boulder, Colorado is renown for its summer hailstorms. The carnage is so bad that you may find your car in the auto shop for a week to get all the dents out. While teaching an evening class one summer night at the University of Colorado, the winds kicked up and sparks of electricity filled the Boulder valley. The classroom shook with each clap of thunder, followed by the sound effects of extremely large hail balls. After the initial excitement, I could tell many of my students were pondering the extent of damage to their cars. So was I. Coming so close to the last hour, I dismissed the class early, and everyone peeled out of the room, taking cover under their textbooks.

Driving home was quite the ordeal. The voice on the radio alerted listeners to the sightings of three funnel clouds. I, on the other hand, could see nothing; my windshield wipers going at warp speed to maintain some degree of visibility.

As I was driving, my thought instantly turned to prayer. Not for myself or even for the other drivers who were all moving at a snail's pace on the road. Instead, my thoughts turned toward my bird feeder. Every year a couple of finches build a nest in my bird feeder. This season there were four chicks, about two weeks old. The bird feeder hangs loosely and moves quite freely in the wind. I prayed that those four chicks would survive the hellacious storm.

When I got home, the first thing I did was run out to the porch. I was saddened to see the four chicks lying dead on the ground. It was a grim sight indeed as I tried to understand this example of nature's balance.

Early the next morning I peered out my window to see not a hail ball in sight. Within seconds, I observed the parent finches land on the bird feeder, staring at the empty nest. If a bird can have a puzzled look on its face, I surely saw it. Baffled, both birds flew away and I moved on to other things, pretty much forgetting the whole episode.

Later that night as I walked into my house, I heard a familiar sound—the chirping of baby birds. I rushed outside to see that two chicks were huddled under my porch furniture crying for help. Putting on a glove, I gently picked up each bird and carefully placed it back in the nest, at which point the chirping stopped. That night I prayed that the parents would return once more so they could finish their job.

I woke the next morning to see that one of the two birds saved, fell out of the nest during the night and this time really was dead. I sat, waited and watched the nest for over an hour. Once again I prayed. To my surprise, the parents did return. Now, getting all the attention, the sole surviving bird flourished. Over the next few days it doubled in size.

This family of finches has been renting out my bird feeder for over four years. I have never been known to name the chicks, but this time was different since I had become so intimately involved.

I named this bird "Hail Mary!"

All thought is prayer. May we keep our thoughts filled with positive intentions in times of stress, for the highest good of all concerned.

5. The Healing Power of Prayer

IN THE SPRING OF 1997, I was asked to make a presentation on mind-body-spirit healing for the American Occupational Health Association's annual meeting in Orlando, Florida. At first, the crowd of about a hundred physicians seemed less than interested as I stood at the edge of the stage, presenting to them information on the vanguard of holistic medicine, as part of a one day stress management seminar. But what appeared at the start of my talk to be an uninterested crowd of general practitioners became a lively group of participants by the end of the session. As I made my way to the back of the room to pick up my slide carousel, I was politely ambushed by twenty-five physicians and nurses, business cards in hand, asking for more information.

One participant, who patiently waited until the group had dispersed, approached me and said, "You were the reason I came to this conference, but I wished you had talked more about the healing power of prayer. Do me a favor and call Dr. John Pfenninger." She quickly wrote down his phone number on the back of her business card, handed it to me, and smiled as she walked away. Intrigued, I placed a phone call to Midland, Michigan a few weeks later. Dr. Pfenninger's remarkable story underscores the dynamic healing power of prayer. That afternoon, he shared these memories with me.

In 1994 John's son, Matt, a high school senior, was diagnosed with an inoperable brain tumor. The diagnosis wasn't immediate. In fact, Matt spent a fair amount of time in and out of hospitals, and if you were to ask him he would tell you that he has seen more than his share of MRI (Magnetic Resonance Imaging) machines. Matt's mother's standing joke is "the only specialists we didn't consult were those in obstetrics." Eventually, the diagnosis revealed a brain tumor. It also revealed cancer cells isolated in the fluid of his brain and spinal cord. Matt began to receive the typical treatment of chemotherapy. Chemotherapy, while effective, is not infallible. It not only can kill cancer cells, it destroys healthy cells as well. And chemo doesn't always work.

In the shadow of nearly every cancerous tumor lays the question of death. Matt's father decided to meet this shadow head on. Knowing how much support the Pfenninger family had in this crisis, the thought occurred to John that if Matt were to die, those in attendance at his funeral would be in the hundreds. Rather than have them come together for a funeral, John decided to utilize the energy and well wishes of their friends, colleagues, and family to heal his son, rather than grieve the loss of his life. John called them all to a meeting.

"I know if Matt were to die right now, you would all come to his funeral, but it makes more sense to me to use your prayers now. I would like to ask if you could pray with me and my wife for our son to be healed, " said John.

So the group of 200 people sat in silence in an auditorium and prayed for Matt's recovery, some for over an hour.

Prayers are said in several ways. There are intercessory prayers where we seek help and guidance. There are prayers of gratitude where thanks are given. Many prayers combine help and gratitude together. Some prayers read like poems. Some prayers are spontaneous, like ad-lib conversations with God. What they all have in common is intention, the desire to work in collaboration with a higher source, a display of devotion to join the will of God, whatever that might be.

Several months later, Dr. Pfenninger made a grand rounds presentation at his hospital. By all measures, it was a short one. "Many of you have inquired about Matt's condition. As you know we had a prayer session for him not too long ago. I'd like to show you something." As he said this, he illuminated two x-rays, before and after pictures. The tumor was gone. A hush fell over the crowd.

John concluded with these words, "To those of you who understand the power of prayer, no explanation is necessary, and to those of you who do not, no explanation will suffice." With these words and a wave of his hand, Dr. Pfenninger left the stage.

Not only can faith move mountains, when our will is aligned with the will of God, faith can make tumors disappear.

6. Dan's Divorce

It is early Sunday morning, late summer. The rays of sunlight on the Colorado Rockies have turned from pink to orange to white. I sit on my porch enjoying what is known as Alpenglow—sunrise on the Rockies. The ring of the phone breaks the silence. I pick up the receiver to hear the shattered voice of one of my best friends calling from Vermont. My first thought is that his wife or children have been seriously injured. Indeed, this was the case, but the damage was emotional, not physical, with Dan himself bearing the brunt of first impact. As he spoke, he tried to hold back the tears, but to no avail. His marriage has capsized and was now shipwrecked on the shoals of infidelity.

Research conducted by Thomas Homes and Richard Rahe in 1967 revealed that divorce is one of the most stressful life events anyone can face, second only to death of a spouse. I had known Dan to go through a great many harrowing ordeals, but this Sunday morning was catastrophic. Sad to say, Homes and Rahe were right!

When we spoke, the story was still incomplete, but the details Dan gave over the phone were enough to see the irreversible demise of what both of us thought was a good marriage. As it turns out, Dan's wife had begun a passionate relationship with another man. The affair became public less than a day before Dan called me. When confronted with the allegations, Dan's wife admitted to her new loyalty and with less than a full explanation, grabbed some items, threw them in the car, and drove off to her new lover, leaving her husband and their two young children behind. Shell-shocked, Dan sat down, trying to make sense of a seemingly senseless life-changing event.

Harnessing my best counseling skills, I validated Dan's anger and encouraged him to feel his frustration rather than ignore it, then let it go. With tongue in cheek, he asked permission to quickly move from anger to bargaining, saying she could have the Enya CDs but the Neil Young collection was staying. We both chuckled. Laughter was, indeed, a good sign.

After an hour or so of sorting through the details, analyzing personalities of the characters involved, and mourning the loss of a ten-year partnership, Dan had to return to paternal duties. I promised I would call him back the next day.

In times of strife, a strong support system of friends and family is essential. I did my best, given the distance of 2000 miles, to "be there," through several phone calls and a barrage of e-mails. When Dan wasn't connecting with his closest allies, he turned inward to do some serious soul searching.

In the course of several conversations over the next few weeks, I was quite moved by Dan's rapid healing process. I have known friends and colleagues who have gone through similar situations only to get stuck in anger, transforming the dark night of the soul into a decade. It became obvious through our conversations that it was Dan's faith that became the metaphorical biceps muscle to pull him through this crisis.

My "Green Mountain" friend shared with me what it meant to him to have faith, an undeniable knowing that it would all turn out all right. In turn, I shared with him a favorite quote from Nelson Mandela in his book, *Long Walk to Freedom*, "Faith is not belief without proof, but trust without reservation."

Dan eloquently described to me his conversations with God in which he offered his surrender for personal desires, his intentions of unconditional love for his wife and children, his release of expectations and outcomes, and his promise to walk with God every day.

A quick business trip to Vermont the next spring brought us together over lunch on the banks of Lake Champlain where the conversation again turned to faith.

"There are a lot of good stories in the Bible on this subject," I said.

"Yeah, sometimes the mustard seed parable works. On rare occasion when I'm feeling low, I have to resort to something smaller, like a photon of faith," he said with a Cheshire cat grin. "Just kidding! I typically start with an avocado seed and work up from there."

Even with faith, no stressful event is without its potholes. In Dan's case, there were custody arrangements to agree upon. The dream house went up for sale. Mementos were boxed up and put in permanent storage, and there were difficult financial adjustments. But through it all, Dan's trust in God—that all would work out—remained constant.

One Sunday morning a full year later, I was again enjoying the sunrise. Again the silence was separated by the phone's ring. The

Green Mountains and Colorado Rockies were once more connected. Reviewing the past year Dan said, "You know, faith is a mystery, but thank God you don't have to understand it to appreciate it." He added, "The body may need carbs, fats, and proteins, but the spirit requires faith and love. There is no need for anyone to go spiritually hungry. Faith and love are always in abundant supply."

Faith is not wishing for things to turn out as we would like them to be, although this certainly may happen. Faith is knowing that no matter how things turn out, we will stand strong through the winds of change and walk away gracefully.

7. Table For Two, Please

As a way for me to get to know my students and workshop participants better on the first day of class, and perhaps a way for them to get to know each other better as well, I introduce a little icebreaker. It's a simple question, one that I thought up many decades ago. It goes like this: "If you could have lunch with anyone, absolutely anyone living or dead, someone whom you have never had lunch with before, and most likely will never have lunch with again, who would you like to get to know better (in a private setting) and why?"

I love this question for many reasons. At some level the question speaks to the nature of role models and heroes. It also speaks to the nature of self-esteem values and curiosity.

I first thought of this question as a conversation piece when I was back in undergraduate school. My answer was Jacqueline Kennedy. I wanted to hear *her* perspective on the Kennedy assassination, particularly since she was right there at the time. As a private person she never mentioned her thoughts on this morbid historic event in public, but since this is a hypothetical lunch date, she would surely confide in me. Over the years, my answer changed to renowned psychologist Carl Gustav Jung, as I have found him to be one of the most fascinating people to walk the earth. Gandhi is not far behind on the list. To be honest, my list is quite long.

In the 25 years that I have asked this question, I must confess that I never cease to be amazed at the answers. Now, you might think that college students would have a shallow mind when it comes to once-in-a-lifetime conversations, but I was astonished to learn that few people ever wanted to have lunch with celebrities such as Madonna or Michael Jordan. Instead the vast majority of workshop students wanted answers to questions from some of history's most notable luminaries including Richard Burton (the explorer who translated the Kama Sutras), Francis Crick (who is credited with co-discovering the double helix of the DNA molecule), Margaret Chase Smith (first woman Senator) and Langston Hughes (famous African American poet). When answers to the cosmos weren't sought after, it was love that prompted the invitation, typically to a deceased family member (usually a grandfather or grandmother) occasionally a deceased parent or sibling. Many of these answers really pulled on the heartstrings.

Before I moved from Washington D.C. back to Colorado I sifted through my belongings looking to see what would make the sojourn to the foot of the Rockies and what would stay behind in the nearest trash bin. I picked up a shoebox loaded with something and peeked inside. There neatly stacked in bundles were packets of white index cards from all my former students and workshop participants. On the back of each card was the answer to the Lunch question. I sat down and read through these and as I flipped over each card I felt a rush of excitement. There in my hands was one of the rare ingredients in the formula of empowerment. Every answer was inspirational. I kept the box and vowed one day to do something creative with all the answers to the now famous lunch question.

One day, while jogging in Boulder, an idea came to me: Write a book. I decided to call it *Table for Two, Please*. I decided that it might make better reading to not only place the answer to the question on the page, but also where possible, place a quote from the person who was extended the invitation so as to create a type of conversation on the page. In several cases, I tried to contact some of the people who were cited as answers to this question in the hopes that they might actually consider writing a response. Tom Landry (Dallas Cowboys football coach), Sophie Burnham (author of *A Book of Angels*) and Mary Chapin Carpenter (singer, song writer), replied. Here is an excerpt from the book that is as powerful today as it was when it was written nearly a decade ago:

"Mary Chapin Carpenter. I have great ambitions to be a singer and Mary Chapin Carpenter is someone whom I really admire. Perhaps she could give me some tips on getting into the business."— Arlene

" I believe it was Lily Tomlin who astutely observed that 'they call it show-biz, not show-art.' That's why a succinct answer to your question is so hard to come by. Is it fame you want, is it art you wish to create, is it the pure joy of music, is it the respect of a few or the adoration of many? There is no one way to pursue a career in music, although resilience in the face of constant rejection and an acceptance of humble living circumstances during the pursuit would be helpful. Go out and find places where you hear music you like. Make friends, contacts. Go out on a limb and ask for a gig. Work on improving yourself daily and don't be arrogant. Above all

work toward your goal as long as it brings you happiness. Don't spend one more day doing something that doesn't make you happy." —Mary Chapin Carpenter (singer/songwriter)

Although I thought the manuscript had the words "best seller" written all over it, *Table For Two, Please* never really became a literary sensation. Every now and then, however, I happen to come across someone who read it and they remark how this was their favorite book.

Since I first posed this hypothetical question many moons ago, it now dawns on me that I have, in fact, had lunch with many of my heroes, role models and mentors. Over the years, since I first conceived this question, I have had the opportunity to have lunch with several notable luminaries including Jessie Owens, Nein Cheng, Deepak Chopra and Arthur Ashe. My most memorable table for two luncheons, however, was with world-renowned primatologist, Jane Goodall. Jane Goodall is the embodiment of grace. As a 26 year-old woman who ventured into the rainforests of Tanzania to study the chimps of Gombe, she was the first person to discover that humans are not the only species to walk the planet that uses tools. In 2000 she was appointed by the UN Secretary General Koffee Annan to be a United Nations Messenger of Peace, a title she takes quite seriously.

Most of our conversation focused on the state of the world today and the many environmental concerns that beg for attention.

"The world is dying," she said to me with a look of sadness in her eyes. When I first arrived in Gombe there were millions of chimpanzees. Now there are only thousands. Everywhere I go around the world I see signs that our lovely planet is under such strain. So, I have decided to dedicate my life to the children, because they are our future," she said.

Jane asked about my work and then invited me to join her in a fundraising project for the restoration of wildlife habitat in Gombe, Tanzania. I agreed without a moment's hesitation.

Despite Jane's sense of urgency regarding the world's ecological situation, first and foremost she's an optimist. And that feeling certainly rubbed off on me.

So whom would you like to have lunch with for an hour, break bread and get to know better? There are no wrong answers. Just be sure to be a good conversationalist, ask a lot of profound questions and remember to pick up the check. Bon Appetite.

I once heard the renowned actor Laurence Olivier say, "Legends are just ordinary people doing extraordinary things." May we all rise to the occasion to become legends.

8. The Stolen Passport

To KNOW SANDI LAWRENCE IS TO KNOW a spiritually minded person. A registered nurse by training and the director of the Student Wellness Office at the University of Southern Indiana (USI), Sandi has dedicated her life to the care and service of others. To know Sandi is also to know an adventurous soul. When she heard that the Mid-American Singers, a choral group from USI, was going to Poland in the summer of 1997, she made a visit to the office of the choir director, and asked, "By any chance, do you need a nurse to go to Poland with you?" Sandi just knew she would be going. He smiled a reassuring Yes. When the choir boarded the plane for Warsaw, Sandi was a welcome addition to the group.

"I felt a little nervous prior to leaving because I didn't know the other people on the trip and I was unfamiliar with the health care delivery system in Poland," she explained. But Sandi did know the potential risks for a bunch of young adults in a foreign country and sought divine help to cover all her bases.

"I have to tell you that I asked many of my friends to pray for me, that I could take care of the forty people in our group and that I could be the kind of witness to my faith that God would want me to be — knowing they were praying for me released me from having to worry about the outcome. I wanted everything to go all right on the trip. And I did my share of praying too," Sandi explained.

So, how was the trip?

"The trip was fantastic, but it wasn't without its moments," she explained.

En route, they had been advised to keep their passports in their possession at all times in a safe place. On the third day of the trip, Sandi recalls, one of the students, Troy, had his passport stolen—pickpocketed, just like you see in the movies.

Sandi quickly surveyed her options. She learned that replacing Troy's passport would require a trip from Gdansk to the American Embassy in Warsaw, causing a disruption of the travel schedule (not to mention undue stress for the thirty-six students and four staff members on the trip). There just wasn't time for unscheduled travel. In her mind, there was no choice, the group had to keep to its original itinerary. Sandi approached Troy and said, "I want you to know that

I will be saying prayers that someone brings your passport back to us." A woman of great faith, Sandy started to pray. Pray and detach. She put the whole matter in the hands of God and waited to see what would happen.

On the fifth day in Gdansk, the group decided to take a thirty-minute boat ride to Westerplatte, one of the sights where World War II started. Troy's passport was still missing. The group was to fly back home in less than a week.

"So there we were on Westernplatte overlooking the Baltic Sea, enjoying a sunny day, climbing on tanks and exploring old bombed out buildings. As I was walking toward the Westernplatte monument, a Polish woman walked up to me and said, "American?"

"At first, I thought she wanted her picture taken with us, or something. I looked at her and said, 'Yes, American!' "

"What happened next took my breath away. She proceeded to open her purse and pulled out Troy's passport, then handed it to me."

"Here," she said, "I think maybe this belong to you." The woman smiled a faint smile and took a few steps backward.

Sandi quickly called to Troy. When he approached, she told him what had happened and placed the passport securely in his hand. Stunned, Troy said, "This is a coincidence!"

Sandi then asked him if he remembered what she had told him on the bus. Troy answered, " Yes! You said you would be saying prayers until someone brought back my passport."

Sandi exclaimed, "This is not a coincidence, this is an answer to a prayer!"

All the while the group of students proceeded to get pictures of Troy and the Polish woman.

"Now some people would say this is quite a coincidence," said Sandi. "I have no doubt that my prayers, and those of my friend back home were answered. I came away from this trip with a stronger faith in God and thirty-nine good friends. I think several students did too."

Faith is a unique inner resource to help us in times of need. If stress is a dark tunnel, then faith is the guiding light at the end of it even if we can't always see it. Faith is a reminder of our divine connection— the assurance that we are neither alone nor abandoned, even in the darkest hour of the darkest tunnel. If there is a recipe for faith, perhaps it is this: one part optimism, two parts confidence, one part wisdom, three parts patience, four parts love and a pinch of mysticism for good measure. Faith and prayer go hand in hand to serve each other. There are exceptions, but generally, this is how it works.

Faith, through prayer can provide some miraculous results, and relieve some stress in the process. An important factor to remember is to detach from the outcome and let whatever may happen do so. Regardless of the result, faith, on the wings of a prayer, can certainly help restore a sense of inner peace.

9. Facing Our Fears Head On

A HOGAN (PRONOUNCED HO-GUN) IS A CIRCULAR-SHAPED HOUSE common among the Navaho and Hopi tribes. Its architectural structure, a dome shaped hut with its only entrance and exit facing toward the east, is conducive for sweat lodges, a sacred healing ceremony among the Native American population. Today, the healing practice of sweat lodges has found popularity among white people as well.

Native American culture contains a depth of wisdom that the Western world has yet fully to grasp, particularly in regards to medicinal healing, involving diseases such as cancer and AIDS. It was such a case that brought Sam to his first sweat lodge, and his first hogan prayer.

How Sam contracted AIDS is not important. His condition was headed downhill as fast as his T4 cell count. Unconvinced that drugs would help, Sam, like so many others who turn to various forms of alternative medicine and complementary healing, signed up for a sweat lodge ceremony.

If you are unfamiliar with a sweat lodge, there is something you should know. A sweat lodge is not an Indian version of a sauna. In a true sweat lodge, spirits come to offer their healing medicine. This is what Sam was looking for, not just a cleansing but a healing—a purification of his soul.

Others present at the sweat lodge ceremony Sam participated in said that they had never seen the rocks so red before and the heat was almost unbearable. The medicine woman leading the ceremony recounted later that the intense heat was needed to purify the sickness. After a short while, a spirit spoke. It was the spirit of the Thunderbird.

Sam was told to walk outside, strip down naked in the rain and pray. He was to converse and pray to the Thunderbird spirit, but in a certain way. He was instructed to pray in the *Hayokah* manner, which means you pray for the opposite of that which you desire. So if you want to get well, you pray to get worse. If you wish to live, you pray to die.

The *Hayokah* prayer is not easy. For when you pray in this style, you must face your fears head on. Simply stated, you prepare to fight the metaphorical dragon (a universal symbol of fear). This style of prayer forces you to get in touch with that which you are most afraid of and deal with it. The aim is to reduce you to your bare essence— washed clear of any doubts, fears, and worries. You begin this prayer alone, and end it knowing you are never alone.

After an hour or so, Sam crawled back into the hogan. Again he received another message from the Thunderbird spirit. He was to stop reading any material about AIDS— no papers, no television, no media that reinforced the message of fear. Again he was instructed to go outside and pray the *Hayokeh* prayer. In the pouring rain, Sam faced his fears again till each faded away, never to return.

Six months later Sam came upon the medicine woman who ran the sweat lodge. His T4 white blood cell count was normal. There was no sign of the AIDS virus. Sam was healed.

Fear is the predominant stress emotion. Perhaps with the exception of anger, all other stress emotions, from doubt and worry to guilt and panic, originate as fear. The most common approach to fear is avoidance, the desire to run and hide. While this may be appropriate for a handful of stressors, it can be devastating with the majority of problems that we encounter, no matter how big or small. To confront fear is no easy matter. It takes courage, a French derivation of the words "big heart." Courage is never used to retreat. It is courage that allows us to move through, or around our problems, and eventually transcend them.

In the words of F.D. Roosevelt, "We have nothing to fear, but fear itself." We must face our fears to make them disappear.

10. Breakfast with Uncle Fred

It's a well-known fact that if you live in colorado, you will find that many long lost friends show up on your doorstep during ski season looking for free lodging. Some people who come to Colorado during the ski season could use a lesson on proper winter attire. No matter what they bring, it never seems warm enough. There have been many occasions when I have lent my down ski jacket (luckily, I have two) to a weekend houseguest as temperatures dipped way below freezing. It has almost become a tradition for my guests to reach for the green and purple nylon ski coat before heading out the door.

Several years ago in the cold of winter, I reached for "the" jacket myself and hopped in my car to drive to Denver to visit Uncle Fred. A wealthy man, Uncle Fred was the kind of guy who took his role as uncle quite seriously. From my boyhood, I can remember he was always there with smiles, bear hugs, magic tricks, winks, and an occasional five-dollar bill stuffed in my shirt pocket as he walked out the door. As I headed south to Denver, I secretly thought to myself in the form of a quick prayer, "Hey God, I could sure use some of those fives right now." I had just left an academic position to try my hand at consulting. A career change always brings about a change in finances, and my savings were evaporating in the thin mountain air.

Fred's wife Ernie had died of cancer the previous year, and within months of her passing, my uncle was diagnosed with cancer as well. So we met for breakfast and over omelets and pancakes, discussed some of the deeper issues of life and death, complementary medicine, and the afterlife. Sipping a cup of coffee, Uncle Fred shifted gears and asked me about my career. I decided neither to divulge my financial precariousness, nor my massive credit card debt. I assured him I was moderately successful. Quite humbly, I pulled a twenty-dollar bill out of my wallet and picked up the breakfast tab. As the waiter went off to get change, I made a trip to the rest room.

About a month later I got a phone call from my cousin Donna. Fred had died peacefully in his sleep. It was sad news, but I knew his days were short that morning at breakfast. He so much as told me so.

Two years and many houseguests later, a frigid air mass hovered over the state of Colorado during the Thanksgiving holidays. My fiancée, visiting from the east coast, grabbed the green and purple coat as we headed out the door for a neighborhood walk. Fumbling around the pockets, Bonnie pulled out an envelope, some tissues, some gum wrappers and a Bic pen, ready to find the nearest trash barrel. Opening the envelope, she saw a wad of bills and stopped in her tracks. "Look at this," she exclaimed. "There must be several thousand dollars here!"

The first thought that occurred to me was a former houseguest had misplaced some travel money. After all, this coat has seen several ski resorts in the past two years. We quickly headed back inside and Bonnie counted the money, a total of $3,500. I was stunned. So was she. I began to make several phone calls to friends who borrowed the coat. No one claimed the money. Trying to make sense of it all, the clue to solving the mystery was soon found inside the bank envelope—It was from Uncle Fred!

Over a Thanksgiving feast that same day, I asked my cousin about her father's philanthropic deeds. "Oh," she said, "Dad was always generous, but he was rather quiet about it. On more than one occasion, He would stuff wads of tens and twenties into a bank envelope and place it in my coat pocket when I wasn't around." Then she paused and looked at me, quizzically. "Why? Did he do that with you too?" she asked.

Bonnie and I just smiled at each other. Then we broke out in laughter. That day, Thanksgiving took on a whole new meaning.

A prayer answered takes time. When we pray, beseeching divine intervention, more often than not, we expect immediate results. Human nature may have always been this way, but the age of high technology has certainly brought with it a tacit demand for immediate gratification. No matter what our troubles, there is a higher order to events. And this point is important to remember. All prayers are answered, but in God's time, not ours.

11. The Black Tie Affair

AS A CHILD, I GREW UP HEARING STORIES TOLD at the Sunday dinner table when my grandmother would come to visit. Although there were countless mythical stories, from the assassination of President McKinley to watching the Hindenburg crash in New Jersey, the ones that stuck in my mind were her adventures as a young woman living in the D.C. area. As it turns out, my grandmother's sister was a socialite, a debutante who often gave parties for presidents, senators, and a host of celebrities from Helen Keller to Charles Lindbergh. My grandmother was invited to a great many of these social events and private dinner parties, so as you can imagine, the stories were anything but boring. The names I read in history books were not just names to her. They were real people. As an impressionable youngster, I took delight hearing these stories; a kind of living history. As young kids do, I fantasized about the day I might be invited to a black tie event in Washington D.C. (even though growing up, I lived hundreds of miles from the place, with a snowball's chance in hell of mingling with the people who might someday find their names in the history books).

After dinner when everyone would saunter toward his or her bedroom for the night, I would lay awake on my bed imagining what it would be like to sit and have dinner with Albert Einstein, Amelia Earhart, or Teddy Roosevelt. At the ripe old age of 8, I had no idea of the concepts called mental imagery, guided visualization or the power of intention, but looking back on those days, there really was no other way to describe this intentional form of daydreaming, nor the potential it seemed to unveil.

As fate would have it, I ended up moving to the D.C. area, not once, but twice. The first time was for a graduate studies program in the early '80s where I completed my Ph.D. program (lots of egos, but no celebrities there). I returned again in 1988 to serve on the faculty of the American University, after a two-year hiatus in Burlington, Vermont, working as the director of Sports Medicine for the Olympic Biathlon team. It was this second time that forces of the universe conspired together to make my wish to attend a black tie event come true. As with a great many adventures, this one began with a burst of spontaneity.

The day was January 21, 1993. I awoke with the sunrise and after greeting the world with my usual round of appreciation, I meditated for about a half hour. Just as I positioned myself to get up off the floor and head into the kitchen to eat breakfast, the phone rang. I looked at the clock; it was exactly 8:00 a.m. I picked it up and said, "Hello."

The voice on the other end was chipper, if not rabid.

"Hi, this is Barbara. Listen, I know it's early, but I have an important question to ask you. Do you have any plans tonight? I hope you're free because I just happen to have one extra ticket to President Clinton's Inaugural Ball. What do you think?"

I paused. Then I gulped. I was ecstatic, yet, at the same time filled with a sense of panic.

"Yes, I am free and I would love to go, but Barbara, I don't own a tux." (in fact, the best I had was a corduroy blazer with elbow patches.) I took a deep breath. This was the social affair I had been waiting for and all that stood between this black tie event and me was a black tie … not to mention the tux to go with it.

"Well, call around" she said, "See what you can come up with. I won't offer anyone else this ticket until I hear back from you." With that she said "good-bye" and hung up, but not before I promised to track down the all-illusive black tux.

Before I continue, there are a few things you should know about living in the D.C. area during such events. First, getting your hands on a ticket to an inaugural ball (regardless of who's being inaugurated) is about as rare as seeing Elvis shaking hands with Bigfoot. Second, finding a tux to rent the day of an event like this is more rare than pork chops at a bar mitzvah.

I quickly got into my car and drove to the nearest shopping mall, whereupon I sat silently, offering several prayers until the Mall doors opened up at 9:00 a.m. I made a beeline from my car to the Men's department of Sears. The man behind the counter looked at me like I had two heads when I inquired about a tux for the evening.

"Do you know what day this is?" he demanded.

"All of our tuxes have been rented for months, since election day last November to be exact," he stated as if admonishing me, yet at the same time resentful that I indeed had a coveted ticket and he did not.

"I know, but could you please look, just in case there might be one left somewhere in the back," I said.

The man did an about face and headed for the storeroom, perhaps just to appease me, perhaps for a cigarette. I am not sure who was more surprised when he walked out with a large plastic bag in his hands containing the last remaining tux.

"What's your size?" he demanded.

"42 jacket, 34 waist, 33 leg length, I replied.

"Well Cinderella", he said sarcastically, "today is your lucky day. Here try this on."

After paying for the tux rental, I quickly headed home (on cloud nine) and called Barbara.

"Barb, I have the tux and it's a great fit.

"Oh how exciting," she replied. "Ok, I'll be ready at 6:00 p.m. See you then."

I had no idea what to expect at an Inaugural Ball. As it turns out, I learned that there are typically about 8 of these events planned all around the city. On this auspicious night, the President and First Lady as well as the Vice President and his wife migrate from ball to ball making extremely brief cameo appearances at each one. Sometimes, because of security motorcades, traffic, weather etc. they never make it to all of them. Translation: You can spend BIG bucks on the ball, and never see the guests of honor.

Our tickets indicated we were scheduled to go to the National Armory, not exactly an exciting locale compared to the Omni Shoreham Hotel downtown or some of the other pristine locations, but as the saying goes, beggars can't be choosers. As it turns out, The National Armory was THE place to be that night.

Now, I could tell you that, in the spirit of my wonderful Grandmother, I mingled with Nelson Mandela, Ethel Kennedy, Magic Johnson and several other notables who were there that night, but why name drop? The real stars of the evening were the musicians up on stage playing live music, including Johnny Rivers and South Side Johnny and the Asbury Jukes (with noted saxophone player, Clarence Clemmons).

In all the excitement of the evening, Barbara upon arrival, sprained her ankle (a casualty of high heels and wet pavement) leaving me without a partner to dance with. Throwing etiquette to the wind, I decided the music (Secret Agent Man, Maybelline, Memphis, Rockin' Pneumonia and the Boogie Woogie Flu to name a few) was just too good to stand still. So I danced anyway—by myself. I didn't care how foolish I might have looked alone on the dance floor, I was having fun. Even though the dance floor was nearly empty, I had a great time rockin' and rolling the night away.

Between every song people waited with baited breath on word of the arrival of our new president. Everyone pushed closer to the stage in the hopes to get a good view of Bill and Hillary when they arrived. I am not sure exactly how I became so well positioned, but at times I felt I was practically on the stage myself. Looking back, I know there is no way they could have planned this, but after the first song played by South Side Johnny, a hush filled the room. In walked the new president and his lovely wife. Clarence Clemmons walked to stage left as Bill and Hillary moved to the front of the platform and waved to the crowd. Clarence and the band started to play a moderate rendition of Hail To The Chief and Bill slow danced with Hillary. When that was done, Clarence took off his sax and passed it to Bill. In the new role of President, Bill waved his hand NO and turned to the mike to thank all of his supporters in the crowd. All the while the band played a slow instrumental song in the background. Once again Bill took Hillary in his arms and danced a little on the stage, then the two bowed and waved good-bye to the crowd.

Clarence Clemmons is a large man. Perhaps he simply wanted the honor to play with the president. Perhaps he ran out of his own songs. We may never know, but as Bill turned to thank Clarence and return the stage to the Asbury Jukes, Clarence politely shoved his sax into Bill's hands and the audience roared. Hillary laughed and motioned him to play. Bill placed the reed up to his mouth and hit a few notes. It sounded great. I was not the only person who was surprised and delighted. The crowd went wild. Clarence quickly grabbed another sax positioned upright on the floor and the two proceeded to play a song together while the band joined in. The crowd was euphoric with sustained applause. It was a magical moment to be sure. At some point during Bill Clinton's solo, I could have sworn he looked directly at me and winked. In hindsight, I realize most likely it was the hot looking woman standing next to me. When the song ended (and for the life of me, I cannot recall what that song was), Bill passed the sax back to Clarence, smiled from ear to ear, waved to the crowd, and he and Hillary disappeared behind the stage… off to the next gala.

I learned the following day in an article in the *Washington Post* that Bill and Hillary never made it to all of the Ball locations, and it was reported, he only played sax at one, the one I was at. I think my grandmother would have been proud. In the several years since that momentous night, I have never attended another black tie affair. Then again, I haven't exactly had the occasion to accept an invitation to one either. But that's OK! Looking back I can honestly say I am not sure that night could ever get better than that. Now I too, have a story to tell at the Sunday dinner table. And if you ever happen to visit D.C. make sure you have a black tie (or the equivalent) because you just never know when opportunity is going to knock.

In the words of Satchel Paige, "Work like you don't need the money, love like you've never been hurt, and dance like no one is watching."

Letting Go Of Stress

"LETTING GO OF STRESS" IS A PHRASE USED TO REMIND US to discard any thoughts, feelings, attitudes, or opinions that no longer serve us. In fact, these perceptions, which at one time might have been quite useful, eventually get in the way of personal goals, cause disruptions with family and colleagues, and limit our own personal growth. Over time, they can become our biggest obstacles in life. In truth, these perceptions are servants of the over-inflated ego. They weigh us down and tire us out, eventually impeding our process on what is known as the journey of life. Perhaps worst of all, this emotional baggage limits our ability to reach our highest human potential.

What do acceptance, forgiveness, gratitude and compassion have in common? These are but a handful of ways in which we are invited to open our heart, temper the ego, and release ourselves from the illusion of control which so often binds us to our problems, perpetuating the stress cycle. Each story in this chapter offers a lesson in letting go and moving on.

"Letting go of stress" is a reminder to do just that, to let go and move on, for to stay put is to whither and rot. No one ever said it was easy to let go, but those who do will tell you, this is where real power and freedom reside.

1. Silver and Gold

THERE ARE MANY DEFINITIONS OF STRESS, but the definition I have come to appreciate the most is this bit of ageless wisdom: Stress is a disconnection from our divine source. While it's true that we are never separated from God, however we may perceive this connection, unresolved feelings of anger and/or fear can become so intense that we actually feel that we have been abandoned by the divine. You know what I mean if, in the midst of a crisis, you have ever said to yourself, "What did I do to deserve this?"

While anger and fear are not bad (they are actually survival emotions), left unresolved, they create what is called in Eastern cultures the veils of illusion. Layer upon layer of these veils eventually obstruct our vision. Ultimately, they create a false sense of separation from our highest Self. This is no mere metaphor. It is interesting to note that research reveals the greater the level of stress we are under, the more our peripheral vision decreases (and conversely, that one great stress reduction technique is when you feel yourself becoming tense, to widen your peripheral vision and peripheral hearing). Stunning, simple, and effective.

In simplest terms, the ego is the bodyguard for the soul. But in what becomes a never-ending story, the ego exchanges power for control to steal the stage and dominate the show. Motivated by fear, the inflated ego can grow like a cancerous tumor. In truth, the real power resides in letting go. "Surrendering the ego" is an expression used to remind us to detach from earthly desires, which impede our spiritual growth process.

As a child, my mother would read to me stories, fables, and myths. Not merely entertainment, each story had a specific message. At the end of the story she would ask me my impressions, and what I would do if I were the story's character. The following is one story, as I best remember, which illustrates the idea of surrendering the ego:

One upon a time, there was a young man who lived in a village surrounded by very tall mountains. On his eighteenth birthday, as was the custom of his people, he packed a sack of clothes and food and, bidding farewell to his family, set out in the direction of the rising sun. As he waved good-bye, he heard his father repeat the words, "Remember the Golden Rule; Do unto others... " but his father's voice faded in the wind. Hurrying off, the young man was eager to get going on his mission, which was to discover the nature of his being, seek his life fortune, and if his fate would so dictate, one day return to his village, bearing gifts of treasure and great wisdom from far away lands.

One day well into his voyage, he heard the cries of an old elfish man, apparently stuck at the bottom of a deep well. Only his feathered cap lay at the well's stone edge. The tiny man had fallen in an attempt to get a drink. With no rope, he could not climb out. "Fetch me out of this well and I will pay you with a piece of silver," he said to our hero. The traveler, assuming this might be a trap, offered no help. Yet, seeing a small heavy sack laying beside the well, he picked it up, placed it in his backpack, and continued on his way, passing through several villages and hamlets. The sack, he was to learn that evening was filled with nuggets of gold. This will be useful, he thought, as he lay down to sleep among the stars, tightly holding his newfound treasure.

In the tenth month of his journey, the young man sat down to rest by a stream. Cooling his bare feet in the water, he was startled by a beautiful maiden picking wild flowers. In their exchange, she offered him a silver ring as a good luck token for his trip. The young man was unimpressed. He had acquired a taste for gold. In fact, in a bet with a French troubadour a week earlier, he won twelve more golden nuggets. Silver is of no real value, he told himself. My mission is to acquire more gold. The Golden Rule as he'd come to understand it, was, "He who has the gold, rules!"

Bidding the maiden farewell, he placed his shoes back on his feet and headed toward the next town. On his way, he met a gnarly old woman beggar on the side of the road with a bleeding face, obviously beaten and left for dead. Only her silver-handle walking stick remained by her side. Hand outstretched, the old hag pleaded for assistance. The young man began to reach for a piece of gold, but sensing this might be a trap, instead pulled a polished stone from his coat pocket, placed it in the her hand and, without wishing her well, continued walking toward the village. Within a fortnight he accumulated twenty more golden nuggets.

On the next leg of his journey, the young man came to a river. The water was moving too quickly to ford himself, so he waited for a ferry to bring him safely across. Within a short time, the ferry arrived and he boarded, paying the old ferry master a modest fare for safe passage. No sooner did the flat boat reverse direction than it hit a large rock under a torrent of waves, and the ferry master was thrown overboard. The young man was about to offer assistance, when the large raft tilted. Burdened with the weight of the gold-filled sack on his belt, he plunged overboard into the river's white water along with the ferry master. Now, the young man was a fair swimmer, but he tired quickly, for his large bag of gold weighed him down. Seeing this, the old man yelled, 'take off your belt and grab my hand.' The young man feared the loss of his treasure, but he feared his death more. So he unbuckled his belt, losing the gold fortune he had amassed, and soon was strong enough to fight the current and climb aboard the boat. As he dried himself off in the sun, he turned to see the aged ferry master climb aboard. Before his eyes, the old man transformed into the beautiful maiden of the forest. In her one hand was the silver ring, the other held the old woman beggar's walking stick. The young man fell to his knees, humbled, for he knew his mistaken behaviors and was filled with remorse.

As the boat neared the shore, the fair maiden once again handed the young man the silver ring. He stepped ashore, gave her thanks for safe passage, and headed west into the mountains toward his village, for now he was ready to go home and share his true fortune—the Golden rule: Do unto others as you would have them do unto you. He vowed to commit his life to acts of service and by sunset that day, he had done three. Arriving in the village the next day, he was greeted by his parents and friends. Behind the crowd stood the fair maiden, whom he married by year's end.

EGO stands for 'Edging God Out.' When you surrender your ego,
you bring the divine spirit back into your heart, and
no matter what is happening in your life, it is easier to bear.

2. The Case of The Delayed Flight

THE ENTIRE RANGE OF HUMAN EMOTIONS CAN BE SEEN every day at any airport, from the exuberant smiles and tears produced at the reunion of loved ones to the hypertensive scowls on the faces of passengers with the news of a delayed flight. Being a frequent flyer, I see the entire range every time I travel, but one day stands out, wing and tail, among the rest.

On a trip from San Jose to Denver, I stood patiently in line for the next ticket agent to stamp my ticket. No stranger to the friendly skies, this employee was determined to share her smile with every customer. Sensing she was a good sport, I engaged in a conversation about professional travel. When she inquired if I had any bags to check, I placed my tongue in my cheek and said, "No, but I do have some emotional baggage."

Without skipping a beat, she said, "Remember, only two carry-ons."

We both laughed. I passed through security and found my way aboard flight #1602. As luck would have it, I was upgraded to first class. Comfortably seated, I reclined with a glass of orange juice and patiently waited for the plane to push away from the gate.

Once all the passengers were seated, the flight attendants began to demonstrate the flight emergency procedures. Then they took their seats and we waited. Twenty minutes later, the pilot's voice came over the speaker.

"Eh, folks, I don't know how to tell you this, but there is a federal agent on board who has lost an item. Consequently, everyone needs to exit the plane and go through security again—including your carry-on bags."

Moans of incredulity swept the cabin. One man in front of me said in all seriousness, "This is a conspiracy. I watch "The X-files," I know what's going on."

No one laughed but me. Perhaps everyone else had connections to think about. Like sheep, we filed off the plane and proceeded to go through the security check-in.

Once back in the terminal, it was easy to see how stressed the secret service agent, a young man about age twenty-five, was. Apparently he was missing his gun, which he had in his possession when he boarded.

Now it was gone. After twenty minutes of standing in line, we were given the go ahead to board the plane again and within an hour of our initial departure we were up in the air. Rumors quickly spread through the line of disgruntled passengers like a game of grade school gossip—he found the gun! I think it was an Uzi.

After the in-flight meal, I walked up toward the galley and struck up a conversation with a flight attendant 35,000 feet above the earth. After making a brief comment about the meal, I inquired about the missing gun.

"Well, we're not suppose to say, but it looks like it was stolen." Yikes, I thought. As if she read my mind, she added, "It could have been scary, but everything is OK."

The threat of a hijacking was over, but the threat of missed airline connections was very real to nearly everyone on board the plane. Tension hung heavy in the air.

If there is one thing I have learned about traveling, it is that when you become a passenger, you relinquish control of your arrival, all you can do is sit back and relax.

God, grant me the serenity to accept the things I cannot change, the courage to change the things I can and the wisdom to know the difference (particularly on airplane rides).

3. Passing Judgment—
Not a Good Thing To Do!

A WHILE AGO, I WAS ASKED BY MY TEXTBOOK PUBLISHER to write a series of human feature stories for a college textbook on drug abuse. I had used the format for my text on stress management and the appeal was so great that my editor decided to use a similar approach for this new book project.

I first approached the idea with hesitation. Never having done drugs of any kind, I felt I was the wrong person for this project. Stress, I knew. Drugs were a foreign concept. My editor was unyielding.

"You teach college, right? Interview some of your students. I'm sure they have a lot of first hand experience," he said with a chuckle, as he concluded the conversation. Pondering the possibilities, I agreed, but not without reservation. The revised edition of this drug book was scheduled to have seventeen chapters, covering the span of drug use, from cigarettes to cocaine. My assignment was to find one person per chapter and write up a human feature story for each.

The next night of my class—I was teaching a course on nutrition—I explained to my students my new assignment, and a handful of students accepted the invitation. Several telephone interviews later; I had come up with about sixteen drug-related stories, one shy of my self-imposed goal. So I returned to my class looking for one more story. Right before I was to start with my lecture, a student came whizzing into the classroom on his skateboard, then flipped the board into his hand as he took a seat in the back row. I knew with one glance I had found my last story. Perched on his chair, wearing a tie-dyed shirt and peering through his wired-rim glasses, Chris looked dazed and confused, and I hadn't even started the lecture. When it came time for a break, I walked over to him and asked if he would see me after class. Bewildered, he agreed to my request.

As the students filed out of class, Chris walked up to me with skateboard in tow. He ran a hand through his long frizzy black hair and stood patiently as I packed up my notes.

"Chris," I said, "This has nothing to do with class." I paused looking for the right words to say. "I need a favor." As I explained my search for one more feature story for the drug text, Chris listened attentively and when I finished explaining, without hesitation, he agreed to be interviewed. I took down his phone number, set up a time to call him, and then we both walked out the door. It was rather hard to tell what Chris was feeling, but I was elated. In my mind, this kid had the word "drugs" written all over his face.

Four days later, I dialed his phone number.

"Hello, is this Chris?" I asked.

" Just a sec, I'll get him," the voice answered.

"Hello, Chris?" I said again.

"Yeah, this is Chris. How ya doing?"

" Good! Are you ready for the interview?"

"Sure, let's start."

"OK," I began, "tell me any experiences you've had with drugs, pot, coke, alcohol." I usually started with this question to see if there was a tendency toward one particular drug.

"Well, I really don't do those kinds of drugs."

I shook the phone for a better connection.

"Did you ever smoke pot?" I inquired.

"Once, but I didn't really like it," came his reply.

"What about booze, are you a beer drinker?" I persisted.

"When I was a kid, I tried a beer, but never liked the taste. Actually, I don't drink at all."

Flustered with how the interview was going, I changed tack quickly in the hopes of finding one more story. "Chris, how about your friends? Do they do recreational drugs?"

"Not really, I don't hang around those kinds of guys, I guess."

"Well," I concluded optimistically, "Chris, I'll try to do something with this, but I can't promise anything."

Chris replied, "OK, but don't you want to know about Ritalin? I thought that's what you wanted to talk about."

I was stymied and somewhat embarrassed. Ritalin? I was so focused on recreational drugs that I stupidly passed over prescription drugs. Worse, I made a judgment about this student, which was totally false. He may have looked like a Grateful Dead groupie, and he might have been for all I know, but a drug user? Definitively not!

The ego loves to judge and evaluate. It's extremely good at this. Perhaps good to a fault. In a sense, judgment is like an internal alarm sensor. While at times this thought process may be necessary, perhaps even life saving, most of the time, judgment just gets in the way of happiness and diminishes our ability to connect with others. But a strong ego is always on guard, ready to judge, particularly other people's looks and behaviors that are different than our own.

Freud called this behavior "projection," a defense mechanism of the ego to protect or minimize our own emotional pain in a given situation. In simple terms, a judgment we place on others is often a projection of our own fears, prejudices, and insecurities. Because it would be painful to admit these to ourselves, we project these perceptions on to other people, often unaware that we are doing it. So in truth, those people we judge are really reflections of ourselves or perhaps more accurately stated, specific qualities of ourselves that, in a candid moment, we would admit are none too flattering. Passing judgment on others is a common stress-prone behavior. It's an area in which we could all use a little reminder to drop the gavel and relax.

I was chagrined at my judgment toward Chris, but if there were any ill feelings on his part, he never showed it. I learned an important lesson that day. I remind myself regularly of its importance. Although it may seem all too easy to pass judgment on scores of people with whom we come in contact, it's definitely not a good idea.

Every face you meet is the face of God. Every face you meet is a reflection of yourself. Accept the beauty and diversity of all people and the beauty of your inner self will shine.

4. Walking in Balance

IN A RECENT SURVEY, TIME AND MONEY (or more accurately the lack thereof) were cited as the two most common stressors in the American culture. As responsibilities increase between work and home, the pressure to do more and do it well can lead to a perpetual feeling of tension and frustration. The end result is a hectic lifestyle best described as "out of balance."

The behaviors of hunting and gathering are as present today as they were for our ancestors; however, there is a slight twist. Living in a competitive consumer society the race is on to accumulate "things," which in turn, only adds to the pressures of time and money. Ideas for time management are as plentiful as grains of sand in an hourglass, but one thing experts agree on is that rather than finding one more hour in the day, we must learn to use time more efficiently, and this often means deleting things so we may live a more balanced life.

Mary is a single working mother of three children, all under the age of ten, and not a day goes by that she doesn't experience some level of stress. She loves her job, and although she admits to being rather biased, her children are quite well behaved. The stress comes from too many responsibilities and not enough time to get everything done in the course of a very long day. "Between walking the dog, dance lessons, swim team, and day care — not to mention my job — at the end of the day I am like the Energizer bunny whose batteries have died," she laughs.

By all accounts, Mary is a spiritual woman and her moments of inspiration come from the Bible. Years ago she got into the habit of using the Bible as an oracle. Opening to a random page, Mary closes her eyes and lets her index finger land on a word, typically loaded with a divine message. "Sometimes," she laughs, "I point to the word *the* or *and* and I have to do it over again.

"But let me tell you something," she explains as her eyes grow wide. "Since my divorce three years ago, things have not been easy, but last month was by far the worse. I was beyond patience and my gas tank of faith was running on fumes. So in my typical fashion, I walked over to the Bible, prayed for a message and this time, I got a doosey. There under my finger was the word *balance*. I knew immediately what the message referred to, and boy did I need to hear it."

Mary proceeded to explain that her life was top heavy in responsibilities. "My life was like a boat ready to tip over on one side. Something had to get thrown overboard so my ship would come back up right again. So I sat down with the children that night and explained my strategy. We all came to an agreement. We would simplify our lives, not complicate the family structure with our rendition of Camp Runamuk. We set limits on watching television. Each kid took only one sport or hobby, not the usual three. We cooked more meals at home and ate out less. I placed better boundaries around my work schedule. It's been three weeks now and my life—our lives—have come to a place of balance. I think I fell into the trap where I was trying to please everyone and, in the process, pleasing no one. There comes a point every now and then when you have to edit your life to regain a sense of balance, and my time was long overdue."

"This morning I picked up the Bible and opened it again. You know what word my finger found?" Mary said with a Cheshire cat smile.

"Peace."

Balance is crucial to nature and fundamental to a healthy life. There are reminders of balance everywhere, and it is not hard to achieve. Make it a goal to strive for balance each day.

5. Life and Death in a Small Town

HOW DO YOU EXPLAIN DEATH TO A LITTLE CHILD? Using words, which parents think their children will understand, they often describe death as a journey or trip where a person just doesn't come back. The death of a house pet often provides teachable moments for children as they try to process the difference between life and death, animate and inanimate, and the here and hereafter. The meaning of death through old age or an accident is already somewhat difficult to explain; death from murder or suicide pushes the limits of grace in a teachable moment. Of all the events played out on the human stage, the death of someone close to you is cited to be the most stressful episode anyone can experience.

In the fourth grade, I had a good friend name Brendan Silly. Brendan was a shy, quiet kid. He never spoke out in class. He never did much to bring attention to himself. He did confide in me that he hated his last name. That was attention enough. He was teased unmercifully. Still water runs deep. What Brendan may have lacked in extrovert qualities, he made up for with intelligence. He was the kind of kid who always knew the right answers. During recess, we would hang out and talk, kick a soccer ball, or just walk around the schoolyard property. Looking back it seemed to me that Brendan was a troubled soul. Decades have passed and I am often reminded that you can see someone every day, at work, at school, and never really know what goes on in their life. Such was the case with Brendan.

One day I came to school and noticed that Brendan wasn't sitting at his desk. He didn't come the next day either. On the third day, the teacher made an announcement. She said that Brendan wouldn't be in class anymore. She never mentioned his name again. I was a little confused, but thought perhaps he had moved away. It would be like Brendan not to say much about this. Getting him to talk about much of anything was like pulling teeth.

I remember shuffling home that day, sad that I had lost a friend. I walked into the house to overhear my mother on the phone. Her voice conveyed a sense of shock. I heard her mention Brendan's last name and the words murder and suicide. At that point she saw me enter the kitchen, said she had to go, and hung up the phone. I stood there with a blank look on my face.

That afternoon I received my first lesson about death. I don't remember the exact words my mother used, but as delicately as she could, she explained to me that Brendan's father had taken his life, but not before killing his wife and two children. I would never see or hear from Brendan again, she said.

I have thought of Brendan many times over the years, particularly when similar events make the headlines. The act of violence makes as little sense to me now as it did years ago. Not long ago, in preparing a presentation on the healing power of humor, I learned this: the word silly comes from the Latin word *'selig.'* It means blessed or holy. I took a moment to reflect back on my friendship with Brendan. I wish I could have told him then what I learned about being silly. I think he would have liked its meaning. From this experience I have also learned much about tolerance, for one never truly knows another person's experiences, which can greatly affect mood and personality.

Perhaps the greatest lesson is that there are many circumstances and catastrophes, which make absolutely no sense. Try as we might, we can find little or no meaning. Some may say "it is God's will," but this leaves us with little consolation. There is still a void where there was once life, pain where there was joy. Devastation such as plane crashes and earthquakes or even that of a murdered child deepens the sense of loss. In time, the wounds will heal, but they lend very little to our understanding of "why." It is fair to say that we will never have the answers to all of life's questions, such as these. Yet the void is never filled by staying still. We must move on.

6. Fifteen Seconds of Fame

IT WASN'T UNTIL ONE OF MY FRIENDS CAME WALKING down the hall of my dorm with the JT album in his hand that I began to see a different side of life than most people see. The year was 1976 and I was a sophomore at the University of Maine. John placed the LP up to my face, called all the guys around. Heads popped out of all the dorm rooms and slowly they all flocked toward us. John then yelled,

"See I told you. Dead ringers. These guys could be twins." Every time James Taylor came out with a new album or did a PBS special, the same comments came flying my way.

James Taylor. Sure I had heard of him. *Fire and Rain. Something in the Way She Moves. Up on the Roof* and *Sweet Baby James.* These are some of the most famous anthems of the baby boomer generation. Everybody has heard of James Taylor. But not everyone looked like him. John was right. I could pass for his brother. If it wasn't for the fact that James was six inches taller than me we could pass for twins. I first saw James Taylor at a concert in Colorado's Red Rocks amphitheater in 1982. I walked to the front of the stage to get a better look. It was a little scary. He didn't just look like me. We actually had the same mannerisms too; smiles, eye motions, hand gestures. For better or worse, our hairlines have receded at the same time too (despite the fact that JT is a decade older than me).

If I had a dime for all the people who told me that I looked like James Taylor, I could retire on some Caribbean island now a very wealthy man. What is it like to look like someone famous? Well, first people stare at you all the time. You can read their mental thought processes as their brain does a mental search of pattern recognition: Is that really him? Being stared at can give you a complex if you're not careful. If you watch their lips, you can tell they are whispering, "Do you think that's him?" I see it all the time.

In 1992 I was on a transatlantic flight to France. Once the plane leveled off, one flight attendant came down the isle and stopped in my row. She bent down and whispered in my ear, "Mr. Taylor, would you like to come up to first class?"

I said, "I think you have the wrong person."

"You're James Taylor, right?"

I said, "If I was James Taylor, would I be sitting here in coach?"

She answered, "You'd be surprised who moves out of first class to stretch out their legs on these red-eyed flights."

I just smiled as my body stretched out over four seats. She concluded the conversation saying that she loved my last album.

The real litmus test came in the spring of 1993. A friend of mine invited me to a concert at the Birchmere performance center outside of Washington D.C. The star of the evening was Livingston Taylor (James' brother). This ought to be interesting, I thought.

When we entered the building the owner greeted me with a wink and tried to seat me close to the stage, but I refused. A man close to my seat nearly fell over backward when he looked in my direction. When I tried to tell him I wasn't James Taylor, he simply refused to believe me.

When the show was over, Abby wanted Livingston's autograph. I simply wanted to go home. We got in line and when it was our turn to approach the singer, Livingston's mouth dropped to the floor.

"God, you look just like my brother. It's not fair, you look like him and I sing like him, " he said. As he reached to shake my hand, I realized I was stepping into a parallel universe.

Over the years, I have had countless people stare at me in restaurants, scream at me at concerts, yell at me on street corners, and beg for autographs all over the country. It's bad enough that it has happened once a week for the past thirty years. I cannot begin to imagine what it would be like to have this all the time!

In 1999 I did actually meet my double. James Taylor came to Boulder, Colorado to give a benefit concert for the NPR radio program called *E-Town*. The entire night was a fiasco. One of the show's producers, Steve Boynton, came up to me and said, "Do you know you look just like James Taylor?" When the concert was over I walked down to the stage to meet JT. I foolishly thought that by meeting him I might break the spell and never hear the comments that have haunted me for the past three decades (that hasn't happened). As he shook my hand, he looked me in the eye, smiled, and said, "Hey buddy, nice hairline."

When I first heard the expression "15 minutes of fame," I didn't quite understand the concept. In a media-based world, I figured it had something to do with stepping into the national limelight. Now with multiple reality shows on television and the proliferation of ego-based websites and blogs I think Andy Warhol was more right than even he imagined. I have had some time to ponder the concept of 15 minutes of fame and as best as I can figure out, it's mostly about ego. With the best of intentions, ego, at best, can make you look foolish. At worst, it can devastate self-esteem. The ego's desire for fame is never satisfied with just 15 minutes. It wants an entire lifetime, perhaps even more. The bottom line is that people, regardless of who they are, want to be accepted. Perhaps at a deeper level, they want to be loved. In truth, everybody wants to be loved. The shallowness of fame (15 minutes or a lifetime), however, is not the path to take for this endeavor. Simply being true to yourself is.

Let there be no doubt, we are living in the day and age of the 15-minute fame society. Considering that most everyone has a personal home page on the Internet, perhaps the better description is the 15 gigabytes of fame society. Egos are running wild, and in many cases making a mess of things. I have decided to gladly relinquish my fifteen minutes. I don't want it. Having borrowed several faux minutes from JT under false pretense I gladly return them and offer mine to him as well. You might do well to do the same.

"Fame is a vapor, popularity an accident, and riches take wings. Only one thing endures and that is character."

—Horace Greeley.

7. A Moving Meditation

THERE IS A LIFE FORCE OF SUBTLE ENERGY, which surrounds and permeates everything. The Chinese call this life force "Chi." To harmonize with the universe, to move in unison with this energy, to move as freely as running water is to be at peace, or one with the universe. The ancient practice of T'ai Chi is a graceful exercise bringing one in harmony with nature and the universe.

I first started practicing T'ai Chi, which is known as a moving meditation, in graduate school, intrigued by what appeared to be its mystical nature. Later, when I began teaching stress management classes, I knew that this was one technique that I wished to share with my students. Perhaps more profound than the exercise itself is the Taoist philosophy that underlies it. In simple terms, the concept of Taoism speaks of balance. It is often symbolized by a circle, one part black, and the other half white. Taoism honors the union of polar opposites (e.g. male/female, hot/cold, day/night), referred to as yin and yang. When these opposites come together, they don't fight in opposition. Rather, they unite to create wholeness; you can't have one without the other. The Tao is the unseen, mystical force, which energetically binds all things together. Taoism gently reminds us of greatness through humbleness, strength through softness, power through gentleness, wisdom through nature, prudence through discretion, and insight through patience. Indeed, the principles of Taoism are identical to the concepts of stress management.

In the practice of T'ai Chi, one learns to move in rhythm with energy, to go with the flow. The same philosophy can be applied to life's daily routines as well. Rather than continually fighting resistance, trying to change things we have absolutely no control over, the implicit message is to flow like water. Internal strength grows from passivity. As a physical metaphor, T'ai Chi reminds us to stand strong, but to go with the flow. But T'ai Chi offers other benefits as well.

Betty Stewart had heard of T'ai Chi over twenty years ago, but it wasn't until September of 1994 that she began to practice it in earnest. In the early '70s, she was intrigued to try this form of relaxation, and even went out and bought a video so she could teach herself, but she said that just didn't work. Then one day years later, Betty noticed that a class in T'ai Chi was to be offered at the Prestige Club, a unique hospital-based health promotion program for seniors in Colorado with a special focus on bridging standard and complementary forms of healing. Betty wasted no time in signing up.

What makes Betty's story so remarkable are the changes she saw after she began taking the class. Prior to beginning the course, Betty, who was seventy-nine, was all of fifty-five inches. To the amazement of her physician, Betty added over two inches to her height since doing T'ai Chi. And unlike most people her age who lose inches to bone demineralization, Betty's bone density has actually increased in the two years of doing T'ai Chi. Recently she told me, "There was a chance to be involved in a bone demineralization study, but I said, I didn't have time in my life to see if after four years of clinical trials, all I got was the placebo. I wanted the real thing; that's why I started T'ai Chi."

Aside from the benefits of bone integrity, Betty says there have been other benefits. "I have a much better sense of balance. Why, one day I tripped on an uneven sidewalk. Because I had learned how to shift my weight, all that happened was a little bang, no fracture. My coordination and concentration skills have also improved, as has my level of energy. You know, you cannot do T'ai Chi if your mind wanders. You lose track of where you are in the progression of movements."

Aside from the physical movements, Betty is attracted to the philosophy of this moving meditation. There is a real poetic quality to T'ai Chi, she says with a smile in her voice. "I can tell you about stress too! Let's just say that both my husband and me have had our fair share of it these past few years. T'ai Chi has really kept me balanced. I think T'ai Chi is phenomenal."

Recently Betty has been more than just a practitioner of T'ai Chi. She is a roving ambassador as well. As part of the Prestige Plus Program of her hospital in Longmont, Colorado, she now travels to assisted living centers and teaches her peers how to do T'ai Chi. Because there are over thirty-seven movements to master in the traditional short program, Betty felt this was too much to learn for seniors, particularly those in wheelchairs, so with the help of her teacher, she created a special short routine, known affectionately as the "Cinnamon Park Form."

"There are people in wheelchairs who wish to do some part of T'ai Chi, but they are limited in their motion because they are seated. So I made up a short form of T'ai Chi they could do."

Over the phone one afternoon, Betty has shared with me that T'ai Chi isn't just another form of exercise; it's become a way of life for her.

Mountains and water may not have much in common, but when combined together; they offer the message of majestic strength and calm gentleness. To be strong, solid and secure during the winds of change, yet to move peacefully like running water over rocks and shoals. This is the message of T'ai Chi, this is the message of the Tao, and this is the message of managing stress.

8. Sweet Forgiveness

MUCH STRESS IS CAUSED BY DEEP-ROOTED ANGER AND RESENTMENT; poisons that, left unattended, corrode our system literally making us sick. That's why part of an effective stress management program involves practicing forgiveness. Forgiveness is a component of the human spirit that acts as a bridge to connect the mind and body. If unresolved anger is a toxin to the spirit, then forgiveness is the antidote. Where anger is an insurmountable roadblock, forgiveness serves as a tall ladder to climb above and transcend the experience. For forgiveness to be complete and unconditional, one must be willing to let go of all feelings of anger, resentment, and animosity. Sweet forgiveness cannot hold any taste of bitterness, as they are mutually exclusive.

Joanne is a physician living in the Southeast corner of the country. Although trained in the science of western medicine, Joanne's intuitive side brought her to the front door of the field of Psychoneuroimmunology (PNI), where mind, body, and spirit meet in the dynamics of human life. Like most people who become physicians, she entered the field because of her desire to help people. Pain is one of the things that physicians try to alleviate in their patients, and Joanne is no stranger to pain.

In 1997, the back and neck pain she had been experiencing for over a decade became so intense that she literally could not sit. She tried a host of known modalities in her profession to cure it—pills, physical therapy, acupuncture, and craniosacral therapy, none of which seemed to work. One day she awoke to find her right hand and arm were numb. An MRI revealed several bone spurs in her neck, distorting the spinal cord. A neurosurgeon detected nerve damage clear down to her feet. On his advice, she reluctantly scheduled herself for surgery.

"I did not want to go through with the operation," she explained to me at a workshop. "I am well aware of the mind-body connection, and as I lay there I wondered why the mind-body techniques I practiced—mental imagery, etc.—didn't kick in.

"One day I was lying on my living room floor listening to the Caroline Myss tape, *Why People Don't Heal* in which she was talking about forgiveness as a key element to the healing process. I asked myself, 'Who do I have to forgive?' I combed my past to see what lay lurking in the shadows, some unfinished business that I had yet to attend to. Then it came back to me."

In 1984, Joanne and her boyfriend, Lee, took a trip to Grand Cayman Island. Toward the end of their stay, they rented a car and drove to a remote beach, a romantic secluded paradise.

Late that afternoon, combing the beach for shells, a man who had murder on his mind accosted them with a knife. In a bloody fight for their lives, both Joanne and Lee were badly beaten and stabbed. A swift kick to the face of their assailant finally allowed them time to escape for help, but the emotional trauma would manifest as Post Traumatic Stress Disorder for both Joanne and Lee.

"I came to see that I was hanging on to some remnant of this event and it had become immobilizing. So I lay there sending thoughts of forgiveness to this man. I prayed for forgiveness and then I sent thoughts of forgiveness to myself. As I did this, I noticed the pain became less severe. I knew immediately this was the connection. So I continued with this. Although I had previously wished my assailant dreadful tortures in prison, what was called for was unconditional forgiveness. I felt that knives would no longer be a part of my life. I believed that the bone spurs had been zapped. As I lay there, I was overtaken by a joy more profound than any I have ever known."

Joanne explained to me that there isn't a doubt in her mind that her condition was related to the feelings of resentment she harbored for her assailant. Now it was time to let go. Once having done so, the end result was, as it always is, wholeness. Her neck pain never returned.

"I would like to thank my forgiveness, which *A Course of Miracles* defines as the realization that we are not separate—that everything is connected. What was once a curse, is now a blessing to which I am forever grateful and I hope to share this lesson with many others."

Forgiveness is one path of the healing process. If unresolved anger is a toxin to the spirit, then forgiveness is the antidote. Every act of forgiveness is an act of unconditional love, and it is through this love that inner peace resides.

9. Making Friends With the Enemy

IN THE EARLY 1980S, I TOOK A JOB AT A HOSPITAL working in the department of Cardiology. As any nurse will tell you, there is an abundance of over-inflated egos within the walls of any hospital. In fact, the tongue-in-cheek definition of M.D. is "Medical Deity." This hospital was no different. Before I even took the position, I had heard mixed reviews of the person I was to work under. However, I was committed to giving him the benefit of the doubt. My doubt soon waned. It didn't take more than a few days to see the truth, even through my rose-colored glasses. Back in the early '80s the expression, "boss from hell" hadn't been coined. Instead, everyone just referred to this guy as the "Antichrist."

Intimidation was his *modus operandi*. His eye contact was piercing. No matter how well you did your job, it was never good enough. He was quick to criticize and even quicker to undermine efforts which did not support his means. There was no room for creativity and no tolerance for different opinions. And, it was no exaggeration to say there was no life outside of work. We were all at his beck and call every hour of the day.

I quickly learned that every conversation on and off the premises was consumed by this one personality. Topics about the weather, sports, politics, and religion all funneled down to the subject of the boss from hell. To make matters worse, I was asked on a daily basis how I could stand him. Some people simply asked, "How do you like your job?" waiting for me to complain about him. To me, pessimism serves little purpose. Constantly complaining never solves anything. In fact, it tends to intensify feelings of anger and animosity. These, in turn, perpetuate the stress response, they don't resolve it. Rather than slip my neck in the noose of negativity, I devised a strategy. I decided to give a standard response. I would answer by saying, "This job has proven to be a valuable learning experience." More than once I saw eyeballs roll back in disbelief, but I held firm to my perception. As it turned out, I did learn a lot from this guy. I learned how not to administrate a program. I learned how not to treat employees. In essence, I learned how not to be a boss from hell.

I often look back on my career, and silently give thanks to my boss from hell. He proved to be a great teacher, perhaps far greater than he'll ever know. From this and many other experiences, I have come to realize that if we can learn from even the most difficult situations, then there is some value to them, and with value, even the most negative situation turns out to have a positive side. Perhaps world renowned mythologist, Joseph Campbell, said it best this way, *"Jesus said love your enemies, he didn't say don't have any."*

Gratitude is the door to forgiveness. By giving thanks to those from whom we have learned, we cross the threshold of forgiveness.

10. Two Monks and A Woman

THERE IS AN EXPRESSION, WHICH SAYS, "where there is ego, there is stress." That's why sages throughout the ages have offered the same advice to deal with ego-produced stress: to detach, release, and surrender the ego. Most of us, however, hang on, and cling to stress-producing thoughts, which, in fact, no longer serve our purpose. Prejudice, guilt, grief and doubt, to name a few, have a heavy gravitational pull on the human soul. Hanging on to old thoughts, attitudes, perceptions, and beliefs stunt our mental, emotional, and spiritual growth. While at first they may be useful to get through a given situation, old perceptions gather weight as we attempt to move forward with our lives. Some perceptions act like roadblocks, disrupting the journey altogether. To break the cycle, we must constantly remind ourselves to let go of the perception, and hence let go of the stress.

To remind myself, I always like to keep this story in mind. Two monks were walking from one town to the next on a humid summer day. In silence, they walked for miles under the hot sun along a graveled path. Late in the afternoon, they sat down on the grass and listened to the sounds of water cascading over stones in a shallow riverbed. If the monks kept their pace, they would reach their destination before sunset. After a short while they got up and resumed their trek. Soon they came upon the remains of a washed-out bridge. Built several years previously, it had been destroyed in the spring floods. Without thought, the first monk stepped into the water and proceeded to make his way across the river, careful of his footing; the second monk followed ever so cautiously.

Upon reaching the far bank, the first monk looked up to see a woman approach him. "The bridge is washed out and I cannot make it across and I must get to my village before dark. What am I to do?" she cried.

The first monk offered to carry her back across the shallow moving water. Picking her up, he carefully secured his step with each foot until he placed her down safely on dry land. Then he turned around and forded the stream once more to join his fellow traveler.

The two again walked for miles in silence until the first monk paused for a moment and then sat down. The second monk joined him by his side and began to talk.

"Brother, we have taken vows of chastity. How could you pick up that woman and carry her as you did? You have forsaken your vows," he admonished.

The first monk answered, "Remember, we have also taken vows of service." Then he paused for a moment and then said, "Brother, I placed that woman on the banks of the river several miles ago. It is you who still carries her."

Carrying around useless stress is a heavy burden to both body and soul. Remember to travel light on your journey of life.

11. Never Again!

ONE DAY, WHILE STANDING ALONG THE SIDE of the swimming pool to start my workout, a man twice my age walked up to me and, with an accent I couldn't place, asked if he could share my lane. His smile was genuine and I could have sworn I saw one of those Hollywood twinkles in his eyes. Getting in the water is by far the worst part of swimming, so, in an effort to stall the chilling effects of immersion just a moment longer, I nodded my head and waved him in ahead of me. In he plunged, and for the next fifty minutes he never paused once to rest along the pool's edge. I was intrigued by his good nature, not to mention his stamina, and hoped to strike up a conversation at the end of our workout. As I approached the wall to do a flip turn, he tapped me on the foot, waved good-bye, and jumped out of the water, heading for the locker room. By the time I finished my workout, he was gone.

Several days passed before I saw him again. Once more he approached me, motioned to my lane, and this time, without saying a word, dove in and started swimming. As he entered the water, I noticed a tattoo on his left forearm. Throughout my workout, I was puzzled by the engraved numbers, distantly familiar, yet beyond my immediate recognition. In fact, it bothered me all day long. Just as fast as he entered the water, he jumped out fifty minutes later, but not without tapping my foot, waving good-bye, and smiling.

My curiosity now heightened, I began an inquiry as to this man's identity. I learned that, like me, he was a faculty member of the American University. His name was Arnost Lustig. But unlike me, he had a very different past.

Originally from Poland, Arnost was about seventeen when he and his family were rounded up by the German Nazis and sent off to the notorious concentration camp, Auschwitz. Like all prisoners who entered that camp, he was separated from his family, stripped of all his belongings, robbed of his essence, and denied his humanity. I was told by those who knew Arnost that the horrors of Auschwitz can never be put satisfactorily into words. The tattoo I observed on his forearm was his official identification number. About a year after he was interned there, the American Forces liberated the camp and hell came to a gradual end. Arnost was a free man in a world riddled in chaos and grieving lost innocence. Like many Holocaust survivors, he emigrated to the United States to start a new life.

The next time I saw Arnost it was in the pool locker room. He approached me and introduced himself to me. We exchanged names and then he gave me a big hug, kissed my forehead, and, with another big smile and twinkle in both eyes, said, "You are like a son to me!" On that day we started a budding friendship, enjoying several workouts and conversations. I later learned that his last name, Lustig, means humor or laughter in German, a name he wears well. Putting his hand to his mouth, he whispered, "It's how I got through that horrible ordeal in Auschwitz." Then he put his arm around me and proceeded to tell me a joke.

Until the day I met Arnost, the Jewish Holocaust was a distant event in history to me. From the film footage I saw in high school to the works of psychologist Victor Frankl to Steven Speilberg's, *Schindler's List*, the stories of the Holocaust were disturbingly moving. Yet on that day, Hitler's "Final Solution" became a living memory. For those who survived, it is said that the atrocities of the Jewish concentration camps were the worst hell on earth.

The same semester I met Arnost, one of my undergraduate students shared with me this story during a classroom discussion about anger and forgiveness. Her grandmother, also a concentration camp survivor, had moved to New Jersey after the war. She returned to Europe two decades later with her daughter. Crossing a street in Poland, she saw the face of a man she could never forget, a Nazi concentration camp supervisor. Filled with emotion, the woman grabbed her daughter's hand, and walked over to the man, with the intention of slugging him. As she got within a foot of the decrepit old man, she looked him straight in the eyes and quickly changed her mind. Instead she said "I forgive you," then slowly turned and calmly walked away.

Recently my intrigue with Holocaust survivors led me to a book titled, *The Triumphant Spirit*, by Nick Del Calzo, a collection of portraits and stories of Holocaust survivors. Although the common theme of hope, the internal sense of a positive outcome is evident amongst all survivors, there emerges another theme as well—and that is the theme of forgiveness. From the thoughts of many survivors, it is explained this way—we had to learn to forgive and move on. To hold disdain and hatred toward a person or people for such horrible atrocities only perpetuates hatred. There are many lessons to be learned, forgiveness is one of them. In the words of Paula and Klauss Stern, Auschwitz concentration camp survivors, "We didn't survive to hate—but to hope that the world learned something from the experience, so that atrocities like these will never happen again."

Yom Kippur is a Jewish holiday, the Day of Atonement. It is a day to make peace with our mistakes, injustices, and wrongdoings. Although not a national holiday, many of my students excuse themselves from class to honor the day. I honor the day too. For me, it is a day of forgiveness, and a day to remember.

12. Compassion in Action

AT THE FIRST SIGN OF STRESS, my sister Gail would not hesitate to light up. The cigarette dangling from her mouth started as an occasional social habit in college. With the advent of her first job as a graphic artist, however, it soon became an adult version of a baby's pacifier. Like most people who smoke, Gail tried passionately to quit, but her efforts met with little success. More than once I would hear her quote Mark Twain, "Quitting smoking is easy, I've done it hundreds of times." Eventually, social pressures at work forced her to take her adaptive coping technique outdoors, yet the habit continued.

As Gail explained to me, "Cigarette smoking is horribly addictive. The craving for a smoke, actually it's the nicotine, is beyond approach. I have had other addictions, which we won't go into, but this has got to be one of the hardest."

When Gail was pregnant with her first child, Ashley, she kept the consumption of cigarettes to a strict minimum. "I would catch flack from some people—the non-smokers who haven't a clue. My friends who smoke were more compassionate." With the second pregnancy she did even better; yet old habits die hard. Within a month of delivery of her son Ian, Gail went back to a pack a day.

"I am very careful not to light up around my children. I know the dangers of second-hand smoke. I don't smoke in the house or the car. And you wouldn't believe the nagging I get from my kids."

One day her four-year-old son, Ian, asked his mom if he could invite a friend to stay over night. As parents do, Gail called the mother of the child to make the arrangements. The answer was a polite but definitive No!

Gail hung up the phone and called Ian over.

"Listen honey," she said. "Curtis can not come over to spend the night. In fact, he cannot come over at all. His mom explained to me that he has only one lung and she is very careful not to expose him to any chance of cigarette smoke or anything else that would pose a threat to his health." At first Ian had a blank look on his face, till the message was fully understood. Then Niagara Falls started.

"The tears from Ian's face continued for three days. He just couldn't understand why I couldn't quit. Looking back, I am sure I probably had a few tears too," Gail explained. "It was one of those, Dammed if you do, dammed if you don't, situations."

"You know you can do a lot for your kids to show them you love them. Most of these require large blocks of time, and a lot of it seems to require money. There are sacrifices and compromises for sure. And to be honest, sometimes there's resentment with these decisions. Any honest parent will tell you so. In this case, there was none of that. I had simply broken my son's heart. Broken hearts are mended with love. I knew there was only one thing to do. I had to quit smoking."

Smoking cessation for Gail was not an overnight sensation. It took several stressful weeks. As any of us can attest, to change habits just for ourselves is hard. Doing it for someone else doesn't make it any easier. But when our actions are motivated by love—for those we love—then we gain footing to a new level. With a good month behind her of smoke-free lungs, Gail made another phone call to Curtis' mom. This time she got the green light. Ian was beaming.

In simplest terms, compassion in action is an act of service. Until love is acted upon, it is merely a theory, a seed set upon inhospitable rocks. Fear is the motivating factor of stress. It undermines much of our behaviors. Compassion in action is a conscious act of love. We do acts of service not to make friends, to win brownie points or earn favors from God. When we engage in acts of service, everyone benefits.

Compassion in action is nothing less than an act of unconditional love. When we give in the name of service, we give to ourselves as well.

13. The Story of the Polite Monk

WHEN GIVING PRESENTATIONS ON THE TOPIC OF STRESS, I often address the concept of acceptance. Acceptance is an inner resource, a muscle of the soul, that we exercise in times of strife with things we simply have no control over. In this rapidly changing world in which we live, many people feel that there are numerous things that defy control. This is where acceptance comes in. To quote the famous serenity prayer: God, grant me the serenity to accept the things I cannot change, the courage to change the things I can and the wisdom to know the difference.

I have met a great many people who bang their head against a metaphorical wall attempting to change things that they have absolutely no control over. There is one thing we always have control over though and that is our thoughts. This is where acceptance plays the biggest role as a muscle of the soul.

There is a parable of a young man who embodied the concept of acceptance. The story goes something like this: In a land far away, it was the custom of the youngest son to leave the family and go to the nearby monastery as an offering to God. Not only would the young man be ensured of food and clothing, but the family would be esteemed as well. Because the eldest son was killed in childhood, this young man waited several years to go to the monastery until he felt his parents could manage without him. As it turns out, his younger sister married whereupon her husband took responsibility for looking after his new in-laws. So on the appointed day, he packed a small cloth with the few belongings he owned and made the arduous trek from the west village miles away to the monastery on the hilltop, where he was greeted warmly and taken in.

Nearly a year passed when one day there was a commotion outside the gates of the Abby. A woman, holding her baby was yelling at the monks. Soon the yard was filled with young men in purple robes. The woman looked at all the men, and then pointed at the young man from the west village and handed him the baby, indicating that he was the father. She said she was too poor to feed and clothe the baby, and he must accept his responsibility. Without a moment of hesitancy, the young man walked back inside the monastery holding the infant close to his chest, accepting his new role as father. He had never seen the woman before in his life, but knew that to say anything would humiliate her. It was not becoming of a monk to cause embarrassment. Besides, who would believe him? Obviously she was so poor she could not care for the baby herself. She reasoned that this was the best means to ensure safety for her baby. Although he was not sure why he was selected from all the monks, he accepted his fate.

Over the next few years, the monk became quite fond of his newly acquired son. Although all the monks participated in the role of father, the monk from the west village held a special bond with the boy. So it was quite a surprise a few years later when the mother of the baby came back to the monastery, pounding on the door demanding to see her child. She was now accompanied by a man, her husband, and he too demanded the return of his son. Once again the monks assembled in the courtyard in a flurry of purple robes. The young mother walked over and hugged her son. She confessed that the monk wasn't the father after all, she was just too poor to feed him and picked out the man with the greatest compassion in his eyes. The monk felt a deep emptiness in his heart. He knew he would never see this little boy again, yet he knew that the child really belonged with his mother. She slowly walked outside the monastery gate and the monks headed back into the courtyard. Later that day when asked how he felt, the monk from the west village explained it this way: "I knew when she handed me the baby two years ago I was not the father, but knowing that there was no way to prove this, I accepted it. When she came in today to reclaim what was hers, I knew I must accept this too."

The moral of the story is this: Acceptance is perhaps the most important muscle of the soul to exercise, particularly with those things we have absolutely no control over.

Palm Springs is a very hot place to be in the summer, as temperatures can reach well above 110 degrees. It was my first time in this desert city and all the rumors I heard of the summer heat were true. I was there presenting at a conference on the topic of stress and human spirituality. Unlike the scorching heat outside, the room was comfortably cool. Typically, I provide handouts when I speak. I arrived early so I could place them on the chairs for people to glance through the material and become familiar with it. As I was getting the projector and laptop positioned, a man walked up to me to chitchat.

"I looked over your list of muscles of the soul. Good list, but you forgot one," he said.

"Oh really, which one," I inquired?

"Acceptance, " he answered. Then he paused, looked down at the ground for a moment and then raised his head to make eye contact and spoke again.

"My granddaughter was murdered last year. It was a terrible loss to my son and daughter-in-law, as you can imagine. It was a terrible loss to us all. I think I had to employ nearly every muscle you have listed, but it came to a point where I knew I also had to accept the situation. There was a lot of anger and a lot of unanswered questions, but after a while the resentment really drains you."

He went on to explain that acceptance isn't a one step process. It is a long journey.

"Just when you think it's all behind you, something surfaces, perhaps a memory, perhaps a news story, and there it is all back in your face again. You can try to fight it, but in the end you'll lose, so acceptance is the only thing that gives your heart peace."

> *"God, grant me the serenity*
> *to accept the things I cannot change,*
> *the courage to change the things I can*
> *and the wisdom to know the difference."*
>
> —Reinhold Niebuhr, The Serenity Prayer

STRESSED is DESSERTS Spelled Backward

Good Vibrations: Healing Techniques

A CONSENSUS AMONG THOSE AT THE VANGUARD OF HEALTH suggests that René (*I think, therefore I am*) Descartes was wrong. The mind and body are not two separate entities. Rather they are one. Although Western science isn't quite sure exactly what the mind really is, this we know: it's not the same thing as the brain. The mind merely uses the brain to function. Our current understanding suggests that mind, or consciousness, in all its wonder appears to have an energy component to it. The laws of physics suggest that energy has vibrations. Bad energy, such as unresolved anger or fear, has what is termed dissonance. Good energy, such as love, joy and happiness, has resonance, harmony and syncopation. Light, sound, food, imagery, and breath are also forms of energy. With regard to effective stress management, each has the ability to heal or make whole. In simple terms, good vibrations bring a greater sense of inner peace, which after all, is what we strive for in this hectic pace of life, right?

Prolonged stress can have serious effects on the physical body ranging from the common cold to cancer. Denied the chance to completely relax, one or more organs or physiological systems will show signs of dysfunction. This is why the regular practice of relaxation techniques is so important. These techniques allow the body to return to a sense of inner peace. In doing so, they help maintain the integrity of all the body's organs and systems. There are hundreds of relaxation techniques, ranging from music therapy and physical exercise to hatha yoga, meditation and T'ai Chi. No one technique is better than the rest. It comes down to a matter of personal preference and time. The purpose of each technique is to calm the body and mind, and this is where real healing takes place.

The following stories explore the nature of relaxation and restoring the body to wholeness through a host of various mind-body relaxation techniques that can best be described as "good vibrations."

1. The Sound of Music

SOUND IS ENERGY MADE AUDIBLE. Music is sound transformed. Some say when we listen to music, we eavesdrop on the thoughts of God. Most people agree there is some spiritual quality to music. Music is a gift from God, or so Orpheus thought. Greek legend has it that Orpheus was given a lyre by Apollo, the God of music, so that he might offer songs of praise. Although Apollo bequeathed this gift, it was the muses who taught Orpheus to play, hence the word "music." You don't have to understand the intricacies of tone, pitch, harmony, timbre, or rhythm to appreciate good vibrations. The sound of music has a healing quality, which can motivate as well as pacify our deepest emotions.

Sound healing seems to work at many levels. First there is the concept of entrainment, the sympathetic resonance of vibrations, which allows for a harmony between the vibration of music and the vibrations of cell tissue. Second, the ear structure is positioned near a lymph node, allowing a unique interaction with the immune system. Finally, through our perceptions, music can heighten our enjoyment to the sounds we hear, resulting in a release of neuropeptides throughout the body, which also have a profound healing effect. Perhaps it's no surprise that a research study conducted by the Mitchum Corporation showed that listening to music was the number one relaxation technique reported by thousands of people to calm their nerves.

Some listen to music, others play it. Recently I was moved by a story of the lead singer/fiddler, Mairéad Ní Mhaonaigh of the Irish group, *Altan*. She and her husband, Frankie Kennedy, formed the group in 1986. Frankie died of cancer in 1992. It was his wish that the group continue on. And it has, with great success.

"The music was a healing force then," Mairéad explained in an interview in the *Boulder Daily Camera*. "It lifted my spirits when things were low. When he actually succumbed to cancer, the music was the only way to express those feelings."

I happen to see *Altan* perform some months after Frankie's death. Mairéad has the most genuine smile and a calm presence about her. When she placed bow to fiddle, she became electric. It was no secret that music was and still is her healing force. She wasn't the only one who benefited, however; the audience did as well.

The sound of applause is not usually considered to be a symphony of sorts, but it is music to the ears of singer, songwriter Naomi Judd who, with her daughter Wynonna, became one of the nation's most popular country music acts, The Judds. Stricken with a potentially fatal case of Hepatitis C, Naomi's singing career was nearly cut short in the summer of 1990. Told she could only have a few years to live, her team of physicians sent her home to prepare to die. As a woman of great faith, Naomi decided to listen to the voice in her heart, more than the voice of her physicians, and determined that she would not be a passive victim to her condition. Instead, she would become an active participant in her healing journey.

A long time advocate of the mind-body-spirit connection, Naomi began to apply what she knew in her heart to be true. Setting her focus on healing, she planned a strategy for her recovery. One day after calling her husband, Larry, daughters Wynonna and Ashley, and her mom to her bedside, she informed them of her game plan. In her heart, Naomi knew that if she were to disconnect from her profession, her colleagues, and her music, she would die in record time.

Naomi decided to fight back. She announced to those around her that she would go back on tour, what soon became known as, "The Farewell Tour." But this would be no ordinary tour. Not only would she give the gift of music, this time she would receive it as well. Knowing how powerful the energy of love was, after performing each song, she would soak up the applause, the whistles, the cheers, and direct this sonic energy throughout her body—asking the vibrations to stimulate her immune system, to heal the cells of her liver and send the virus in remission. In her own words, she said, *"I would turn each standing ovation, this applause into prayerful support."* And it worked! Nine years later, she is the picture of health. Naomi makes no bones about sharing the message of faith, hope, and love with a little music thrown in, as essential components of the mind-body-spirit equation.

In 1996, Naomi invited me to join her as a speaker on a panel at the National Wellness Conference in Stevens Point, Wisconsin. As panel moderator, Naomi asked me to speak of human spirituality as an integral part of the healing process. I cannot recall if music therapy entered the conversation that day, but it could have certainly fit in nicely.

Two years later, I was a guest at Naomi's annual celebrity auction in Nashville to raise research funds for the American Liver Foundation, of which she is the National Spokesperson. It was there I heard her say that for the past two years, she has tested negative for the Hep C virus. The complete remission of Hep C is virtually unheard of, but Naomi just winked. She knows what it took to get there - good vibrations of all kinds. A decade later, she is still free of this disease and shows no signs of slowing down.

Music has always held a soft spot in Naomi's heart and that spot continues to grow as she shares her message of the healing journey that we must all take part in to nurture our souls and become whole.

In 2004 I was invited by the Eversound Music Label to make a compilation CD of what I considered to be the most relaxing music from their entire collection. The result is an instrumental CD titled, *One Quiet Night* and it is wonderful (I can say this because I didn't compose or play one note on the entire CD). Every now and then someone who has purchased One Quiet Night emails me to express his or her gratitude. What can I say? When you listen to good music, you eavesdrop on the thoughts of God.

Medicinal therapies are available in a great many ways.
Music not only soothes the savage breast,
it brings peace to the heart and soul as well.

2. When The Pupil is Ready...

JOAN HAS BEEN MEDITATING FOR YEARS, but not long after she began to practice insight meditation, a technique she learned from Jon Kabat-Zinn, director of the Stress Reduction Clinic at the University of Massachusetts Medical Center, an insight came to her that had been waiting to be revealed and resolved for decades.

Meditation is a practice of cleansing the mind. Although it is often associated as a religious practice, the premise of meditation is non-denominational, and is increasingly being used in the West as a stress reduction technique. In fact, the American Heart Association now advocates meditation as stress prevention for coronary heart disease.

Meditation is increased concentration leading toward increased awareness. The purpose of meditation is to still the mind and quiet the voice of the ego, so that a sense of inner peace may permeate our being, bringing peace to the body as well. Mental homeostasis promotes physical homeostasis: decreased resting heart rate, blood pressure, muscle tension, and metabolic function. Meditation is not only good for the mind; it's wonderful for the body as well. When the mental chatter is stilled, unresolved issues residing fathoms below the conscious mind, often bubble up to the surface, uncensored, to be reconciled.

One day, Joan was in such a relaxed state. Up to the surface came a voice, "You didn't save me!" Following the instructions she was taught, Joan took a deep breath and tried to dismiss this thought as she had the others before it. But twice more she heard the same voice, bearing the same message. It took several moments for Joan to pull the pieces together, traveling back seventeen years, reconstructing the memories.

The year was 1980. Joan had completed nursing school in Chicago with a specialty in intensive critical care, coupled with a very short term in the Dominican Republic performing rural health care. This became the stepping-stone to her next assignment the same year—as a nurse in the American Refugee Center acute care hospital unit at Khao-I-Dang, Thailand. Across the border from Thailand, lay the killing fields of Cambodia. Looming within earshot were Vietnamese troops, poised to attack. As Joan will tell you, this was not a re-creation of the television series M*A*S*H: "We, the Americans, had Hospital

One. Across from us was the German Red Cross, down the row, the French, the English, and the Japanese. Our hospital was one large open room with about 100 plywood platform beds. It was always crowded with medical staff, assistants, translators, patients, their families, and visitors."

One afternoon, Joan was asked by a physician named Bob to escort a female patient across camp for a chest x-ray. The woman was diagnosed with Chinese Liver Fluke Disease. One look told Joan this woman was in serious pain. Her abdomen was grossly distended and stretched tight with fluid, ready to burst. Most likely she contracted this disease from unfiltered water. It struck Joan odd that she traveled safely over one hundred miles of land mines to find shelter at the Thai border, only to succumb to this. The disease was quite advanced, but with her labored breathing, the physician wanted to see if it had progressed to her lungs. The best they could do was treat the symptoms and minimize the pain.

The woman was transported from a cot to a gurney to the back of a dusty pick-up truck. As the vehicle pulled away, Joan saw three young girls run behind to catch up with their mother. From the young faces she turned to view the refugee living quarters; over 240,000 Cambodian, Vietnamese, and Chinese refuges cramped in a two by two mile perimeter. Returning her glance inside, Joan wiped her patient's brow and tried her best to kept the flies away from her face.

"I prayed that she would not die en route," Joan said. "I tried a couple of Hail Mary's. I prayed, 'Mary, please don't let this woman die now. Not in the middle of camp, not with me along to attend to her, and especially not with her children watching.' But I was in Khao-I-Dang, Buddha's territory and he is a brutal realist. His miracles are performed through insight, not some miraculous recovery."

The patient's breathing slowed considerably. Joan weighed her options. No crash cart, no ambulatory bags, no medical team, nothing! Was CPR even an option? Suddenly it was too late. The woman died. The annoying flies landed repeatedly on the corpse, as her three children, now orphaned, looked on with unyielding eyes.

"Back at the hospital, after seeing how upset I was, Dr. Bob and the rest of the team calmly assured me I had done the 'right thing.' But I was still plagued with questions. Had I played God? Had I made the wrong decision? If I had done CPR, how much longer would she have lived? Had I failed in my role to save and respond? Did I for one minute have the power to give the breath of life and refuse it? I wondered if her spirit lingered or did she move swiftly toward the light to welcome the pure freedom of breath without pain?" These questions remained unanswered in Joan's mind for seventeen years.

There is a Chinese proverb that states, "When the pupil is ready, the teacher will come." It refers to the idea that when we quiet our minds very still, wisdom rises from the depths of our unconscious mind to offer insight and illumination. We are both the student and the teacher. Knowing this, sitting quietly, concentrating on her breath, Joan awaited the voice of the teacher. It said, "All breath moves toward wholeness."

Again came the woman's voice, "You did not save me." This time Joan answered, "No, I did not save you. I could not save you." Joan took several more slow deep breaths; the teacher spoke once more, "How does it feel not to have control? How does it feel to let go?"

Remember: When the pupil is ready, the teacher will come.

3. The Healing Power of Nature

ELIZABETH ROBERTS IS A MOST EXTRAORDINARY WOMAN. A teacher, philosopher, humanitarian, and social activist, Elizabeth is no stranger to the vanguard of social change. In the early '60s, she marched with Reverend Martin Luther King to promote civil rights. Years later she launched a crusade for television reform. Her resumé lists her as a former program director for National Public Radio, and it was she who coined the title for the now renowned afternoon news program, "All Things Considered."

"Most likely that will be my epitaph," Elizabeth says, jokingly. However, her most lasting legacy may be her awareness of the healing power of nature.

I had been given her book, *Earth Prayers*, in 1992 by a very dear friend of mine in Vermont. So moved was I by the prayers and poems that I began to use several of them in a relaxation slide show I produced titled, "Mother Gaia: The Healing Power of Nature." Word circulated about the tremendous impact of the slide show and one day I received a phone call from a conference coordinator wishing to team Elizabeth and I up to do a joint presentation, with Elizabeth reciting the poems from her book. As it turned out, we both live in the same town, so we arranged to meet at her house one afternoon. Over a cup of tea, she shared this story:

"How did the book come about?" she said, repeating my inquiry. "Let me tell you. I had been sick for quite some time with Chronic Fatigue Syndrome. It got so bad that I was bedridden for about nine months. It was horrible. I was so exhausted I could barely lift my hand up to my face. About the only thing I could do was read, but I was too tired to hold a book. The most I could hold up was a piece of paper.

"While I was sick, I had many conversations with God, many times not believing in a God anymore. My theology became a cosmology as I turned to the earth for help. And I got it.

"Elias, my husband, had sent the word out to my friends not to call because I couldn't hold the phone to talk. Instead, he said to them, 'Write letters.' So they did. Knowing how much I loved poetry, and knowing my love of nature, several friends sent me poems to read. In nine months time, I had quite a collection."

Elizabeth explained how her dark night of the soul became a womb of creation. She decided to edit the collection of poems into a book called *Earth Prayers*. The project became her *raison d'être* and the energy to edit this project became a healing energy itself. "Elias and I sent out invitations for our friends to contribute a poem as well. And oh, the permissions to use some of these poems, you should see the folders in my office," she exclaimed.

Through her illness, Elizabeth came to see the powerful metaphor nature is. "Nature speaks to us in seasons. There is a time to produce and a time to lay fallow. In hindsight, I saw my down time as that which my body needed to heal. Although I knew of the concept of laying fallow, it took chronic fatigue to make me realize I was not honoring this aspect of life. Now I have learned my lesson."

In 1990, Elizabeth and Elias formed The Boulder Institute for Nature and the Human Spirit, a social activist organization, which organizes grass root ecological projects as well as small group vision quests in the quiet surroundings of Colorado's southwest corner. When Elizabeth speaks about the vision quests, her whole face lights up. "We have so much to learn from nature. Nature in all her infinite glory speaks to us, and we must listen."

Elizabeth is one who walks her talk. It is not uncommon for her to be found in the calls of nature, partaking in a vision quest. There she listens to the wisdom of the rocks, the songs of the trees, the lullabies of the streams, and the energies of the earth. And if you were to hike the many trails in Boulder's park system, you might see Elizabeth out there. She partakes regularly in the healing process of nature. Her example is one to follow, for in this high-tech age it is all too easy to distance ourselves from our primal environment and lose contact with the heartbeat and resonance of Mother Nature.

There is a right time for everything. A time to be quiet and a time to speak up, a time for keeping and a time for throwing away (Ecclesiastes: 3). May we often reconnect with the rhythms and healing energies of nature.

4. Inherit The Earth

ONE DAY OVER LUNCH, Elizabeth Roberts and her husband Elias shared with me a new book project they were working on.

"Have you noticed how much gloom and doom there is with the coming millennium?" Elias asked me. "So we are inviting several hundred people to write prayers, poems, and messages for the new millennium. It is our hope that these prayers will be read throughout the world to create a critical mass of conscious thought and pull humanity in a positive direction.

"We want to get a message to the world's people that there is hope, that there is faith to get us through the crises looming over our heads. You know we are not going to make it if our only attitude is despair. We have contacted the Dalai Lama, Vaclav Havel, Joan Baez, Jane Goodall, Jimmy Carter, Thich Nhat Hanh, Desmond Tutu and several others.

"Wow," I said, "this will be an impressive work." Reflecting on their two anthologies of collected poems and prayers, I felt this work would be a positive statement.

"Are you going to have any letters from children and young kids, perhaps even college students? I asked.

"Oh," said Elizabeth, "that's right. We need the voice of children as well. Perhaps that can be its own chapter?"

Elias then turned to me and said, "Here. We'd like you to write one too. This is your formal invitation."

In my hands Elias placed a letter with the heading, "*Prayers for 1000 years: Invocations for the New Millennium.*" I was honored.

For well over a week I pondered what I would say to the people of tomorrow, about the earth, about love, and about community. Hundreds of ideas circled in my mind. I continually asked myself, what message could I leave that would make a difference?

While it's true that children have an innate talent to live in the present moment, it would be unwise to think that today's younger generation lives a stress-free life. To the contrary, both children and teenagers face stressors similar to their parents and grandparents. And while the problems of youth may seem trivial compared to adult "real world" stressors, feelings of pain, fear, frustration, anxiety, and depression are identical to their grown-up counterparts. At some level, kids are quicker to adapt to the quickening speed of change in the world they stand ready to inherit; yet at another, bombarded with pessimistic headlines and newscasts, they too face the ever-present reality of global pollution, ethnic conflict, refugee migration, and financial crises, to name just a few foreseeable problems. However, if there is one attribute the youth of every age have, it is resiliency—the ability to bounce back.

Resiliency is a unique spiritual muscle. Like a special flower, it is a hybrid of several coping skills, which culminate to overcome the winds of change, the odds against us. The fibers of resiliency are humor, creativity, persistence, and optimism, and their roots reach well below the surface, ready to rise again and again when needed. Perhaps its greatest facet is the ability to stay focused in the present moment, rather than stuck in the past or focused on the future. We enhance our resiliency when we galvanize these resources in the face of adversity. Each time we rise from the metaphorical fall, we come back stronger, and what was once considered a mountain now becomes a molehill.

A week after meeting with Elizabeth and Elias, I sat in a restaurant in Boulder after a long hike in the mountains. To me, like Elizabeth, the mountains always serve as a point of inspiration. I ordered my food and pulled out my notebook, ready to start my poem/prayer. No sooner did I put pen to paper, than three high school-aged kids came into the restaurant and were seated across from my table. I had momentarily forgotten that these kids were the audience for this book. My concentration was interrupted by the commotion and I placed my pen on the table. What initially started as a distraction became an inspiration, as I eavesdropped on their conversation. Here is the poem that came of that experience:

Inherit the Earth

I overheard a conversation among three teenagers yesterday.
They were discussing crime, pollution, and human values,
particularly the work ethic.
"The system appears to be corrupt," said one.
"Perhaps Earth is a prison and we are stuck here
until we wake up," said a second.
The third just shook her head is disgust.
This thought came to my mind:
It is said that the meek shall inherit the earth.
But after all we have done to it, will they still want it?
Soon, their conversation turned to giggles and laughter.
The energy shifted as did the topic, then more laughter.
In their mirth I heard defiance, resiliency, and faith.
Laughter, like hope, springs eternal.

5. Seize The Day!

AT TIMES, STRESS CAN NOT ONLY SEEM OVERWHELMING, it can seem very disempowering, if for no other reason, it can make you feel like you have no control over a particular circumstance. One of the basic human fears is the fear of losing control in any given situation. The consequences are paralyzing. One of the ironies of human nature is a desire to manipulate things we have no control over, and neglect or abandon the things we have complete control over.

So what do we have control over? First and foremost, we have control over our own thoughts. But we also are empowered to use our inner resources, or muscles of the soul. These muscles include but are not limited to: humor, creativity, optimism, patience, persistence, integrity, faith, courage and compassion. When you acknowledge the amazing potential of these resources, your wealth is immeasurable. These are the attributes that we recognize, consciously or unconsciously in the people we call our heroes, role models or mentors.

Empowerment and mentors, along with support groups and uniqueness, constitute the four pillars of high self-esteem, and high self-esteem is paramount in dealing with stress effectively. Reflect for a moment on a person or persons whom you would identify as your mentor or role model. Once you have a specific person in mind, ask yourself what is it in them that you admire? Lastly, ask yourself what steps can you take to enhance these same qualities in yourself? That's empowerment!

Barbara Abromawitz is a marriage and family therapist in Houston, Texas. I met her in 1999 on a visit to Houston. She was interested in my work, and I was equally interested in what has become her remarkable healing story. It wasn't her outcome that was astonishing (although it truly was), but rather what Barbara did to ensure the outcome. This is a most compelling story of a woman who embodies the concept of empowerment.

In February of 1998 Barbara was diagnosed with uterine cancer. You should know that Barbara took years to cultivate her powers of assertiveness and now she was determined to do all she could to turn this condition around. So well before her physician scheduled Barbara for surgery, she took matters into her own hands. She knew to heal herself she had to reclaim her personal power, not hand it over blindly to her team of physicians at M.D. Anderson Hospital and wait passively in the hopes for a positive outcome.

Her empowerment strategy to healing mind, body and spirit was grounded in research; articles from various peer-reviewed journals to prove what she was doing had scientific merit because she wanted the docs on her side.

"I took a proactive stand and made some audacious requests, but how else are you going to get the care you really want," she asked? "It was my intention to heal not only at the physical level, but the mental, emotional and spiritual levels as well. I also felt that I needed to be on solid ground with my team of physicians, which is why I backed everything I did scientifically." The following is a brief outline of her winning strategy:

- The day she was diagnosed she went into meditation and prayed. She wrote in her journal the images and vision she saw while in meditation that would guide her. Then she went out for a walk to ground herself in nature.

- She contacted a physician herbalist who recommended various herbs to help her cleanse out any toxins in her body, and prepare her for surgery.

- She created a small altar in the surgery room that day to honor the sacredness of life.

- She held a healing ceremony in the surgery room prior to anesthesia asking doctors, nurses and interns to hold hands and be a community of healers. Barbara also said to them, "No matter the outcome, I am grateful for all of your expertise and experience, something which I can never repay."

- She wrote a script that she asked her physician to say while she was under anesthesia, a dialogue of encouraging healing suggestions and affirmations to enhance the healing process of mind, body and spirit. "The unconscious mind hears everything during anesthesia, and I only wanted to hear encouraging words for my healing process," Barbara explained.

- She requested that she be in complete control of her pain management— studies show that patients who tend to use less medication, recover quicker.

- She requested a hospital room with a view of the flower garden because studies prove people recover quicker from hospital stays with a view of the natural world.

"I have been cancer free for five years now, and I know that this whole process was a collaborative effort. I am sure I changed a few paradigms in that operating room, but when it was all said and done, everyone involved was more empowered, being highly professional in the context of real community," she said.

Barbara is one of my heroes. She is the epitome of someone who seized the day so she could live to seize another. Barbara is the epitome of empowerment. Carpe Diem!

So here is a question for you: What actions do you take to feel empowered?

"You may never know what results come of your action, but if you do nothing there will be no result."

6. The Body Flame

As a professor, i discovered that life in academia is comprised of three parts teaching, four parts research, and one part service to the community. For students, the academic life consists of three parts studying, eight parts partying, and four parts stress (usually from partying too much and studying too little). So part of my service to the community was to go to the residence halls during the most stressful times (e.g. mid-term and final exams), and teach relaxation techniques.

Most evening sessions were similar. A receptionist would meet me at the front desk and take me to the floor where the students were to congregate. I would walk into the lounge area and greet everybody. At the appointed time, somebody, usually the Resident Assistant would formally introduce me to the crowd, then we would form a circle on the carpeted floor and I would give a quick ten-minute presentation on the merits of relaxation during times of stress. At this point, I would invite the students to lie down on the floor and participate in a twenty-minute session of various relaxation techniques.

There are literally hundreds of techniques to promote relaxation, many of which fall into the category of mental imagery and visualization. After beginning each session with some diaphragmatic breathing, I would lead the group through a host of imagery exercises and close with some positive affirmation statements. Although the format was consistent from event to event, I would vary the imagery exercises, usually doing whatever came to mind that particular session.

One fall evening I shared with the group an exercise I call the Body Flame. In this particular visualization, you picture an image of a flame hovering above the center of your body (about an inch or two below your belly button). The flame represents your body's stress level. A high torch-like flame is symbolic of a high stress level, whereas a small flame, like a pilot light in a gas stove represents a state of relaxation. During this exercise, one is encouraged to allow random thoughts, excess energy and toxic emotions to pass from the mind to the stomach and up through the flame so as to burn off one's excess energy and return the mind/body to a greater state of homeostasis.

Throughout the exercise, I would gently remind students to take a comfortably deep breath, concentrate on the image of the flame (e.g. the color, the size, the shape, and movement), and ask them to continually send any thoughts and feelings that are no longer needed as fuel for the body's flame. Toward the end, I would invite the students to imagine their body flame as low maintenance flame, indicative of a peaceful state of tranquility. Perhaps because of the anticipated stress from their looming exams, these students were quite receptive to this exercise.

When the lights came back up this particular evening, I was greeted with smiles and relaxed faces of those students now ready to return to their books. One fellow, a young man with deep black eyes walked up to me, shook my hand and told me this was the most profound experience he had ever had. He thanked me profusely, then slowly turning toward the door, gave me an authentic salute and walked away. I stayed to chitchat with the remaining students who hung around. When everyone had left, I walked to my car and drove home.

About a year later, I was asked back to the same dorm. Again I began the session with some diaphragmatic breathing and then slipped into a visualization exercise I call the Rainbow Meditation, matching each color of the rainbow with a specific body region. When the meditation exercise was over, the lights came back up and students slowly made their way back to their rooms. As usual, I hung around to chat with students and then picked up my things to go home. In the corner of the lounge stood a young man with black hair, a goatee, and deep black eyes. He waited until the crowd had left and then approached me, extending his right hand.

"Great session, Dr. Seaward," he said. "I really enjoyed it, but you didn't do the Body Flame this time. How come?"

Not recognizing him at first, I was caught off guard by the question.

"Well, there are so many mental imagery exercises, I just do whatever comes to mind," I answered. As I looked into his eyes, I remembered our encounter the previous year.

"I was hoping you'd do it again," he said. "You see, I have been doing that particular exercise every day on my own since I learned it from you. Several years ago I was diagnosed with a severe stomach ulcer. The medications have been as bad as the problem itself. That first night, when you talked us through the visualization, I placed the body flame over my stomach, and it was the first time I felt complete relief. I am happy to say that within three months, the ulcer disappeared. I am off medication and I feel great. Thanks!"

This technique is really quite simple—and useful. Here's how to do it.

1. First, lay down, with your arms comfortably at your side. Try to keep your spine aligned, from your head to your hips. Gently close your eyes and focus your attention on your breathing. Feel the air come into your nose and mouth, down into your lungs and as you do this, feel your stomach rise up, and then descend back down as the air begins to leave through your mouth. Make each breath comfortably deep and relaxed.

2. Now, with your eyes closed, try to locate the center of your body; your center of gravity. If you are like most people, it will be about an inch or two below your belly button. Place your attention there just so you are aware of this body region.

3. Next, imagine a flame hovering over that point, the center of your body. Metaphorically speaking, this flame is a symbol of your state of relaxation. It feeds off your body's energy. When the body has an abundance of energy: nervous or negative energy, this flame will be quite tall. Perhaps even like a blowtorch. When you are completely relaxed, your flame will be quite small. I call this a "maintenance flame," like that which you would see as pilot light in a gas stove.

4. Using your mind's eye, imagine the size of your flame. See its size relative to your body's level of energy. What color is your flame? Is it an intense brilliant yellow/white color? Now look at its shape. Is the bottom round or oval shaped? What does your flame look like? As you look toward the top of the flame, you will see it comes to a jagged point. Your flame may even dance around a bit. As you look at this flame, feel it feed off the excess energy in your body. Let your flame burn off any excess energy you feel detracts from your ability to relax. If you happen to have any wandering thoughts that pull your

attention away from the image of the flame, try to send these up through the flame and redirect your thoughts back to this image. With each breath you take, allow any excess energy or draining thoughts to move from your head down to your stomach and become fuel for the body's flame. In doing so, you release the tension in your mind and body to become more relaxed.

5. As you continue to watch this image of the flame, feel your body slowly become calm and relaxed. As your body becomes tranquil, notice the flame decrease in height. Soon you will notice that your flame is decreasing in size; about only a quarter to one half inch tall. Continue to notice the color, shape and size. And feel your body relax as your attention is affixed to this image. Continue to keep your mind's eye focused on your body flame.

6. When you feel completely relaxed with your flame very small, very still, allow this image to fade from your mind, but retain this feeling of relaxation.

The mind and body work as one entity in the healing process. As we release excess or toxic thoughts that no longer serve us, we bring the body back to a greater sense of relaxation and restored health.

7. Dreams Revisited

IN THE FALL OF 1986, I WAS INVITED TO BECOME A MEMBER of the sports medicine council of the U.S. Olympic Biathlon team. Biathlon is a winter sport that combines cross country skiing with marksmanship shooting. The sport evolved from the practice of winter hunting in the Scandinavian countries. The Europeans were genetically programmed for this sport, with over 1000 years of practice to brag about. We, the Americans, on the other hand had only about twenty years under our belts. To be honest, our team needed a lot of help.

The financial windfall of the Los Angeles Olympics in 1984 trickled down into the coffers of each sport. While some teams bankrolled their million-dollar bootie, the Biathlon team chose to spend theirs in hopes to earn the ever-elusive gold medal. An elite coach was hired from Norway, and a council was formed to offer the best sports medicine services our athletes could receive.

My job was to introduce and integrate several aspects of mental training, primarily skills to promote relaxation. During various training camps, I would fly in and set up shop in the hotel. My routine was like this. I would put a sign-up sheet on my hotel door with hour-long slots for sport psych sessions. Athletes would come into my room, sit and talk for a few minutes about various stresses of amateur athletics, then lie down on a bed and be taken through a series of relaxation exercises.

On a trip to Lake Placid, New York where the team often trained, I arrived at the hotel and once settled in, placed a sign-up sheet outside my door—open for business. On the second day, I walked back to my room from lunch to find the coach's name penned in for the seven o'clock hour. Coaches are not exempt from stress, but I was a bit surprised, thinking that my responsibilities were solely to the athletes. At seven o'clock, Hans walked into my room, his gregarious smile long absent.

In a thick Norwegian accent, he humbly asked, "Do you have time for me to come to you now?"

"Yes, please come in, " I replied.

Hans approached the spare bed and sat down. Placing his hands to his eyes, he rubbed his face and sighed. He began to explain a recurring dream he had had for several weeks. It was obvious to me before he even began how disturbing its message was. In a dream state, Hans would return home to Norway to find two open coffins in the family room. In the first was the body of his wife, in the second lay his newly born daughter.

"What does it mean? Can you help me?" came a disparaging voice.

In *Man and His Symbols*, Carl Gustav Jung spoke of recurring dreams. Dreams, Jung wrote, were the language of the unconscious mind. Dreams rich in color, symbolism, and meaning are meant to be explored, not ignored, in a conscious state. In particular, recurring dreams, it was his opinion, related to unfinished business of the soul. Jung proposed an exercise called "Active Imagination," where in a relaxed lucid state, a person could re-enter the dream and "finish the script," in effect completing the unfinished business which in turn allows one to move on. By doing this, the dreamer begins the resolution process of the unfinished business, and in most cases the episodes of the recurring dream cease. I had had great luck myself in practicing Active Imagination to resolve a recurring dream of my own involving a huge black ferocious dog months earlier. So it was Jung's wisdom I drew upon for my answer.

"Let's try something, Hans," I said. "Let's recreate the dream right now, but let's finish it. Lie down and get as relaxed as you can. Take a few deep breaths. I am going to share some images with you. Use your imagination to make these images as real for you as possible. Embellish them with rich detail to make the image as real as possible."

Once Hans appeared relaxed, I described the scene in his family room as he described it to me. After having him take a slow deep breath, I invited Hans to imagine that the coffins were transformed into a really large bed. I asked Hans to approach the bed, lie down next to his daughter and wife, cuddle with them, and feel the warmth of their skin.

"Listen to the rhythmical sounds of their breath," I said. "Your wife and child are very much alive, just sleeping, waiting for your return."

Next, I invited Hans to speak softly to his wife, telling her he was home for an extended time now, telling her that he loved her, how much he missed her, and how glad he was to see her and their daughter.

"All is well," I said, "All is well."

Within moments, Hans appeared completely at ease. He slowly opened his eyes and smiled. Something inside him had changed. He thanked me, rose to his feet and said he had to make a phone call.

The next morning at the breakfast table Hans came up behind me, placed his large hands on my neck and began to massage my shoulders.

"I had the best night sleep in two months," he began. "You work miracles! I called my wife early this morning; we had been out of touch for several weeks. Everything is OK, now," he said, slapping me on the back and laughing. Then he turned to the six Olympians and said in Norwegian,

"Ardi Fardi,—Let's Go!"

Carl Jung once said, "The dream is a little hidden door into the innermost and most secret recesses of the soul." If you listen and decode its message, your stress will dissipate like a faded memory.

8. Curiosity and the CAT Scan

AN AGELESS PROVERB REMINDS US THAT CURIOSITY KILLED THE CAT. I don't know cats well enough to comment, but from my experience as a teacher and therapist, I can say that curiosity is one of the more commonly used muscles of the soul in times of stress. And while too much of anything can be unhealthy, searching for answers to life's more threatening questions is considered by many to be an essential coping tool. Academically speaking, curiosity as an inner resource is termed "information seeking." When the red light of stress goes on, all senses are on alert for information on how to best get to safety.

So perhaps it came as no surprise when the phone rang at 6:00 a.m. sharp Mountain Time one Tuesday morning. A friend from the East Coast was in high gear seeking some indispensable information. Although I immediately recognized her voice, there was a peculiar dissonance coming through the line. Within seconds, Susan explained that a routine mammogram a day earlier led to a suspicious CAT scan. The diagnosis was breast cancer, and her physician suspected it has metastasized to her spine and lymph nodes as well. Susan said she was taking it well, but her voice was not convincing.

I had met Susan at a conference a few years earlier. A wellness director at a small New England college, she was attending a workshop I gave on mind-body-spirit healing. Sitting in a circle with fellow participants, Susan, like others, was taking copious notes as a strategy to incorporate the information into her own campus wellness program. At the time, she confided, the material presented was purely theoretical. Now Susan wanted 100 percent application.

"Luke, can you help me design a healing program? I am open to anything." she said bringing calmness to her voice.

"Sure," I replied. "Let's see," I stalled staring into the darkness, as I composed my thoughts. "OK, got paper and a pen? Here we go."

Drawing on the wellness model of healing that I learned from Dr. Elizabeth Kubler-Ross, I sketched out a list of ideas, suggestions, recommendations, and some local contacts in her area. The healing template covered everything from nutrition and mental imagery to acupuncture, music therapy, affirmations, prayer, and a "healing Treasure Map." Susan was all ears, and she repeated, with great frequency, my comments to make sure she heard every word correctly.

"Just a minute," she said, "I'm writing everything down, let me hear it again."

Her behavior was far from unique. Canceled air flights, stock market fluctuations, or midterm exams can all activate the curiosity antenna. In my opinion, however, cancer (or any life-threatening diagnoses) pushes the button with the greatest force. "How did I get it?" and "How do I get rid of it?" are typically the first two questions asked. After a few hours on the phone, Susan's voice was much better, and heartfelt laughter replaced the nervous giggles I heard earlier in the conversation. "I'm going to bounce back from this, I just know it," she said with confidence.

Two days later, I learned that Susan's lumpectomy occurred without incident. It was the bone marrow transplant that had her a little more concerned. She was scheduled to fly to Houston in a few months. She was told by her physician to use this time to regain all her strength. To Susan this meant not only physical, but also mental, emotional, and spiritual fortitude as well. She promised she would keep me updated regularly on her progress.

In addition to her chemotherapy and radiation, Susan pulled together many different resources to create her own personal holistic healing program. This is the template of her healing process (Please note: these are suggestions and it would be to your advantage to include the involvement of your physician in this program, just as Susan did. However, if your physician is not open to holistic healing practices, you do have a right to change physicians. It is important to have a doctor on board whose health philosophy is similar to your own.) This template of ideas and recommendations comes from my mind-body-spirit healing workshop and is considered to be a stepping-stone to optimal health. As you will see, most if not all of these recommendations either directly or indirectly affect the efficiency of your immune system. The standard holistic approach involves the four components of optimal well-being: body, mind, emotions and spirit. Let's start with the body, since it is the most tangible of the four.

Physical Well-Being

Good nutrition is essential for good health. Today there are hundreds of synthetic substances in our food to preserve shelf life and hence corporate profits. In simple terms, these substances are toxic to the your body's physiology. The American Cancer Society states that between 40-50 percent of cancers are the results of a poor diet. Hippocrates, the father of modern medicine who said "First, do no harm!" also said, "Let food be your medicine and medicine be your food." Great advice! So here we go:

1. **Eat a large amount and variety of vegetables**, preferably at the noon and evening meals. Veggies are said to have phyto-nutrients, which help boost the immune system. Soy products have a substance called phytoestrogens that is thought to be very helpful for women with breast cancer. Fresh organic veggies contain more nutrients (vitamins and minerals) than canned or frozen veggies. They also contain fiber that is thought to reduce the risk of colon cancer, and possibly remove toxins from other foods that might enter the blood stream. Fruits are good, however, cancer cells thrive on a high content of sugar. Use fruits in moderation. Fresh, local, organically grown fruits are considered the best source.

2. **Consume good sources of vitamins and minerals.** Vitamins A (beta carotene) C, and E are anti-oxidants that help fight free radicals and boost the immune system. The best source of vitamins is the natural source, not synthetic. Also, do a test on your vitamins to see if they really are bio-available to healthy cells in your body. Some products are synthesized with insoluble binders, making them pass completely through your GI track undigested and absorbed, resulting in expensive urine. To test your vitamin, place a tablet in an 8-ounce glass of water with one teaspoon of vinegar. If it does not dissolve in 20 minutes, find a brand that does.

3. **Eat foods that are whole and natural.** Avoid highly processed foods, especially foods that contain hydrogenated oils or partially hydrogenated oils (e.g. baked goods, snacks, cereals, etc.). These contain transfatty acids and are toxic to cell tissue. It's not a bad idea to cut down your consumption of fats, because an increased consumption of fat is thought to decrease the efficiency of your immune system. The more processed food you eat, the harder your immune system

has to work to clean up the toxins. As Andy Weil, M.D. states in his book *Spontaneous Healing*, this is energy better spent on working to dismantle cancerous tumors. Eating whole organic (pesticide free, hormone free, herbicide free) foods allows the immune system to attend to areas in greater need.

4. **Reduce your consumption of milk products.** Milk today is far different than it was years ago. Today milk contains hormones, pesticides, herbicides, and antibiotics in doses, which, over time, significantly weaken the immune system. Ice cream, butter, and cheese are no different. Where you can, buy organic dairy products. If these are not available, try mixing rice milk with your milk to cut down on the level of toxins. For a change, try almond cheese, and yogurt is a great source of nutrients.

The American diet is extremely low on essential fatty acids, those that the body cannot produce and must acquire from outside sources. The essential fatty acids are Linolenic (Omega 3) found in cold-water fish (salmon, tuna, trout, etc.) and flax seed oil, and Linoleic (Omega 6) found in nuts, safflower oil, corn oil and Canola oil and eggs. Not only is there a dearth of Omega 3s in our diet, but the imbalance of Omega 3s to Omega 6s is thought to be bad as well. It would be an excellent idea to include the intake of Omega 3s on a regular basis.

5. **Avoid artificial products** such as MSG and Aspartame (Nutrasweet®), as these negatively affect the functioning of neurotransmitters in the brain. There have been more complaints about Aspartame to the Food and Drug Administration (FDA) in the past ten years than all other food additives, but for political reasons, nothing has been done.

6. **Stop using the microwave oven.** Microwaves employ ELF's (extremely low frequency) vibrations and these are known to increase the proliferation of cancer cells.

7. **Try acupuncture**, specifically five-element classical acupuncture where the practitioner takes pulses before inserting tiny needles. Five-element acupuncture is a holistic approach, not merely symptomatic relief. It is based on the ancient Chinese concept of the body's human energy field and meridian system. A good practitioner has gone to school for three to four years to study acupuncture. Many physicians in the United States become eligible to practice by taking a two-week

seminar and watching 40 hours of videos; some physicians have no training whatsoever. So check the practitioner's credentials before you get treated. If you do not like your first session, find another practitioner. It's always a good idea to seek references.

8. **Schedule regular full body massages** according to your schedule and budget. Actually, there are many different types of bodywork, massage is just one of many. But muscle tension is the number one symptom of stress; so getting a massage is a good place to start. Many types of bodywork include energy healing, such as Reiki, zero point balancing, Therapeutic Touch, Healing Touch, bio-energy, etc. Energy work is new to Western culture, but it is an ancient practice of healing, based on the premise that we are comprised of layers of energy. It is based on the idea that disease doesn't start in the body, that's where it ends up. Energy healing works with the immune system that extends well beyond the physical body. If this is something you wish to explore, ask around for a good practitioner or call the office of the International Society of Subtle Energy and Energy Medicine (ISSSEEM) and ask them if they can refer someone to you in your region (See the Appendix.)

9. **Physical exercise is part of living a balanced life.** The regular secretion of the stress hormone, cortisol, is known to destroy white blood cells. Exercise utilizes cortisol, as well as other stress hormones such as epinephrine, nor epinephrine, thyroxin, and aldosterone, thus helping to keep the body's physiology in balance. Research shows that lack of exercise tips the hormonal scale out of favor of an enhanced immune system. Regular rhythmical exercise (brisk walking) for as little as twenty minutes a day, helps restore this balance.

10. **Get adequate amounts of sunlight, full spectrum sunlight** (about twenty minutes per day). Light is an essential nutrient. Today most people don't get an adequate supply of full spectrum lighting. You don't need much, but you do need some, every day if possible.

11. **Drink chemically free water.** Tap water has lots of chemicals including chlorine and fluoride. Although they are used to keep water clean, they are not without problems. Filtered water is great, but it may filter out minerals, so be sure these are replenished. Bottled water is good, but there are no FDA regulations on bottled water, so ask lots

of questions at the health food store. Drink plenty of good water as this helps aid the detoxification process of your body.

12. **There are many herbs that are good for healing.** Try to find a good source on herbal therapies. Several herbs help boost the immune system including echinacia, goldenseal, and astragulus, however there are caveats with each one (for example, echinacia should be taken for short periods of time, not every day). Also, taking milk thistle to help cleanse the liver is a good idea. If you are on antibiotics, you may want to ingest some acidopholus (good intestinal bacteria), which is killed off in the small intestine through the use of antibiotics. This can lead to candida and again this will compromise the immune system. For more information you can buy a good reference book, or try calling the Herb Research Foundation (See the Appendix.).

13. **Try to keep your sleep, eating and exercise habits on a regular schedule.** The body responds well to a healthy 24 hour cycle, such as meals at regular scheduled times, or always going to bed by 10:00 p.m.

14. **Allocate about ten to twenty minutes per day to some type of relaxation technique.** In this time, allow yourself quiet time to relax and do absolutely nothing.

Emotional Well-being

1. Creative Anger Management: There is a large aspect of grieving in the healing process and the initial stages of grieving involve anger. Not feeling anger may prolong the grieving process, thereby making one less emotionally healthy. First, realize that it is OK to be angry. Anger is a healthy emotion, however it is most healthy in very small amounts. Suppressed anger can suppress the immune system and hence become toxic to the body. Venting anger is considered good when it is vented toward the aggressor, however, sometimes just yelling at the sky helps. Set aside some time each day, to feel and creatively release your anger. A good book on anger management is Harriet Lerner's book, *The Dance of Anger*. Anger is also related to fear. If you are not feeling any sense of anger, check your fear barometer. Talking, writing and acting out feelings of fear act as a catharsis to relieve the accumulation of these toxic feelings.

2. Music Therapy: The body has a natural rhythm of about 7.8 hertz (cycles per second). Healthy musical rhythms are said to entrain the body to a homeostatic level of 7.8 hertz. Not all music does this. Classical music is said to, some new age, some (slow) jazz. Music with lyrics typically does not. Dolphin and whale music is said to be at 7.8 hertz, which is why you will find these types of sounds, mixed with relaxing nature sound tracks. The bottom line is to find acoustic music you like to relax to and let it do its thing. Music therapy can most certainly have an effect on your emotions, which is why personal preference is so important. Listening to music to relax is a great way to promote healing, but mixing your own tape of "healing, upbeat" music works as well. This can be played in the car while driving or anywhere. Good sources of relaxing music (without lyrics) include Kay Gardner and Steven Halpern and can be found in your local music store, or have them special order it. There is a lot of great music out there. Go explore and have fun.

On another note, when you turn the stereo up, turn the television off (due to the proliferation of negative newscasts). Andy Weil, M.D. recommends a news fast. I think this is an excellent idea. If there is something really important going on, trust you will hear about it. Television has an addictive quality to it. Try to wean yourself off it periodically.

3. Humor Therapy: Laughter is good medicine. Try building a humor library! Put out the search for funny audiotapes, books, movies, and videos. Anything that will increase your humor quotient to a minimum of 20 laughs per day. Expand your humor venues beyond television. Making a tickler notebook is a good idea as well. Start collecting comics, photos, cards, poems, letters—anything that lifts your spirits. There is also a wonderful humor conference put on by Joel Goodman's The Humor Project. See the Appendix.

Mental Well-being

1. Mental Imagery & Visualization (healing images): Mental imagery and visualization are mental training techniques to use the power of the mind to heal. Years of research suggest that it is best for the individual to come up with a healing image rather than a therapist or counselor to suggest one. This way the image you come up with is unique to you and for this reason, the most powerful. Susan used an image of her chemo drugs acting like gardeners who were helping her. Using mental imagery to aid drugs, radiation, and surgery is a wonderful idea.

Mental imagery can be done along with positive affirmations (see below) or it can be done while meditating. It can also be done several times in the course of a day, a simple constant reminder to have your conscious and unconscious minds working together rather than in opposition to each other that is often the case.

Visualization is best described as a conscious choice with intention, whereas imagery can be defined as a spontaneous flow of thought originating from the unconscious mind toward consciousness. Pick an image which you find to be relaxing or healing and using the imagination of your five senses make the image as real and powerful as possible. The possible images for healing and relaxation are limitless.

2. Positive Affirmations: Think of a word or a phrase you can repeat to yourself many times a day. Some people even suggest writing it down 15 times a day. Make it a simple phrase, and begin with the words I AM....

A positive affirmation statement should be positive, (e.g. I am healthy, rather than I am not going to die as this is interpreted unconsciously as "I am going to die"). And a positive affirmation statement should be stated in the present tense.

3. Art Therapy: The purpose of art therapy is to let the unconscious mind speak to the conscious mind while you're awake (as opposed to i.e., a dream state). The unconscious mind uses the language of colors, shapes, and symbols. Everything you draw on paper has meaning. Even if you drop the crayon and it makes a mark, this has some meaning, which hopefully will be revealed to you. It doesn't matter what your drawing ability is, whether it is at the third grade level or that of Michaelagelo. It makes no difference!

Once you get a box of crayons or pastels and a pad of large paper, draw an image of your illness, what it seems like to you. Your image can be either symbolic or representational. For example, a cancerous tumor can be drawn like Casper the friendly Ghost or like an actual cancerous tumor. White blood cells can appear like angles, white sharks, space ships or white blood cells with a nucleus and cell membrane. Let your mind speak to you as to how to draw the image. There are no wrong images.

After you draw the first image of how things are and how you feel, next, draw an image of how you wish to be—the end result of your cancer. Drawing this image sends a strong message to your unconscious mind of your intention to orchestrate your health in this direction. Post the second picture on the fridge, bathroom mirror or some place you can see it often, like every day, as a reminder of your optimal health goal.

4. Treasure Map: This is a fun exercise. Pull out about 10-20 magazines on a host of different topics. Next, get a large piece of paper (oak tag or newsprint), a pair of scissors, and a glue stick. Then start gazing through the collection of magazines looking for images, photographs and words of healing image (e.g. organic vegetables, a flower garden, joggers on a beach, etc.). If you don't see specific words, then cut out letters or print a word, phrase or poem from a computer file.

By collecting and arranging an assortment of images, photos and words you begin to work with the unconscious mind as well as the conscious mind to move in the direction of optimal health. The unconscious mind speaks a language rich in color, symbols and images. When you are done, place your treasure map in a place where you can see it every day, often. The treasure map acts like a compass to guide your mind and you to inner peace.

Spiritual Well-being

1. Prayer & Meditation: Regular conversations with God, however you conceive him/her/it to be are always good. Talk to God. If you must, yell at God, ask questions. Make demands. Make specific demands. In her book, *A Book of Angels*, Sophy Burnham describes the steps on how to pray. These steps are identical as those suggested for mental imagery and guided visualization. They include:

1. Honor the present moment: Speak in the present tense.

2. Accentuate the positive: Speak in a positive (not negative) light.

3. Send a clear transmission: focus and concentrate on your intentions.

4. Detach from the outcome.

5. Practice an attitude of gratitude. Give thanks.

Meditation is a means to clear the mind. A clear mind promotes a clear body, as the two are really one. Take some time each day, as little as 5 minutes, to sit quietly with no interruptions. Allow the thoughts and feelings that come to mind to leave with each exhalation.

2. Journaling: Journaling is a great way to get thoughts and feelings down on paper. It can be very cathartic, and this alone is quite healthy. It is also a great way to do some soul searching—the search for meaning and purpose. Start by getting a notebook dedicated just for this technique and make it confidential (for your eyes only). If a blank piece of paper is too overwhelming, try picking up a book on journal writing. There are many good books and hundreds of themes on which to write. Knowing the importance of stories, perhaps one journal theme to start with is to write your own story.

3. Connections to Nature: A walk in the woods, an hour in a garden or a seat on the beach serve as great ways to cleanse and renew the spirit. Becoming in touch with the seasons, the cycles of the moon, the oceanic tides, the migration patterns of regional birds, the names of trees; these are all part of our connection to nature. By getting out in nature, away from the hectic rush of life (the voice mail, e-mail, pagers, photocopiers, radio and television) we begin to resonate with the healing energies of the planet and in turn, bring our mind-body-spirit back to a greater state of homeostasis.

4. Support Groups: Make a list of your friends and family. Who on this list is available to sit and talk, to be there when you need someone to listen? If your list is short or skimpy, find a local support group of people with a similar background (gardeners, cancer patients, single parents, mystery books afficionados, bungee cord jumpers). If there appears to be no group, start one and meet at least once a month.

5. Practice Forgiveness: Holistic healing means coming to a sense of inner peace. Forgiving those who we feel have done us wrong. Forgiveness also means forgiving ourselves for whatever injustices we may have done to our friends, family, acquaintances and neighbors. The word remission has several meanings, one is forgiveness. It's something to think about.

As Susan soon found out, doing all these things is nothing less than a full time job, and many behavioral changes done at once can lead to severe rebound effect. So try to modify your health behaviors accordingly. The best definition of optimal wellness I have come across is the following: Optimal wellness is the integration, balance and harmony of mind, body, spirit and emotions. A good healing program honors the concept that the whole is greater than the sum of the parts, with healing coming to a greater sense of inner peace, not necessarily alleviating or reducing the symptoms of disease or illness. Ultimately, a holistic approach to healing is one where you take responsibility for your healing process, rather than give your power away to a medical staff or holistic care practitioners.

On a Saturday morning several weeks later the phone rang again. It was Susan.

"I want to give you a progress report," she said, calmly. "First, I'm feeling much better. Second, the affirmations have helped a lot. Third, I have cut out all processed foods, transfatty acids, MSG, Aspartame, and I'm taking loads of anti-oxidants—I feel great! My support group is wonderful! I stopped using the microwave. I've started regular acupuncture sessions, and I go for long walks in the woods and talk with God. If the weather is bad, I sit in my room and pray."

"Let me tell you about my visualizations," she exclaimed with joy. "I am on two drugs, Cytoxin and Andromyosin. This may sound crazy, but I have assigned a cute old man to the first and woman, his wife to the second; Uncle Cy and Aunt Andri. They are gardeners and they help me by going through my body and weeding out the bad cells, so the flowers and fruits can grow and bloom. Everyday, several times a day, actually, I say hi to Uncle and Aunt, knowing full well they are busy at work and doing a great job. I feel great!"

"I made some goals, too. I've scheduled a trip to Europe about three months after the bone marrow transplant. I have always wanted to go to Europe! My doctor said it was OK. Say, what do you know about Italy and France? Ever been? "

When Norman Cousins rebounded, with the use of humor therapy, from a life-threatening disease, his premise of holistic healing was that each person must take responsibility for his or her own health. Susan has done just that and her example reminds us to do the same.

9. Huge Footprints?

It's summer time as I write this. A blistering heat wave covers the entire continent. The thought occurred to me as I jogged early this morning (to avoid the desert-like heat) that this weather could serve no better advertisement for Al Gore's movie, *An Inconvenient Truth*. Global warming is here. Some say here to stay. News reports suggest that we should start getting used to prolonged heat waves each summer hence. As an avid skier, I dread to think what this will do to our beloved ski seasons, although I think I have a pretty good idea (sigh). I'm lucky. I live at 5,000 feet above sea level. I know a lot of people who will be owning beachfront property on either coast very soon, if this keeps up.

I loved Al Gore's film and like movie critic Roger Ebert, I too, feel that every American owes it to himself or herself to see this movie! If you haven't seen it, consider renting it at your nearest video outlet. Global warming is not a theory, it's a fact. It's no longer about our grandchildren or children. It's about us. I don't say this to alarm you. Fear is not a positive motivating factor for change. Having said this, the time to act is now. To repeat a phrase I often use in presentations: "To know and not to do, is not to know." We can no longer act ignorant about this issue. While it's true that humans are not the sole cause of global warming (the earth has natural cycles) it is totally ignorant to think that our industrial lifestyle has had no direct effect on the planet. In the words of Chief Seattle, "Man did not weave the web of life he is merely a strand in it."

I feel compelled to write about sustainability in this new edition because I come across so many people at various conferences and workshops that have that glazed-over look when they hear this word "sustainability." I am urged to write about this topic here (and any chance I get) because the environment is one issue I feel compelled to champion. In simple terms, if we don't do something about this now, we only have ourselves to blame. It's time to rise to the occasion and put the earth back in balance. Sustainability isn't just good for the environment; it's a philosophy that underlines the basis of good stress management skills.

Sustainability means living a simple life, taking only what you need for resources and giving back to the earth whatever you can to maintain a sense of balance. Sustainability means recycling whatever items can be recycled, from glass bottles and newspapers to car tires and cardboard boxes. Sustainability means walking, carpooling, or riding a bike rather than driving a car all over town. It means conserving energy rather than wasting it. Sustainability means conserving all resources, including water and food, rather than wasting these as well. Sustainability means living consciously in harmony with the earth rather unconsciously toward reckless abandon.

Perhaps we cannot be perfect in every action toward sustainability, but we can certainly shift our consciousness in that direction. I recall sitting down to lunch with Jane Goodall in the spring of 2004 as we formulated plans for a fundraising event for her organization to save wildlife habitat for the chimps of Gombe. Sitting and talking with her about global warming and sustainability had a huge impact on me. As if inspired by a bodhisattva, for the next several months and well beyond that, I found myself running every thought, every action and behavior through the filter of planetary sustainability. It's a whole different mindset than "the keeping up with the Jones" mentality. My goal is to leave as small a footprint as possible on the planet earth. Right now, Americans have pretty big footprints. Huge Footprints. Sasquatch size footprints. King Kong size foot prints. OK, you get the idea.

So here is my question to you: How big a footprint do you leave on the planet? For a country that contains a fraction of the world's population, we consume over 25% of the worlds natural resources. This is irresponsible. SUV's! Closets overflowing with clothes! McMansions! The impact we have on the planet comes in many ways. Perhaps the biggest way is by purchasing an abundance of consumer products that provide a quick fix for a long-term addiction to stuff! Americans are notorious for attempting to fill the spiritual void (in vain) with consumer goods. I think we are all guilty of this. The next time you pull out your wallet or credit card, ask yourself do you REALLY need this item? Sustainability isn't a guilt trip. It's a philosophy of life. To see ourselves as part of the natural world, not separate or detached from it. Please join me in adopting this philosophy.

Walking out of Al Gore's movie I noted a take home poster describing things we could do to help. Like a kid who needs to be told repeatedly to pick up his or her room, we need to be reminded of these daily chores. This is what the list said:

1. Replace a regular light bulb with a compact energy efficient fluorescent light bulb

2. Drive less! Walk, ride, carpool, use mass transit.

3. Recycle more! (ideally all household waste)

4. Check your tires (keep car tires properly inflated to save on gas)

5. Use less hot water. Consider installing a low flow shower-head

6. Avoid products with lots of packaging

7. Adjust your thermostat by 2-5 degrees

8. Plant a tree to absorb carbon dioxide

9. Be part of the solution. Learn to get involved with www.climatecrises.net

10. Use less water for your lawn. Consider xeriscape plants

11. Consider using a re-usable shopping bag when grocery shopping.

Driving through town one day I saw a bumper sticker that made me laugh: Clean Up the Earth, It's not Uranus. Yup! Pluto has been demoted, downsized in the solar system and Earth is on the list for home improvements. You can help, and in doing so, help yourself as well.

In the words of Mohandas Gandhi, "There is a sufficiency in the world for man's need but not for man's greed." And here is one final note: Save the earth, it's the only planet with chocolate.

10. The Remarkable Story of Garret Porter

PATRICIA NORRIS IS A RARE NATIONAL TREASURE in the field of health promotion. Long before the field of mind-body-spirit healing was given the name, Psychoneuroimmunology (PNI), Pat, a psychologist working at the Menniger Clinic in Topeka, Kansas, was engaged in the integration of mind, body, spirit, and emotions in the successful effort to promote healing in people with chronic diseases.

Pat comes from a family of scientists and practitioners in the allied health fields. Her mother Alyce and stepfather, Elmer Green pioneered the work of biofeedback, making it a household word. Their explorations into human consciousness laid the groundwork for what is now known as PNI. "Growing up under the roof of two very curious-minded parents," Pat explains, "the concepts that influenced my childhood had much to do with mind-body unity."

She became fascinated with the research her parents were conducting on yogis from India who had what appeared to be uncanny control of various body functions, including heart rate, ventilation, blood pressure, blood flow, and temperature regulation. Some could breath less than once a minute—comfortably. Others could shift all the blood in their body to the right side, leaving the left stone cold. This wasn't magic; it was incredible mind/body control. Western science was of the opinion that this aspect of human physiology was autonomic and that human thought had little or no influence over it. As her parents came to learn, the mind is not separate from the body; rather, it works in unison with it. Self-regulation is the term Pat likes to use when describing the mind-body link.

I first met Pat at a biofeedback conference in Colorado Springs in 1990. It was there I heard her tell the remarkable story of Garrett Porter.

In July of 1978, at the age of nine, Garrett was diagnosed with an inoperable malignant brain tumor, an astrocytoma located in the right hemisphere of his brain. Although radiation was used, it appeared to be ineffective as the cancerous tumor grew. The doctors gave Garrett less than a year to live. But Garrett refused to believe his death sentence. Never once did Garrett choose anything but life. In an attempt to seek help, his parents sought the assistance of someone who understood the mind-body connection. Their trail led them to the door of Dr. Patricia Norris.

Pat met with Garret and the two formed a bond of everlasting friendship. As her first cancer patient, Garret was exposed to several different mind-body techniques. It was Pat's intention to create a program for Garrett similar to that designed by fellow colleague, Carl Simonton. Garrett's weekly sessions consisted of a specially designed relaxation tape, mental imagery and visualization, some art therapy and biofeedback. In only a matter of days, Pat knew she had someone special in her midst, a little boy with a tremendous imagination and an incredible will to live.

One day, while doing a session of art therapy, Garrett drew his tumor as Planet Meatball and several white blood cells in the shape of Pacman ready to devour it. Each white blood cell had a squiggly line. When Pat asked Garrett what that represented, he answered, "Aw, gee, Dr. Norris, don't you know, those are antennas, that's how they talk to each other." It would be a few years later before neurophysiologist Candace Pert would discover the mind-body link is created through neuropeptides and a vibration, which acts like an antenna for various cells to communicate to each other.

In October of 1979, Garrett informed his father one night that he couldn't visualize his tumor. Garrett could only conclude it was gone. All he could see in his visualization was a tiny white dot where the tumor had been. It would be a matter of months before a CAT scan could prove what Garret knew. In February of 1980, clinical tests revealed no cancerous tumor (the doctor assumed Garret had undergone surgery). In its place was a small calcium deposit—the small white dot Garrett viewed in his visualization. Indeed, the tumor was gone.

For some, those who see, believe. For others, those who believe, see.

11. The Breath of Life

APPROACHES TO MANAGING STRESS ARE AS VARIED as the people who use them. Perhaps because of the complexity of human nature and the daily events we find ourselves in, it is fair to say that no two people will deal with stress the same way. Yet if there were one relaxation technique that could be described as "one size fits all," belly breathing would win hands down. The long deep sigh, the epitome of taking a moment to relax is really what belly breathing is all about. Unlike most techniques, it can be done anywhere, at any time, and no one is the wiser.

Breathing is easy, and we pretty much take it for granted because it doesn't require a whole lot of thought. But by and large, Americans are chest breathers (whether you are a man or a woman, I guess it looks good to have a big chest.) The problem with chest breathing is that it places pressure on a bundle of nerves under the chest bone and can actually trigger the stress response. Of course, when we sleep, the ego is off duty and we revert back to belly breathing—the style most conducive for relaxation.

Ancient mystics tell us that the word breath and spirit are synonymous, suggesting that divine energy is found within the precious movements of inhalation and exhalation. As such, the breath of life is no mere metaphor. Interestingly enough, every technique to promote relaxation employs some aspect of breathing and this is the technique I begin each class with. A wise sage once said, "There are forty different ways to breath." Here are two styles I use in class:

1. Breathing Clouds:
This technique can be traced back to the origins of the eastern philosophy and religion in both Asia, with the practice of yoga, and Japan with the practice of Zen meditation. It was introduced as a cleansing process for the mind and body, the end result being complete relaxation. You can do this technique either sitting or laying down.

To begin, close your eyes and focus all your attention on your breathing. Focus your attention to draw air from the belly. Try inhaling through your nose and exhaling through your mouth. Visualize the air that you breath in as being clean fresh air, pure and energized air, like a white puffy cloud.

As you breath in this clean pure air, visualize and feel air enter your nose and circulate up through the sinus cavity, to the top of your head, and down the back of your spinal column. As you end the inhalation, image the air circulating throughout your entire body.

Now, as you exhale, visualize that the air leaving your body is dirty hazy air, which symbolizes all your stressors, frustrations, and toxins throughout your mind and body. With each breath you take, allow the clean fresh air to enter and circulate and invigorate your body, while the expulsion of the dirty air helps rid your body of its stress and tension.

Repeat this breathing cycle for five to ten minutes. As you repeat this cycle of breathing clouds, you may notice as the body becomes more relaxed through the release of stress and tension that the visual color of the air exhaled begins to change from black, to gray, perhaps even an off-white, a symbolic vision of complete relaxation.

2. Energy Breathing

Energy breathing is a way to vitalize your body, not only by taking in air through your nose or mouth, but in effect, breathing through your whole body as well. In essence, your body becomes like a big lung taking in air and circulating it throughout your entire body.

There are three phases of this exercise and you can do this technique either sitting or laying down. First get comfortable allowing your shoulders to relax. If you choose to sit, try to keep your legs straight. Now, as you breath in, imagine that there is a circular hole at the top (crown) of your head, like a dolphin. As the air enters your lungs, visualize energy in the form of a beam of light, entering the top of your head. Bring the energy down, from the crown of your head to your abdomen as you inhale. As you exhale, allow the energy to leave through the top of your head. Repeat this five to ten times, trying to coordinate your breathing with the visual flow of energy. As you continue to bring the energy down to your stomach area, allow the light to reach all the inner parts of your upper body. When you feel comfortable with this first phase, you are ready to move on to the second phase.

Now, imagine that in the center of each foot, there is a circular hole that energy can flow in and out of. Again think of energy being like a beam of light. Concentrating on only your lower extremities, allow the flow of energy to move up from your feet into your abdomen as you inhale from your diaphragm. Repeat this five to ten times, trying to coordinate your breathing with the flow of energy.

Finally, as you continue to bring the energy up into your stomach area, allow the light to reach all the inner parts of your lower body. Once you feel you have this coordination between your breathing and the visual flow of energy with your lower extremities, begin to combine the movement of energy from both the top of your head and your feet, bringing the energy to the center of your body as you inhale air from your diaphragm. Then, as you exhale, allow the flow of energy to reverse from the direction of which it came. Repeat this for ten to twenty times. Each time you move the energy through your body feel each body region, each muscle and organ and each cell become energized. At first it may seem difficult to visually coordinate the movement of energy coming from opposite ends of your body, but with practice, this will come very easy.

One summer day while grocery shopping, I ran into a former student of mine, Tom, now a lieutenant in the Navy. His conversation reminded me just how useful belly breathing can really be.

"You know, I used to think that all that breathing stuff you taught us in class was a crock," said Tom, with a smile on his face. "But I don't anymore!"

Peering over a pyramid of apples, I inquired, "What changed your mind?"

"It was about a week before graduation, right, and I'm packing to move to Florida with my wife, to start flight school. Did I tell you she was eight months pregnant? OK, so I'm packing these boxes in the basement and Kathy tells me she's started going into labor. Not exactly good timing, know what I mean?"

Tom takes a step closer, grabbing an apple off the pyramid.

"Yup! you could say that my life was beyond the optimal stress point right about then. So here I am rushing to get Kathy to the hospital, but low and behold, we get in the car only to find I have a flat tire. No problem, I tell her. Take a few deep breaths. I'll have this fixed in a jiffy.

"So now we're in the car headed to the hospital and guess what? Another flat tire, except this time I have no spare. I could go off to get help, but I can't leave my wife alone in the car. So you can only guess what happened.

"Man, that breathing stuff really worked. I kept telling her to take a deep breath, keep breathing, slow and deep, from the stomach, it will be all right. I was breathing right along with her. I'm not sure who it helped more, me or her. What an event! So now I'm the proud father of a little baby boy, Jonathan."

"Congratulations," I said, extending my hand.

"Thanks ! You know you always hear about babies being born in the back seat of a car, but I never thought mine would be one of them. And now, I'm doing that belly breathing technique every day."

*It is said that the soul enters the body with the first breath
and each breath after invigorates the spirit.
Remember to breath—from the belly!*

12. Animals With Souls

THERE ARE THOSE PEOPLE WHO BELIEVE THAT THE SOUL is a divine gift reserved only for humans; all other living things function at the level of basic instinct. The famous theologian Thomas Aquinas believed this. Of course he also said that only men, not women, have souls. Every woman I know would take issue with this. Perhaps given the chance, animals would too.

Souls or not, there is something very calming about having a pet around. Current research reveals that pet owners typically have lower resting heart rates, lower resting blood pressure, quicker recovery time when ill, and, for the most part, are just basically healthier than non-pet owners. In looking for answers to explain the phenomena, researchers suggest that it is the pet owner's ability to express love, which may be the significant factor in pet therapy. No hypothesis suggests that animals may themselves play an active role. That might presume that animals could think and even quite possibly have souls themselves. Perhaps they do!

It is a well-known fact that dogs seem to know when their owners are about to come home. Perhaps you've seen a dog sit patiently by the door ready to greet their master the moment he or she walks in the house. (By the way, it's thought that cats also are aware of their masters, they just don't care.) This fact sparked the attention and intrigue of several people, including British scientist Rupert Sheldrake.

Sheldrake designed a study to see if dogs really knew when their owners were coming home. The data apparently defies Western thought. With a split-timed video screen monitor, one camera on a dog at home with the owner's parents, the other on the owner an hour away, it was shown that the moment the owner made the conscious decision to return home and indeed did so, the dog got up off the floor and sat patiently by the door, awaiting the arrival of his owner. This was replicated several times with several different dogs and their respective owners. Equally interesting are the anecdotal stories of cats and dogs who have been known to travel hundreds (some thousands) of miles of unfamiliar territory in France, Australia, Canada, and the United States to be reunited with their owners.

So how do pets know? Perhaps animals have a divine connection that we are simply unaware of, which manifests at times when we need to see it.

When it comes to animal heroics, there is no shortage of good Samaritans. From dogs and cats to horses, canaries and dolphins, the animal kingdom is rich with compassion. One of my favorite stories involves a little boy named George who stayed too late at the local public library one night reading books on basketball. When he walked out the door to leave, it was dark. George knew his way home, he had traveled this route hundreds of times. On this night, though, as he passed the cathedral church on North 10th street, the hair raised on the back of his neck. His intuition sensed danger. Sure enough he was being followed.

George purposely crossed the street and tried to thwart the advances of this stranger, but he couldn't shake him off his trail. Several blocks from the library with less than a mile to go, George suddenly noticed a large dog walking at his heels, as if guarding him from danger. After a few blocks, the man was nowhere to be seen. As George opened the gate to his yard, he reached his arm out to pet the dog on the head. Once inside he begged his mother to come and look at his new companion. But having accomplished its mission, the dog was nowhere to be seen.

Pets have a lot to offer (and perhaps teach) in terms of sharing joy, love, and relaxation. If you are looking for a reason to adopt a pet, keep this in mind.

13. Going For The Gold

IN THE DOOR FRAME OF MY OFFICE stood a tall daunting muscular man about twenty years old. From the dimly lit desk lamp, all I could see was a rather large silhouette. Not until he spoke did I recognize the voice. It was one of my advisees, Pedro, a transfer student from Spain.

"Do you have a minute?" he asked in quiet voice.

"Sure, come on in," I said, as I got up to greet him.

By nature, Pedro was a happy-go-lucky fellow. Perhaps because of his European culture, he was more mature than most of his American contemporaries. Although his English was excellent, his Spanish accent was undeniable. And with his ever-present smile, framed by a groomed beard, he was a unique fixture on campus.

Closing the door to my office, Pedro asked to sit down. I could tell by his manner that he was quite upset by something. "Can I trust you? I am about to tell you something that no one else knows. If you tell anyone, I will...."

Shades of *The Princess Bride* came forth to my consciousness as I heard one of the movie's most famous lines: "My name is Inigo Montoya. You killed my father. Prepare to die!"

"You cannot tell anyone!" Pedro said.

"OK, Pedro. I promise," I replied with my most serious tone. "What is the problem?"

He pulled a sketch from his coat pocket and unfolded it. There lay a diagram of the Sanskrit chakras placed over an illustration of the anatomical male. "Do you know what these are?" he inquired.

"Yes, they are chakras, the major energy centers of the body, part of the human energy field, " I said casually. This was a topic I had begun to introduce as a theory to my students regarding the not-yet-understood model of stress and disease. The word *chakra*, a Sanskrit term for spinning wheel, is not common to the American vernacular. I was impressed Pedro knew of this.

"Good!" Pedro said, slapping his hand on my desk. "Now we begin. I explain everything."

The story Pedro explained was none like I had ever heard before, certainly nothing that can be explained scientifically.

Pedro won the bronze medal in the 400 meter Butterfly in Seoul, Korea in 1988. The victory took several teams by surprise including the Americans, but not Pedro. His determination was as strong as his movements in the water. Now with a bronze medal under his belt, he set his sights on the gold. As a common course of events with Olympic athletes, Pedro relocated to the United States to train with a new coach. Within a few months time, Pedro began having some serious health problems—heart palpitations, blood in the urine, muscle aches, and an overwhelming sense of fatigue. Pedro took every clinical test available. Each result came back negative. Doctors threw up their hands in defeat, not knowing what to make of his situation. Yet the symptoms continued for well over four months.

One day Pedro's mother had called from Madrid. It appears that she had just come from the grocery store where she overheard a conversation in the produce section. One of the two women speaking was the wife of Pedro's former swim coach. The wife confided to her friend that she placed a spell on Pedro to make him ill. It was his fate for abandoning his coach, the coach that won him an Olympic medal. Pedro's mom gave him specific instructions: Find someone who understands these spiritual matters and have them help you. That afternoon, Pedro appeared at my door.

It was not uncommon to have people from all walks of life come to my office and inquire about matters of human spirituality and health, aspects which Western science has yet to understand and quite often dismissed as nonsense. I had acquired a national reputation for creating a model of human spirituality with regards to relationships, values, and a meaningful purpose in life. Not all of human spirituality, however was so neatly packaged as such. On campus, I had a reputation as well, if nothing more, at least to listen to people as they explained everything from near death experiences and past life regressions to alien abductions. This, however, was the first time I had ever heard about witchcraft, a practice I was to learn was not uncommon in Spain. While Pedro's condition was not fatal, there was no telling how serious the events could turn. So far, the spell had done its work. At the rate of deterioration, Pedro would never make it to the next Olympics, let alone win a gold medal.

With the look of a lost tourist, Pedro said, "So, can you help me?"

"To be quite honest," I said, "this is out of my league." (Boy, was that an understatement!) Before I could continue, Pedro lowered his head in despair. "But, I know someone who can."

119

"Really? Who?" Pedro said, bouncing back to life.

As it turned out, I had just finished taking a yearlong course in bio-energy medicine with a world-renowned healer named Mietek Wirkus in Bethesda, Maryland. A Polish emigrant to the United States, Mietek has the ability to see chakras, auras, and disease states in the human energy field. Better than a CAT Scan, his accuracy rate is about 95 percent. Using a technique he calls bio-energy, Mietek works to clear the distortions in the energy field, bringing the body back to a sense of balance and wholeness. In one aspect, bio-energy would be no different than Western medicine if there wasn't the responsibility on the part of the client to do some internal work too. For the client, meditation, visualization, and prayer constitute the dynamics of bio-energy as well.

At first Pedro's situation seemed unique, if not bizarre. But as I mulled it over, I realized that at some level, it was no different than any other. We all encounter some aspect of darkness or fear, whether our own or others. Perhaps distilled fear is best labeled as "evil." Every time, it is fear which we must learn to overcome—with love. Sometimes we can do it ourselves, sometimes we need the help of others. Always with God's grace.

I called Mietek's office, talked to his secretary, and made an appointment. Mietek took him right away. Mietek never mentioned an evil spell. In his terminology, there are only disturbances and congestions in the human energy field. This is what he worked on with Pedro. After two sessions of bio-energy, Pedro's symptoms disappeared, never to return again. Within weeks he was back to his arduous training routine.

"Let me teach you some Spanish," he said one afternoon outside my office. "I'm gonna teach you how to say, gold medal. Repeat after me, 'Medalla dé oro.'"

Fear, even in its worst form, evil, can be dealt with and reconciled over time. We must take the first step toward decreasing the toxic effects of distilled fear. And there is strength in numbers, for there are always those who can help us.

Working the Funny Bone

HAVE YOU EVER FOUND YOURSELF SAYING, right after hell breaks loose, "A year from now, this *might* be funny, but right now, it's not funny!" I say, why wait a whole year to laugh?

Spiritual muscles attach to spiritual bones, and let there be no doubt, the funny bone is a crucial one! Ask anyone who has undergone a personal crisis and most likely they will tell you at some point, a ray of humor, from a quantum sliver to a Disney rainbow, appeared. Perhaps it's no surprise to learn that many Nazi concentration camp survivors and Vietnam POWs each cited humor as a critical component of their path to freedom. We would be wise to follow their lead, regardless of our situation, whether it be a flat tire, a game of phone tag, locking your keys in your car, or having your child accidentally flush your wallet down the toilet. How about traffic jams? We could all use a good laugh then. The following stories are reminders of what we already know, that humor is essential to deal with stress.

Freud called humor a defense mechanism for the ego. Others refer to comic relief as "the grand coping technique." Regardless of what you call it, you get more bang for your buck when you crack a smile in the face of adversity. And besides, just think, at the very end, how many new pearly gate jokes St. Peter will tell you before you walk in to collect your wings.

"So there were these two poets at the gates of heaven and St. Peter says, "Hi guys. Sorry, but right now, we only have one vacancy. The one with the best poem gets in…. And you have to use the word TIMBUKTU."

1. Laughter Is the Best Medicine

To SEE THE TWINKLE IN HER EYES and the genuine smile that graces her face, you would never know that Donna was a recovering cocaine addict, an addiction that nearly killed her. The twinkle and smile reveal what the mask of cocaine hid for years. As faculty members of the University of Colorado's Center for Human Caring, we met for lunch one day and discussed how humor had been our saving grace in times of trouble.

Humor comes to us from the word fluid or moisture. "Humor is about having a fluid spirit," explains Donna, and she would know, because humor therapy has become her calling.

Right up front, Donna will tell you she is an over-achiever. By the age of nineteen, she had earned a bachelor's degree in nursing. By the age of twenty she had received her master's degree. Perhaps it was an attempt to please her parents. Perhaps it was an attempt to fill a void, but whatever Donna did, she excelled at—exceptionally well. But the road to success was not without its potholes. During her junior year in college, she began to take speed, which then led to alcohol, which in turn led to cocaine—a downward spiral toward the edge of death.

"Back when I was in school, you could get a doctor's prescription for amphetamines. A lot of people took these to lose weight. I took them so I could stay up late and study." As Donna describes it, where there is speed to bring you up, there is alcohol to bring you down, and soon she found herself becoming dependent on both substances to achieve a false sense of balance in her life. By twenty-three, Donna was married and her professional career in nursing was skyrocketing. However, alcohol became a constant friend and it was soon joined by cocaine as her drug of choice for what she calls the last three years of her eleven-year addiction history.

"Where did I get the cocaine?" she asks with a giggle. "I got it from several of the physicians whom I worked with. You know, one out of every five cocaine addicts is a white collar professional. We're not all street bums." "The first time I used cocaine, I loved it. But what it was doing was filling a void. Cocaine was a magic bullet. It took me away from my childhood pain. It also ruined my life. I knew eventually I was going to die."

Ironically, even though she was a psychiatric nurse working with the chronically mental ill, her colleagues never even suspected she had an addiction problem. "As a rule, health care professionals who are addicts tend to be overachievers. Even on a bad day, we still look pretty good. It never occurred to anyone that I had a drug problem. Everyone loved me and cared for me. My friends and colleagues were enablers. They thought I was depressed because I was going through a divorce, so they helped me by covering for me and doing some of my work. It kept me sick longer."

Donna put up a good front, but eventually the habit began to take its toll. Having spent over a quarter of a million dollars in a three-year period, she looked run down and depressed (she lost thirty pounds, slimming down to ninety pounds), and the quality of her work performance suffered dramatically. As the signs and symptoms of an addiction became more than evident, a friend began to see through the lies and deceptions and one day called her on the carpet. Sensing she was suicidal and ready to die, her friend called Donna's parents in a successful attempt to get her some help. Almost by force, Donna quit her job and entered a thirty-day treatment program. It was a very long road to recovery. From the month-long treatment program, she entered a half-way house for three months (a humbling experience, she admits) and then continued as an out-patient for the next nine months, all the while undergoing psychoanalysis treatment and attending Alcoholics Anonymous and Cocaine Anonymous meetings, which years later, she still attends regularly.

"It was my sister who taught me the importance of silliness. It was my grandmother who gave me strength, hope, and inspiration." This special alchemy turned to gold in the course of her recovery. "This may sound silly," she said, "but in treatment, we did meditation and visualization. Three times a wizard came to me with a message either on a scroll or in a crystal ball. The message was one word—humor. It was then I knew I needed to pursue the issue of laughter as a means to cope. I needed to learn to lighten up. So I studied with Annette Goodheart, Steve Allen Jr., and Bernie Siegel." With a natural talent to speak in front of a crowd, Donna's future was cast in mirth. Today she is considered an expert in the field of humor therapy, traveling extensively throughout the international community to share the benefits of humor and laughter.

The twinkle in her eyes, the smile on her face and the laugh in her voice say it all.

God gave us humor so we could laugh at ourselves,
and not take ourselves too seriously.

2. You Know You're Having a Bad Day When...

SOMETIMES MAKING LIGHT OF A BAD SITUATION helps take the edge off. That's what humor therapy is all about. When we can separate ourselves from our problems, we can gain a much better perspective of it. Humor can help us get to that perspective much quicker. One of the elements of humor is the art of exaggeration and this technique is used by most every stand-up comic: "My mother-in-law is so frugal, if you look up the word cheapskate in the dictionary, you'll see her picture there."

It seems that by taking things to the extreme, we gain a proper perspective on the truth, especially those embarrassing moments where humor may be the only relief. In several of my workshops, I invite participants to exaggerate what a worst possible day could look like by filling in the blank. It doesn't take long to realize by doing so, their day doesn't look so bad after all. Here are some of their responses: You know you're having a bad day when...

1. More than two cops pull you over for a speeding ticket.

2. Strange lights start flashing on your dashboard, and you know you're not driving Chitty Chitty Bang Bang!

3. You get called into the boss's office and within moments, there are two security guards at the door to escort you.

4. You get a letter from the IRS inviting you to an audit— yours!

5. Your girlfriend says she's pregnant and you've had a vasectomy.

6. The bank calls to tell you they mistakenly credited your checking account with $2500 a few months ago, and they want their money back.

7. You sit down to enjoy a night of television and when you start surfing you see your name and photograph on America's Most Wanted.

8. Your boss catches you after hours sitting on the photocopy machine—butt naked, about to hit the start button.

9. Your son calls asking for money to go to college and to the best of your knowledge, you don't have any children.

10. You get up early, shower, fix breakfast, and head to work only to find out it's Saturday.

11. You go in for your yearly physical exam and your doctor asks if you'd like to be an organ donor.

12. The car you got for graduation turns out to be a lemon rather than a pumpkin.

13. Your wife comes home from work and tells you she's in love, but as she goes into detail, you quickly realize it's not with you.

You know you're having a good day when you can't think of a bad day to compare it to.

3. Test Anxiety

PICTURE THIS. YOU'RE A COLLEGE STUDENT SITTING IN A CLASSROOM taking a midterm or final exam. This is not your only exam this week. Perhaps you even had two this very same day. You're tired and the information you crammed into your brain last night is leaking out uncontrollably with each breath. All you want to do is take this exam, go home, and sleep.

The professor passes out the exam. Tension hangs heavy in the air. You glance at each page. Anxiety sets in as you realize there are things you just don't know. You didn't study this stuff! You go back to the first page and start with what you do know. Part I: Multiple choice, then multiple guess. Done! Now on to Part II: Definition of Terms. Again you do the ones you know first. Then you backtrack and stare at the others in which you remain clueless. An idea strikes you. Put something down—anything. If you don't know the real answer, make one up. If you really don't know, be even more creative. Maybe you'll get points for imagination. Who knows? Give it a try. Don't forget the final essay!

Now picture this. You're a college professor who has just given a midterm or final exam. You drive home with a stack of forty, sixty, perhaps even eighty exams to grade. The initial thought does not excite you. This will wait till the weekend, you think. The weekend comes and you pull out a red pen and start with Part I: Multiple choice. That was easy. Just match the letters (a, b, c, d) with the key. Now comes Part II: Definition of Terms. On the third exam, you break out laughing. You laugh even harder on the fifth exam. Entirely wrong, but creative answers are your salvation for the next few hours.

Einstein once said that imagination is more powerful than knowledge. He must have thought this after grading some college exams. The following are some answers to exam questions by students in moments of creativity, imagination, and desperation that I have collected over the years. The laughter they have engendered has been my saving grace during the long midnight hours of grading exams.

Nutrition, Health and Performance Exam:
Define the following terms with one or two sentences and give an example where appropriate.

#1: Free Radical
Real Answer: An aberrant oxygen molecule associated with disease and the aging processes. Example, transfatty acids.
Student's Answer: A liberated politician, ex: Nelson Mandela (ha ha!)

2: BMR
Real Answer: Basal Metabolic Rate: the number of calories one burns at complete rest in a twenty-four hour period, approximately 2000 calories.
Student's Answer: Bowel Movement Reaction? Boy, could I use one right now to relieve some stress. (I wasn't here that night in class.)

3: Circle of Poison
Real Answer: Illegal pesticides manufactured in the U.S. are sold to other countries, which use them on various produce and sell them back to U.S. markets.
Student's Answer: The food my wife servers me every night for dinner.
Student's Answer: The food court at the local mall!

#4: Peristalsis
Real Answer: A wave-like muscular contraction moving food from the mouth to the rectum.
Student's Answer: I think this is a fatal disease from eating too much junk food.

#5: Echinacea
Real Answer: An herb used to boost the immune system for colds and flu.
Student's Answer: A deadly bacteria second only to the e-boli virus. This should be avoided at all costs!

#6: Healthy Food Guidelines
Real Answer: A list of suggestions to improve eating behaviors. Example: Decrease consumption of saturated fats like cheese and butter.
Student's Answer: Don't eat the yellow snow- FDA(?)

#7: Aspartame
Real Answer: Artificial Sugar substitute found in Nutrasweet.
Student's Answer: Wild Guess: The guy who discovered broccoli?

#8 Homogenization
Real Answer: The process by which fat molecules are equally distributed in milk.
Student's Answer: This is when two lesbians or a gay couple decide to have a baby. Example: My sister and her lover adopted a little boy.

#9: Candida:
Real Answer: A yeast infection in the gastro-intestinal tract, which can lead to cravings of sweets and weight gain.
Student Answer: The country north of the United States (smile!)

Stress Management Exam
Define the following terms with one or two sentences and give an example where appropriate.

#1: Entrainment Theory
Real Answer: The mutual phase locking of like vibrations. Example: music therapy for relaxation.
Student's Answer: This is a typo. It should be Entertainment Theory. Entertainment Theory describes being entertained to relax. Example: the movie, "Scream."

#2: Hardy Personality
Real Answer: A composite of personality traits to make one hardy against the pressures of stress.
Student's Answer: A fictional personality to overcome stress. Example: The Hardy Boys.

#3: Koan
Real Answer: An unsolvable puzzle used in meditation to reach enlightenment. Example: What is the sound of one hand clapping?
Student's Answer: The Ark of the lost covenant. Example: "Indiana Jones."

4: Glucocorticoids

Real Answer: Hormones secreted by the adrenal gland during the fight or flight response.

Student's Answer: A nutritious food supplement for a well balanced diet—high in sugar, low in fat. Example: Twinkie— I eat these all the time (smile!)

#5: Synestasia

Real Answer: An experience in meditation where sensory crossover occurs. Example, one can see sounds and hear colors.

Student's Answer: Isn't Synestasia the hit sequel to the Disney movie, "Anastasia?"

Perhaps Einstein was right; imagination is more powerful than knowledge. It's definitely more amusing.

4. Grace

I AM FREQUENTLY A DINNER GUEST at my good friend Holly's home. She has two adolescent boys, Steven and Shane. Steven is a rebel without a cause; Shane is the embodiment of joy and wonder. They complement each other quite nicely. Since her divorce, Holly has tried to introduce several new rituals to her boys. The one I observed and on several occasions have participated in is the ritual said before the evening meal — grace.

Spiritual, but not religious, Holly purchased the books, *Earth Prayers* and *The Little Zen Book* as the catalyst for this ritual. The tradition begins with selecting a poem from either book. Each person takes a turn. Typically, the boys, ages ten and twelve fight, not to go first, but last, and this too has become part of the ritual.

One night after each of us had read a poem, I asked if we could join hands. Reluctantly, each boy gave Holly and myself a pinkie and I quickly said the word, "Amen."

Without missing a beat, Steven said, "What does amen mean?"

I replied, "It's a way of saying thanks," hoping not to instigate a fight, but it was too late.

"Who are we saying thanks to?" he inquired with angst. "We're not saying thanks to God, because there is no God." With a voice of complete defiance and fork in hand, he yelled, "I don't believe in God!"

Not wishing to start an argument, I refrained from delving into the topic. But it was too late. Steven was just getting started.

"There is no God," he said. With a brazen look that would have stopped the crusades, he continued, "There is a name for this you know." Looking at me dead in the eye, he stated, "My friends call me…" then he paused, "My friends call me,…" and he paused again. Then breaking character, his eyes rolled left up to the ceiling, searching for the word he so desperately wanted. After a moment, he regained his composure, fixed a stare in my direction and said with the utmost confidence, "My friends call me *an amethyst*."

Art Linkletter, quoting a passage from Proverbs, often said, "Out of the mouths of babes, oft times come gems." Children may be the source of stress at times, but they are also a mine for precious gems. Keep an eye and ear open for gems each and every day.

5. The Infamous Tickler Notebook
Makes the Rounds

HUMOR IS INFECTIOUS, LET THERE BE NO DOUBT. When I give presentations I always include a little humor. People seem to crave it. They drink it up like water on a hot, dry day. Living in these fast and furious times in the start of the twenty-first century, everyone needs a respite from the pressures of life. Humor helps bring things back into perspective, if only for a moment. Sometimes that's enough. Humor, it is said, is a welcome distraction to life's problems. In the words of President Lincoln, "If I didn't laugh at my problems, I would cry."

There is a wonderful proverb that says, "To know and not to do, is not to know." Many people know how beneficial humor is, but often forget to apply it in their lives. Perhaps that is why there is so much depression in the world today. We haven't reached our daily quota of fifteen laughs per day. Consequently, our scale of emotions is weighted heavily to one side with what are known as the negative emotions: Anger and fear. Humor is just the antidote to balance this scale, but knowing this fact is not enough. We have to do! We have to seek out mirth and engage in life with a smile on our face and a chuckle in our heart.

Enter the tickler notebook project: a collection of funny photographs, JPEGS, jokes, Quicktime movies, Dear Abby Letters, Dave Barry columns, birthday cards — anything and everything to warm their heart and bring a smile to your face. I first assigned this project to my undergraduate students at the American University, but today when I give presentations, I give out this homework assignment as a humor Rx to everyone: corporate executives, physicians, nurses, school teachers—anyone within earshot. That is how important humor is in our lives. No one escapes being given this homework assignment.

I'll never forget the first person outside of a typical class setting who asked me to grade her tickler notebook assignment. I was invited to be a dinner speaker for an event in Colorado Springs. The topic of my presentation was The Healing Power of Humor. Everyone seemed to like my talk. They laughed at all my jokes and gave a thunderous applause at the end. As I autographed books in the back of the room after my talk, a woman in a yellow wheel chair approached me and yelled, "Your talk wasn't funny." She then wheeled away out the door in a huff.

A year later I encountered the same woman at a conference. I recognized both her and her yellow wheelchair. She approached me with a huge smile on her face. In her hands was a beautiful gilded page book, her tickler notebook. "If you have a moment I would love to see what you think, and if you are willing, I would like a grade, too. You see, I used to be a curmudgeon. I have fibromyalsia. I saw myself as a victim. But your talk on humor changed my way of thinking. I still have fibromyalsia, but I am not a curmudgeon any more. The tickler notebook has been my salvation. Thank you."

Even my tickler notebook (which grows daily) has made the rounds; a gift of sorts for dear friends who found themselves admitted to a hospital unexpectedly. The first to see my notebook was my friend, Stan. He called me to tell me that he was being operated on for prostate cancer. The day after his surgery, I made a visit to his room. He was glad to see me. I presented him with a copy of the Tickler Notebook and jokingly said that this was his humor Rx. He smiled as I placed the manila envelope containing pages upon pages of jokes on his nightstand. In less than 24 hours I received a voice mail from Stan. "Hey you crazy guy! That packet of jokes was a riot. I nearly popped my stitches laughing so hard."

I also presented a copy of my Tickler Notebook to my next-door neighbor upon learning that he was headed into surgery for a bone marrow transplant as a result of having Hodgkins Lymphoma. I made Steve promise not to read the contents until after the operation. My advice went unheeded, which may have been the best thing. His wife, Candy met me one day as we walked our dogs in the neighborhood. "Oh my God," she said. We have never laughed so hard in our lives. Both Steve and I want to thank you." Did my tickler notebook contribute to Steve's healing process? We may never know for sure, but my intuition tells me it was surely a part of it.

Here are a few of the jokes my editor allowed me to include in this edition of Desserts. My intention in including them here is so you can photocopy them as a kick-start to building your own Tickler Notebook. Enjoy.

Downsizing

A company, feeling it is time for a shakeup, hires a new CEO. This new boss is determined to rid the company of all slackers.

On a tour of the facilities, the CEO notices a guy leaning on a wall. The room is full of workers and he wants to let them know he means business! The CEO walks up to the guy and asks, "And how much money do you make a week?" Undaunted, the young fellow looks at him and replies, "I make $200 a week. Why?"

The CEO hands the guy $1,000 in cash and screams, "Here's a week's pay and benefits, now GET OUT and don't come back!"

Surprisingly, the guy takes the cash with a smile, says "Yes sir! Thank you, sir!" and leaves.

Feeling pretty good about his first firing, the CEO looks around the room and asks, "Does anyone want to tell me what that slacker did here?"

With a sheepish grin, one of the other workers mutters, "Pizza delivery guy from Domino's."

The Good Son

An old man lived alone in Idaho. He wanted to spade his potato garden, but it was very hard work. His only son, Bubba, who always helped him was in prison for armed robbery. The old man wrote a letter to his son and mentioned his predicament:

"Dear Bubba, I'm feeling pretty low because it looks like I won't be able to plant my potato garden this year. I've gotten too old to be digging up a garden plot. If you were here, my troubles would be over. I know you would dig the plot for me. Love, Dad"

A few days later the old man received a letter from his son: "Dear Dad,

For HEAVEN'S SAKE DAD, don't dig up the GARDEN! That's where I buried the GUNS and the MONEY!

Love, Bubba."

At 4:00 am the next morning, a dozen FBI agents and local police officers showed up and dug up the entire area. After finding nothing they apologized to the old man and left. That same afternoon the old man received another letter from his son:

"Dear Dad, Go ahead and plant the potatoes now. It's the best I could do under the circumstances. Love, Bubba."

Final Exam

An eccentric philosophy professor gave a one question final exam after a semester dealing with a broad array of topics. The class was already seated and ready to go when the professor picked up his chair, plopped it on his desk and wrote on the board: "Using everything we have learned this semester, prove that this chair does not exist."

Fingers flew, erasers erased, notebooks were filled in furious fashion.

Some students wrote over 30 pages in one hour attempting to refute the existence of the chair. One member of the class however, was up and finished in less than a minute.

Weeks later when the grades were posted, the rest of the group wondered how the first student to leave could have gotten an A when he had barely written anything at all.

His answer consisted of two words: What chair!

The Lottery Winner

A woman gets home, screeches her car into the driveway, runs into the house, slams the door and shouts at the top of her lungs..."Honey pack your bags. I won the damn lottery."

The husband says "Oh my god!!! No kidding! What should I pack, beach stuff or mountain stuff?"

The wife yells back "It doesn't matter, just get the hell out!!!"

This is the bell curve of life:

At age 4 success is…. not peeing in your pants
At age 12 success is…. having friends
At age 16 success is…. having a driver's license
At age 20 success is…. having sex
At age 30 success is…. having money
At age 50 success is…. having money
At age 60 success is…. having sex
At age 70 success is…. having a driver's license
At age 75 success is…. having friends
At age 80 success is…. not peeing in your pants!

6. Jesus With a Smile

THERE ARE MANY THEORIES THAT TRY TO EXPLAIN THE REASONS why we laugh and giggle, ranging from Plato's superiority theory (laughing at others to make ourselves feel good, such as Dan Quayle jokes), to Freud's release/relief theory (laughter as a sexual release, such as Bill Clinton jokes). Then there are those who insist that humor is simply a gift from God, hence the name, the Divinity Theory. Human spirituality is based on relationships and humor certainly creates a bond between those who laugh together. Humor, it is said, is the shortest distance between two people. The Divinity Theory is alive and well, when you consider the humorous nature of the Dalai Lama, who promotes laughter as a means to cleanse the spirit. A study into indigenous cultures reveals that the role of a healer bears traits similar to those of the American circus clown. Does God have a sense of humor? Most theologians think (and hope) so.

I first came across this idea in a book by Cal Samra, titled *The Joyful Christ: The Healing Power of Humor*. Inside, I found something I had never seen before— illustrations of Jesus actually smiling. To be honest, most depiction's looked more like my college roommates, but nonetheless, I was amused.

Samra and others like him highlight specific references to the mirth and merriment in the New Testament (somehow I must have missed this in church). Whereas it is written that Jesus wept, to my knowledge there is no direct passage citing Jesus having a good belly laugh. However, between the lines are inferences and suppositions leading one to believe such an event must have occurred at sometime in his life. If not in his first thirty-three years, perhaps sometime after...

One person who shares this perspective is Gladys Taylor McGary, M.D., affectionately known as the grandmother of alternative medicine. Raised in India by two American physicians, Gladys was destined to become a physician herself. Perhaps it was the mysticism of the Eastern culture, but Gladys knew there was more to healing than the standard Western medical approach of drugs and surgery. Upset by what she saw as uncompassionate health care, she helped form the American Holistic Medical Association in 1978, an organization founded on the belief that to be healthy, all aspects (mind, body, spirit, and emotions) must be considered in the treatment of each individual.

Gladys will tell you that humor is one of the most important healing agents for optimal well being, even in the face of death. This story is one she shared with me over dinner one evening at the National Wellness conference in Steven's Point, Wisconsin.

"I often tell my patients not to fear death. Death is a transitional stage. It is nothing to be afraid of, I say. One day during my rounds, one of my patients told me this experience," Gladys said with a gleam in her eye.

" 'I was lying on my bed just waiting to die. I prayed and prayed for God to take me. Just then I saw a vision: It was an apparition of Jesus on the cross, as big as life—right in front of me. He opened his eyes and looked at me. I could tell he was suffering. I was suffering too. I looked at Jesus and said, "Can you help me?"

'The next thing I knew, I saw Jesus reach his hand down to me. I was surprised because his hands are supposed to be nailed to the cross. So I said, "Jesus, how can you reach your hand to me when you're nailed to the cross. How do you stay up there?"

'And with a smile, Jesus said to me, *"Velcro.'* "

If Jesus can smile at his plight, so can we with our own!

7. Laughing at Myself

IT HAS BEEN SAID THAT MOST OF US TAKE OURSELVES TOO SERIOUSLY, especially at work, but generally speaking, in every aspect of life. An ancient proverb says that God gave us humor so we could laugh at ourselves; however, I come across a great many people who seem to have cashed in this divine gift for a perpetual frown. While it may be easy to laugh at other people's misfortunes, we are not so likely to do the same with our own. As a rule, we don't share "most embarrassing" stories until the ego's bruises are well healed, various people involved are deceased, or we can embellish the details for an added effect.

My sense of humor had definitely grown over the years. It was my roommate in college who first gave my funny bone a workout. A kid at heart, Tom typically would fill his quota with over 500 laughs a day. Gladly, I followed his lead. Today, my humor muscle is seven times its original size. Now, like everyone, I have had my share of embarrassing moments, some which I am sure I have repressed deep into my unconscious, but here is one that I gladly repeat:

Three months into my first book tour, I stopped in Columbus, Ohio to visit Tom, my former college roommate at the University of Maine. To no surprise, he was still filling his humor quota daily—even with two infants. The second day of my visit, Tom drove me to a local bookstore where I was to do a presentation and book signing. Moments after I walked in the front door, I pulled out my fountain pen, which I used to autograph books, only to have it bleed all over my hands. Feeling foolish (you don't get a second chance to make a first impression), I quickly ran to the bathroom to wash my hands, but it was too late. The ink had dried and nothing I did removed the mess. While in the bathroom, I decided to make use of the facilities, but when I looked around I only saw stalls, no urinals. The first thought that hit me was that this was one of those new bathrooms. Then it dawned on me. In my haste, I ran into the wrong rest room. Just as soon as I realized my mistake, a woman entered, looked at me in horror and let out a scream.

I could have panicked, I suppose, but in my moment of embarrassment, I opted for humor. In the thickest European accent I could muster up, I explained, *"I no speaka anglish,"* and quickly ran out the door.

A half an hour later I began my discussion as people filed in and took a seat in the back of the store. At one point in the talk, I looked up to see the same lady I encountered in the women's room. I waved my ink-stained hand and she smiled at me, for the entire duration of my talk. Inside I was smiling too!

The ego reacts, the soul responds. Allow yourself permission to respond rather than react so that you may be guided by spirit always.

8. Room Service With a Smile

NOT ONLY ARE THERE ALL KINDS OF REASONS why we laugh and smile, there are all types of humor, from self-parody and double entendres, to satire and black (gallows) humor. Although there is no consensus why we laugh and smile, there is no doubt that humor, as comic relief, surely reduces stress. Is there a humor quota for good health and emotional well-being? Perhaps! Research indicates that children laugh as many as 400 times per day. Adults are lucky if they get between 15-20 chuckles. With all the evidence that supports the notion that laughter really is good medicine, particularly the release of wonderful neuropeptides, you would think that we would be striving for more than twenty laughs a day. In fact, there are those who have learned the secret that "she who laughs, lasts." Just ask Fran.

Fran is an emergency room nurse who flew to Estes Park, Colorado from South Florida to attend one of my workshops last spring. A former smoker who stands all of four feet, her acclimation to Colorado's altitude was not a smooth one. Upon arrival, the depravation of oxygen nearly did Fran in. So, in an effort to rest up, she flopped on the bed in her hotel room and quickly fell asleep. Hours later when she awoke she was famished. One look at the alarm clock by her bed and she realized the restaurant had closed. She picked up the phone, called the front desk and ordered her dinner through room service. Her meal came right before 11:00 p.m. Soaked in grease, it looked anything but appealing. With one glance at the food, she immediately lost her appetite.

Fran placed the tray on the table, got into bed with just her panties, which she describes as "liberating from the waist up." She removed her dentures and turned off the light. She awoke at midnight to find the odor of the food bothersome and decided to put the tray in the hall. As she pushed the food outside, the door closed behind her locking her out. Fear immediately struck in her heart. In Fran's own words: "It's midnight. I am in the hall shoeless, topless, toothless, breathless, and now homeless. What's a naked woman to do? Here I was at a stress management workshop, and I needed help! So I banged on all the neighboring doors hoping someone would help, but no one answered. Maybe they couldn't see me through the peephole, or worse, maybe they did! Finally, fifteen minutes later, a man came through the hall, perplexed — no shocked — at first, then through his laughter, offered to call down to the front desk. I told myself a year from now this will be funny, but then I thought to myself, why wait a whole year- ha ha."

He or she who laughs last.... didn't get the joke!

*Let a smile be your umbrella when the skies look threatening
(or if you forgot your sun block).*

9. A Good Day in Hell

LIFE IS FULL OF TESTS, but in college the tests are of a different nature: the grade shows up on your report card, etched in stone for life. There is always that one student who after getting a bad grade, will beat your door down to get some extra credit in the hopes to resurrect the GPA. The offers range from writing a twenty-page term paper to washing your car for a whole semester—anything to expunge the failed grade.

One of my colleagues, Robert Schambaugh, Ph.D. at the University of Oklahoma's Department of Engineering, is renown for asking an open-ended essay on his exams to see just how well his students can synthesize information, rather than simply regurgitating it back. He has been known to ask such questions as "Why do airplanes fly?" One day, our phone conversation turned toward the occasional student who sits and stares at the exam unable to write much of anything. Stunned, they walk out of the classroom seeking some hint of insight, and some academic mercy. Perhaps walking across the campus quad, the idea struck; Hey! Maybe there is another way to resurrect the failed grade!

Was it extra credit that prompted one student to reorganize his thoughts and give it another go to one of Dr. Schambaugh's "alleged" essay questions, perhaps even with a wider audience? What better way to vindicate oneself from the embarrassment of academic humiliation? Dr. Schambaugh could only guess at the motive.

Now this may be a case of *extra* extra credit, or it may be some goodhearted fun, but an answer to this now infamous essay test question has recently circulated well beyond the halls of academia on the Internet.

"I have gotten phone calls and emails from all over the world on this. I'm sorry to say that it never happened. Yes, it's true I ask open ended questions, but this is not the kind of question I would ask." Then, with a pause, he added, "Perhaps it's a former student trying to make amends. I don't know."

Did the Professor think the effort was totally in vain. "No!, it is clever and pretty funny," he added, laughing on the phone.

Extra Credit:

Essay Questions: "Is *Hell exothermic or endothermic? Support your answer with proof.*"

"First, we postulate that if souls exist, they must have some mass. If they do, then a mole of souls also must have a mass. So, at what rate are souls moving into hell and at what rate are souls leaving? I think we can safely assume that once a soul gets to hell, it does not leave.

"Therefore, no souls are leaving. As for souls entering Hell, let's look at the different religions that exist in the world today. Some religions say that if you are not a member of their religion, you will go to Hell. Since there is more than one of these religions, and people do not belong to more than one religion, we can project that all people and all souls go to Hell. With the birth and death rates what they are, we can expect the number of souls in hell to increase exponentially.

"Now, we look at the rate of change in the volume of Hell. Boyle's Law states that in order for the temperature and pressure in hell to stay the same, the ratio of the mass of the souls and volume needs to stay constant.

"[A1] So, if Hell is expanding at a slower rate than the rate at which souls enter hell, then the temperature and pressure in Hell will increase until all Hell breaks loose.

"[A2] Of course, if Hell is expanding at a rate faster than the increase in souls in Hell, then the temperature and pressure will drop until Hell freezes over. "So which is it? If we accept the postulate given to me by Theresa Banyan during my freshman year, that 'It'll be a cold day in Hell before I sleep with you,' and taking into account that I still have not succeeded in having sexual relations with her, then [A2] cannot be true, thus, Hell is exothermic."

A good day in hell beats a bad day in hell anytime.
Go for the extra credit!

10. Making Andrew Laugh

As PART OF AN EFFORT TO EXPAND THE CURRICULUM in our department of Health and Fitness at The American University in the fall of 1990, I was asked if I would create a new elective. I knew immediately what course I wanted to teach. A firm believer in the positive power of humor, I decided to create a spin-off from one of my stress management lectures on humor therapy and create a course titled, "Humor and Health." At first I was laughed at by fellow faculty members and upper level administrators, but within weeks the course was approved.

No sooner did the course appear on the registration catalog than the enrollment filled up. For the next several weeks my phone rang off the hook with students offering me their first-born to get into the class. Their efforts were in vain. As it was explained to me that because of space limitations, there was a ceiling of thirty students (and thirty chairs.) No exceptions! A lot of students hung up disgruntled. This part was not funny.

One day the phone rang and a voice on the other end said, "Hi, this is Andrew. I'm calling because I want to enroll in your humor class and it's booked up. Is there anyway I can get in?"

I replied, "I'm sorry Andrew, I can't help you. There is only room for thirty people and thirty chairs. My hands are tied. There is no more room."

"Fine," said Andrew, "I'll be right over." And with that, I heard a click and a dial tone.

About ten minutes later, I heard an electronic buzz outside my office door, and wondered what it was. Seconds later a wheelchair came cruising into my office. The man in the chair held up both arms and said, "Hi, I'm Andrew."

Impressed by his persistence, but adamant about the situation, I said, "Andrew, I'm sorry, but things haven't changed in the last ten minutes. There is still no room in the class."

He said, "Do you have time to hear my story?" Without waiting for a reply, he began.

"The day after I turned thirteen, the day before school was to start, I was swimming with my brother in the backyard pool. It's not like you think. I didn't hit my head in the shallow end. To this day the physicians can't explain it. All I know is that the angle in which I entered the water in the deep end was wrong. My neck snapped and at the age of thirteen, I became a quadriplegic. I was in the hospital rehab wing for almost a year.

"Every day after lunch, a nurse would come in and say to me, 'Do you want to hear the joke of the day?' If I could have used my arms, I would have pulled the sheets up over me, but all I could do was turn my head away. I thought she would give up and go away, but no, she proceeded to tell me the joke. This went on for several months.

"One day she came into the room and I, of course, turned my head. But this time I must have had my guard down, because when she told the joke, I laughed. I laughed for about twenty minutes. I think I laughed for all the times I wanted to laugh, but didn't.

"And you know what?" Andrew asked. "On that day I realized that I was on the road to recovery." As he said this he raised his arms up off the chair bars. "Now I am not going to say that humor has cured me, but it sure has helped in the recovery process.

"I'm a first semester senior and life is extremely tough. I'm applying to medical school, but I am having a tough time getting in. My funny bone has atrophied considerably. Is there any possible way I can get into your humor class? I really need it."

By now, my eyes looked like a miniature version of Niagara Falls. Wiping a tear, I said, "Andrew, for you I'll make an exception."

And with that he said, "Good! And I even have my own chair!"

As it turns out, Andrew was a much better teacher than a student in that course. On the last day of the semester, Andrew drove his wheelchair up to me and said, "I want you to make me a promise."

"OK," I replied, "What is it?"

"Raise your hand," he said.

I raised my right hand as if I was in a court of law and waited to take an oath.

"Promise me that whenever you teach people about humor, you will try to make them laugh. People take themselves way too seriously. We all need to laugh more. Look at me, if I can do it, anybody can. There is no excuse."

"Andrew," I said, "I promise!"

So to honor my pledge to Andrew, I share with you this joke that I heard told by Garrison Keillor on his show, *Prairie Home Companion*. And yes, it did make Andrew laugh.

Three couples signed up at a local church for the pre-marriage counseling workshop. As they sat down in the church auditorium, the pastor greeted them and then started with these words, "Before we continue any further I must tell you that to be a member of this church in good standing, there must be no sexual relations prior to the marriage ceremony. Is that understood?" All three couples nodded their heads in agreement, and the minister proceeded with the content of his workshop. Before he dismissed the group, again he reminded each couple of their promise of chastity, and told them he would see them again in two weeks.

Two weeks later, the three couples were seated in front of the minister, ready to continue the second of a two part pre-marriage workshop.

"Before I begin, I must ask you in good faith, did everyone abide by my rule?" he asked.

Then the elderly man spoke, "Well pastor, it really wasn't a problem. Although we are living together, we simply slept in separate bedrooms for the past two weeks. We barely even kissed."

"Good!" said the minister, "Now what about you?" directing his question to the second couple in their forties.

"Well," the woman replied, "it wasn't easy. Like the first couple we are living together. We ended up sleeping in separate beds. It was a stretch for two weeks, but we did it.

"Good!" said the minister. Then turning to the youngest couple, he inquired, "Now how about you two folks?"

There was a long pause. Then the twenty-two year old man responded. "Well sir, we were doing rather well the first week. We didn't even hold hands. Then one day I saw my fiancée reach up on a shelf for a light bulb and to be honest, I got rather excited. All of a sudden she dropped the package and bent down to pick it up. I couldn't help myself, sir. For the next half hour we made passionate love on the floor." As he said this he looked down to the ground.

The minister looked extremely disappointed. Holding his anger, he stood up and said, "I am sorry, but you are not allowed in this church."

And the young man answered, "You think that's bad, we're not allowed in the grocery store either."

Angels fly because they take themselves lightly.
When we do the same, we allow our spirits to soar.
(Follow Andrew's advice, lighten up.)

11. American Graffiti

RESEARCH SHOWS THAT A CHILD TYPICALLY LAUGHS between 300 and 400 times a day. By the time we reach adulthood the number drops below fifteen. Hospital patients, it is noted, never reach the threshold of one laugh per day. Humor may be the best medicine, however comic relief is in critically short supply in our health care system.

Rather than assign a term paper to the students taking my humor and health class, I decided to be more creative and have them do a more functional, meaningful project. In trying to instill some life-long health behaviors, I created an assignment called the Tickler Notebook. The premise of this project was to have the students compile a collection of jokes, comics, cards photographs and stories—anything that would put a smile on their face.

"You never know," I said. "One day you might just find yourself in need of this, if you ever end up in the hospital. So have it ready to pack up with your tooth brush and PJs." The project was met with tremendous success. Ten years later, I still get cards and letters from students telling me they are on their fifth or sixth notebook.

Metaphorically speaking, humor is a two-way street. While humor may be a perception we take in, it is also something we can share. Such was the case, I was to learn, with the Tickler Notebook.

Christine Flanagan, R.N., an oncology nurse at Shady Grove Adventist Hospital, in Rockville, Maryland, was a guest speaker in my class one night. She told the class how she had applied and received a grant to create a humor cart for the Oncology ward, which she supervised. The cart, a red wagon, was filled with videos, cassette tapes, cartoon books, and various items to lift the spirits of the cancer patients. Her intention was to integrate humor into the healing process and do something about the dearth of laughter at work. The students were mesmerized by her story. Inspiration struck the class like a bolt of lightening. Like a modern version of the classic fable Stone Soup, students began to offer items from their tickler notebooks as a donation to the humor cart.

Aside from the many humorous items collected, a drive was organized in class by one student to find the funniest graffiti and compile a list to include in the Tickler Notebook compendium. The following are excerpts to tickle your funny bone (and possibly add to your own Tickler Notebook):

On Education:

— Lately, there has been an alarming increase in things about which I know absolutely nothing.

— You can be a business major and be cool, but there aren't too many of us.

— I thought drugs were fun, till I started studying pharmacology

— Linguistics is the exact opposite of screaming

— Graffiti may be funny, but it won't get you tenure

— God created the world in seven days, but it took him four years to graduate from this place.

— God didn't create the world in 7 days, he partied for 6 and pulled an all-nighter

— Riddle me this all you existential Med Students:

Q: How many amino acids can dance on the head of a pin?
— A: It depends on the music
— A: Would it be acid rock?
— A: How about "pro-teen angel"

— Please Remember! Today's lesson: Bullwinkle is ...
Answer: — How a cow knows for sure.

— If you took all the students that sleep in class and laid them down end to end, they'd be a lot more comfortable.

On Politics:

The trouble with America is that so many jokes get elected!

— If "Pro" is the opposite of "Con,", what is the opposite of progress?

The difference between capitalism and communism is that in capitalism, man exploits man. Under communism, it's the other way around.

On Philosophy:

Old Plato saw both mind and matter
Thomas Hobbes saw but the latter
Now Thom's soul doth rot in hell
Quoth God, "It's immaterial"

Q: Why is there air?
A: Have you ever tried breathing Cool Whip?

— Adam was God's rough draft!

— Did you know that ignorance and apathy are the two biggest problems on college campus?
— I don't know and I don't care

— God is love,
Love is blind,
Ray Charles is blind,
Therefore...

On Life:

— It's better to be rich and happy than poor and unhappy.

— Are the poor so unhappy? Are the rich so happy?

— I've been rich, and I've been poor. Believe me, the rich are happier.

— No man is an island, but when you piss urination.

— I complained because I had no shoes until I met a man who had no credit cards.

— Abstain from wine, women, and song, mostly song.

— All I ask for is the chance to prove that money cannot buy happiness.

— Why is it that when you talk to God, it's called praying but when God talks to you, it's call schizophrenia?

World's shortest list:
a) Creative accountants
b) Honest politicians
c) Good American cars
d) Graffitiests who kan spell rite
e) Consecutive winning seasons at Iowa

On Sex:

— Panties may not be the best things in the world, but they're next to it!

— Grapenuts is not a venereal disease!

— If I told you you had a beautiful body, would you hold it against me?

— Contraceptives should be used at every conceivable moment.

— It's hard to find a good man, but oh, it's good to find a hard man.

— The sexual life of a male: Tri -weekly, Try weekly, Try weakly.

There once was a gaucho named Bruno
Who said sex is one thing I do know!
Sheep are just fine
Women divine
But Llama are numero uno

In the Garden of Eden lay Adam
Complacently stroking his madam
And great was his mirth
For he knew that on earth
There were only two balls, and he had 'em

A timorous Viking named Kord
Got sea sick when aboard
Until Princess Vale
Enticed him to sail
His long boat the length of her Fiord

There once was a monk from Algeria
Whose knowledge was somewhat inferior
One night of fun
With a comely young nun
And now she's mother superior

Odds and Ends

— Graffiti - the poetry of the simple minded.

— Human: An erudite ape with less hair and more money.

— College student: A pre-erudite ape with more hair and less money.

— You exist, it's this place that is unreal.

— There is no gravity, the earth sucks!

Imponderables ?????????

• If a sheep is a ram, and a donkey is an ass, how come a ram in the ass is a goose?

• How come there's no ham in hamburger?

• Why do we drive on a parkway and park on a driveway?

• If Jesus was a Jew, how come he has a Puerto Rican name?

• Why is the Octoberfest always held in September?

• Can a blue man sing the whites?

• Is Dogma the mother of all dogs?

• Why do people from England sing with American accents?

• If corn oil comes from corn, and coconut oil comes from coconuts, where does baby oil come from?

• I've been all over this universe, and take my word for it, Earth makes the best popcorn!

— For those of you who think that life is a joke, consider the punch line.

— I was here, where were you? Be back soon. — Godot

— You only go around once, but if you work it out right, once is enough!

Humor (Vitamin H) is an essential nutrient for mental, spiritual, emotional, and physical well-being. Be sure to take your supplement today and get your RDA of laughter.

STRESSED is DESSERTS Spelled Backward

Silver Linings and Lemonade

IT HAS BEEN SAID THAT THE SUBTLE DIFFERENCE between an optimist and a pessimist is just three letters. In truth, the difference is perception. Driving down the street one day, I saw a bumper sticker that read: One's attitude is the real disability. It turned out that the driver was physically impaired; Multiple Sclerosis (but not disabled)! At the grocery store, she parked her car and limped, ever so gracefully, toward the entrance.

When I first ran the Boston Marathon in 1978 on a cold wet day, like so many others around me, I began to moan at the anticipation of Heartbreak Hill, a seven-mile incline toward the end of the race. Just as I was about to turn to my college roommate and complain about a cramp in my left leg, I was passed by an athlete in a wheelchair who had no legs. Four more wheelchair athletes followed him in pursuit. At that same moment, the sun broke through the clouds. The symbology was powerful. Attitude is everything! It turns lemons into lemonade, and at the end of any race, this is truly the thirst quencher.

One component of optimism is healthy self-esteem—believing the good about you. So in addition to stories about simple pleasures and healthy attitudes, this section highlights self-esteem through four components: mentors and role models, uniqueness, empowerment, and connectedness. Perhaps as you read these chapters you might consider how you can begin to augment your self-esteem, so that life's problems will be inclined to roll off your back. And when you cross the finish line of your particular challenge, you too can enjoy the lemonade and sunshine.

1. Positive Affirmations

ONE SHOULD NEVER UNDERESTIMATE THE POWER of high self-esteem when dealing with stress, for when your self-esteem is high, then everyday problems, both big and small, roll off your back. However, when self-esteem is low, it's as if you become a bull's-eye target, begging to be hit.

Our self-esteem is hard to keep high when we badmouth ourselves. Like an obnoxious radio host, the ego babbles incessantly, constantly giving us a subliminal negative feedback that we are 'never good enough.' One of the first methods of effective stress management is called 'positive affirmations,' where you learn to turn down the volume of your ego's negative voice (which can so easily whittle down your self-esteem) and replace the negative chatter with positive reinforcements, which in turn, helps boost self-esteem. Using positive affirmations, particularly during times of duress help you gain composure and balance, and not succumb to the internal voice of negative critic. It is thought that these affirmations unite both conscious and unconscious energies of thought to help accomplish a goal. This is a common practice noted among actors, artists, and particularly, athletes.

At the time I became involved with the U.S. Biathlon team, it had been in existence for only about twenty-five years, a short time compared to the millennium that the Scandinavian countries had been practicing this hunting practice turned sport. We Americans, were lost babes in the woods covered in snow.

Of the six team members, one, named Raymond, was a defector from the U.S.S.R. Raymond's presence definitely made for rather interesting team dynamics. In short, Raymond had a defiant streak in him a mile wide, something I should have suspected from a defector—he didn't get where he was by going along with authority. In my attempts to improve the athletes' mental skills such as concentration, confidence, visualization, and team dynamics, I struck out over and over with Raymond. He turned a deaf ear to nearly all my endeavors—often cracking jokes and making snide comments under his breath, just loud enough for all to hear.

During my efforts to introduce the premise of positive affirmations, Raymond turned up his nose. Despite my best efforts, Raymond would have no part of it. On more than one occasion, he stuck his face in mine and with an air of defiance, he said in a thick Latvian accent, "I don't believe in affirmation statement!" Then he would walk away in a huff.

When the world championships came to Lake Placid in 1987, the biathlon team was in the best position in its history to have one of its team members receive a medal.

I watched the race with much anticipation. In what looks like orchestrated chaos, hundreds of skiers with rifles strapped to their backs cross the starting line, jockeying for position to take the lead for a ten-kilometer distance before they arrive at the shooting range to fire five shots. Then they would ski off to repeat the process all over again three more times.

Raymond approached the range, grabbing the rifle off his back as he skied into his designated spot. Right as he took aim, he noticed that positioned next to him was a former Russian teammate. Remembering this athlete's skill, Raymond's confidence fell a few notches. Pondering his first shot, Raymond's attention then turned to a competitor on his other side, also a fellow Russian of equal standing. The pressure was on. Raymond, who was renown for missing his first shot, aimed and fired. To his surprise, he hit it. He proceeded to clear the remaining four shots as well.

Back on the shooting range after another grueling trek around the ski course, Raymond cleared another five rounds. He became ecstatic, as did the entire American contingent. He did better than he had ever done before.

Soon after his race, Raymond skied up to where I was standing. With a smile from ear to ear, he looked me in the eye and said in a thick accent, "I have new affirmation statement!" A bit surprised, I inquired, "Congratulations! What is it?"

With as much pride as he could muster, he said under a puff of cold air, "I still got the goods!"

Positive affirmations give balance to the negative airplay of the ego and make our lives more stress free. And you don't have to be a champion athlete to gain from the benefits of positive self-talk.

2. Simple Pleasures

I HAVE HAD THE PRIVILEGE to stay in five-star resort hotels, dine at exclusive restaurants, and attend riveting rock concerts, but to be honest, these really can't compare to many of the greatest moments I've experienced that cost absolutely nothing. The other day, while I was out jogging by the creek, a little boy called me over to show me the collection of crawdads he had caught. His excitement was exhilarating. Hummingbirds at my feeder can brighten a dark and dreary morning, while watching a gaggle of Canadian geese pass overhead—in Colorado, this could be 200—has a way of vanquishing any remnants of sorrow I might have. In academic terms, these are referred to as "emotional uplifts." I just call these "simple pleasures."

Simple pleasures can best be described as those times when we find ourselves living in the present moment and enjoying its simplicity. So often our minds are preoccupied with past failures or future problems that leave little or no time to enjoy the present. Simple pleasures are neither lavishly expensive, nor incredibly time consuming. They don't cause stress; they reduce it. It may be an overused phrase, but it's often true that, the best things in life are free.

Ageless wisdom often reminds us of the universal law of attraction, that which you set your mind on you attract to you. Also called the self-fulfilling prophecy, the law of attraction is such that if you focus on all things negative, you will attract more negativity to you. Similarly, putting your attention on the positive will open your mind to a greater source of positive aspects to enjoy. That's what simple pleasures are all about—focusing on the positive side long enough to restore a sense of equilibrium to your life.

In teaching the concept of simple pleasures to my college students and workshop participants, I ask them to make a list of those simple things that give pleasure to an otherwise stressful day. Here are some of their answers:

1. When I get down in the dumps, I head to the nearest grocery store and start reading several greeting cards. I often find myself laughing out loud and this is definitely pleasurable.

2. Here is what I suggest. I suffer from SAD (seasonal affective disorder). My self-prescribed cure is to go to a florist greenhouse and smell the plants and flowers. This always puts me in a better mood.

3. Have you ever heard a recording of Ella Fitzgerald. Her voice is amazing. To hear her sing Cole Porter's "Night and Day" is a one-way ticket to heaven.

4. My favorite simple pleasure, and I have many, is to pick up the phone and call a friend. Sometimes we just talk, but more often than not we meet for coffee or scones. With all this technology, I need real people contact. Friends are the best simple pleasures.

5. Go to a pet store. It's hard to feel bad when you're holding a cute puppy or kitten, even watching the goldfish is therapeutic. (I never have to worry about spending money because I can't have pets in my apartment.)

6. My suggestion is to fill the tub with hot water and add some bath oils, light a candle or two, turn the lights off and soak. Sure works for me!

7. Some people may go shopping (as in retail therapy), but what I do is pack up items in my closet that have not been worn in a while and bring them to Goodwill. There is something about helping others that tends to lift my spirits.

8. My greatest simple pleasures is listening to music, and perhaps more so, hearing new music. I just discovered Dvořák's Slavonic Dances. Where have these been all my life? Opus 72, number 2 in E minor is just incredible!

9. If I want to take my mind off some problems from either home or work , I fill the bird feeder with birdseed and watch the chickadees and finches come in to eat. I think doing this reminds me of childhood, which was pretty damn good by comparison.

10. This simple pleasure cannot be done until nighttime with no cloud cover, but I pull a blanket out on the lawn and search for shooting stars and familiar constellations. It's amazing what can be found in a night sky. Staring out in space always brings my problems back to a manageable size.

11. A single red rose in a bud vase does it for me every time, even if I buy it myself.

12. I take my car in to get washed. A clean car is heavenly and its pleasure just cannot be put into words.

A hot shower on a cold wet day, a phone call from a dear friend, or the lick of a dog's tongue on the hand (or face), are reminders of life's simple pleasures. These delightful interludes not only pull us into the present moment, they also remind us to practice the art of gratitude. Each brief passage brings the mind and soul to a point of balance, and as such, gratitude comprises the last essential component of each simple pleasure.

It doesn't take much to lift one's spirits, and simple pleasures abound everywhere. All we need to do is prepare the mind, look, then enjoy.

3. Dinner with Merlin

SAVORING THE AROMA AND TASTE OF DELICIOUS MORSELS OF FOOD is thought to be one of nature's best automatic relaxation techniques. That's because sensations that seduce the taste buds and massage the gastro-intestinal tract also calm the central nervous system. Salmon à l'orange. Risotto. Swiss fondue. Crêpes. Strawberries. Chocolate. And lest we forget, ice cream therapy. Food serves as a pacifier, a fact of which both babies and mothers are well aware, a habit that begins the moment we exit the womb and continues for many, many decades.

The art of eating does require an element of patience, so as to relish the flavor and texture of each bite. Inhaling one's food, albeit a common practice, does not promote the relaxation response. And while a hectic day at work may dampen the romance of practicing culinary arts at home, it is nothing that a night out on the town can't remedy. As the line in the Disney movie, *Beauty and the Beast* states, "When you're stressed, it's fine dining we suggest. Be our guest, be our guest, be our guest."

Caught in the fast-paced lifestyle that we are all so accustomed to, I am embarrassed to admit that eating fast, dare I say "wolfing down food," is a behavior that I acquired in college. With the exception of eating in a classy restaurant, it is a habit that I had yet to correct. That is until I met Merlin, in the rite of passage called getting a family dog.

One look at Merlin and you know he comes from the species *canine lupine*: wolf. Merlin is not a first generation timber wolf, but close enough to the original gene pool that once you meet him, you can skip the trip to Yellowstone National Park to get the feeling of dancing with this species. It would be fair to say that Merlin has a touch of husky and shepherd, and perhaps it is this mix that cultivated, if not refined, his eating habits. He certainly doesn't wolf down his food.

We picked up Merlin at the animal shelter hours before he was destined to join Rip Van Winkle in Sleepy Hollow. One look in his eyes and you could tell he was ever so grateful. I have no doubt that animals know these things. They can smell death. We were told that he was a stray, about two years old, and from the looks of his protruding rib cage, mighty hungry.

In an attempt to bond with Merlin, I held him on my lap for the entire two-hour car ride home. Once inside the house, I gave him a bath and fed him, first with a few dog biscuits, then his own bowl of food.

Holding out a biscuit, Merlin first sniffed the peace offering and then ever so gently, opened his mouth and extending his tongue as if in slow motion, reached for the food, bringing the piece into his mouth. Then with the grace of royalty, began to chew, slowly. He looked up, making eye contact with me and in his own way saying "thanks." Moments later he walked over to his bowl and repeated the whole process with the food in his dish.

Later that evening Merlin joined us for dinner, again eating very slowly, chewing every bite before swallowing. I was stunned, because in all my exposure to dogs, I had never seen anything like this.

Eating is surely one of the finer aspects of life. In this culture, people eat so fast, they hardly taste what they place in their mouths before they gulp it down into the depths of their gastro-intestinal tracts. Eating dinner with Merlin is a constant reminder to enjoy the simple pleasures of life.

Perhaps it's rare that humans can learn positive behaviors from their pets, but I have learned something from Merlin; eat slow, taste each piece of food in my mouth, and savor the flavor before I swallow. How relaxing!

4. Stepping Out of the Void

It is a misconception to think that human spirituality is the metaphorical equivalent of a trip to Disney World. While it is true that there are many joyous moments we associate with the journey of our lives, the stressful episodes are also part of the same voyage. The most difficult of circumstances led us to the edge of the void, what I refer to as the "emptying process," the winter months of the season of the soul. It is also known as the dark night of the soul. We have all been there. The void is where loss occurs and its lesson is a difficult one. It is in this season where we are gently reminded to "be in this world, but not of it."

It is ironic that when most people come to the precipice of the void, fear holds them back. They don't budge. But the nature of life is dynamic, not stagnant. Energy must flow. I am convinced that if we do not move forward, we are first nudged, then pushed in by some unseen, yet divine, force. Let there be no doubt; the void contains moments of grief and sadness. To grieve a situation is not only normal, it's healthy. But prolonged grieving suffocates the soul. In times of stress, the emotion of pity is plentiful, but everything is relative. If there is a lesson to be learned through moments of loss, it is to grieve fully, and move on. The dark night of the soul is only a night, not a lifetime. Just as winter turns to spring, so too does the night become day.

Perhaps it's human nature, but our first response in the void is to want to fill it up in an attempt to give ourselves a sense of security. I think this is where the term "retail therapy" originates. Yet filling the void with material possessions, or even addictive behaviors, just results in the act of spinning our wheels. Sage advice reminds us that, to step out of the void, we must first step into it. In truth, the void is not the black pit of despair. It is really the womb of creation, what some call the realm of possibilities. However, there comes a time when it's right to exit the void, to rejoin the world, hopefully wiser. One of the best ways to take the first step out of the darkness of the grieving process into the light of the new day is to engage in service. To give of oneself to others in times of need, even when you feel there is nothing to give, lessens our own need for sympathy and evaporates self-pity.

A dynamic colleague of mine, has a world reputation for bringing out the best in people. A leader in the human potential movement, Jean Houston has counseled the likes of kings, presidents, and corporate executives, as well as blue-collar workers and the poor. Not long ago, an episode of national acclaim involving First Lady Hillary Clinton, was falsely exaggerated in the press, resulting in a tarnished image. What could have been a high point quickly became a crushing blow to her career, as she lost several consulting offers and speaking engagements. The event became her dark night of the soul. The whole affair created a large block of time for some deep self-reflection.

Left with much free time on her hands, she stepped back to look at the big picture, sized up her own potential, and pondered her options. In one of her conference workshops I attended, she shared these comments:

"I felt vulnerable," she explained. "But vulnerability lead to availability and I decided to make myself available to those who were in a much worse situation than I. So I did some volunteer work with cancer and AIDS patients. I sat with them by their bedside. I listened to their stories. I prayed, I laughed, I cried, and I smiled with them, " she explained. "It was healing for all of us."

Service is a word that often falls on deaf ears, particularly in times of stress, but this need not be the case. While it may seem that in our own troubled times, we have nothing to give anyone, the truth is that there is always someone we can be of service to, particularly as we emerge from the grieving process. The most effective teacher, therapist or counselor is one who has been there. Empathy creates a sound foundation for genuine service.

A line in the poem, Desiderata, by Max Erhman reads, "For there are always greater and lesser persons than yourself. Strive to be happy." Times of stress may turn our head to those whom we deem to be greater and ask why do we have it so bad. But in times of stress, we should count our blessings and share those as best as we can with those in greatest need.

5. The Glass Is Half Full

SO MUCH OF EFFECTIVE STRESS MANAGEMENT is harnessing the winds of a positive thought in a sea of negativity. In these days of rapid change, that's not always easy to do. Negative thoughts feed upon themselves, making mountains out of molehills. The end result distorts our vision; we see only gray clouds, where there's also a deep blue sky. Worse, negative thoughts tend to attract more negative thoughts, turning gray clouds black and keeping them overhead for a very long time.

Research studies reveal that an optimistic outlook on life is not only good for the mind, it's good for the body as well. Optimistic people are noted for getting fewer colds and flus than those hiding under a black anvil of thought. Moreover, unresolved negative thoughts suppress the immune system, setting the stage for illness far worse than the common cold. While perpetually viewing life through rose-colored glasses is considered by many to be a form of denial, relocating to the darker side of human emotions serves us no better. Optimism gives balance to moments of fear that immobilize the human spirit. For this reason, optimism is essential for our health and well-being.

I have always considered myself an optimist. Perhaps knowing my background as a child of two alcoholic parents would make one wonder how this is so. Yet optimism was something I knew I had inside and I continued to nurture it throughout my life, every step of the way experiencing the power of positive thinking, from my dealings with a loan officer, as I purchased my first house, to getting off with a warning for a potentially expensive speeding ticket. Rose-colored glasses not withstanding, optimism has gotten me through a lot of difficult situations. As a young boy, I would often read the biographies and autobiographies of scientists, explorers, statesmen, and heroes. I learned that optimism was a common factor in their lives. In many cases, optimism paved the way on a rough and narrow course. I also learned that optimism is not a genetic characteristic. It is a birthright for everyone, but it must be attended to, or it will surely atrophy.

Optimism is spirit in motion; pessimism is spirit in constipation. I am of the opinion that everyone has the potential to be an optimist, for I believe it is an inherent human trait. In the words of lyricist Johnny Mercer, all we have to do is accentuate the positive and eliminate the negative. This is step one in turning curses into blessings.

As an exercise for my students, I ask them to define the terms optimist and pessimist, and then, as best they can, explain to me where they see themselves in the continuum. Here are some of their definitions of an optimist.

An Optimist is:

- Someone who sees the positive, even in the worst of all situations.
- Someone who is carefree and seems to enjoy life without reservation.
- Someone who doesn't let failure limit their growth as a human being.
- Someone who can find redeeming qualities in just about everyone, even a pessimist.
- Someone who sees lots of clouds in the sky and describes the day as mostly sunny.
- Someone who takes a personal setback as only a *temporary* inconvenience.
- Someone who counts their blessings instead of their misfortunes.
- Someone who loses a job and says there is a better one waiting.
- Someone who has the ability to re-evaluate their expectations so as not to become depressed when they fall short.
- Someone who is generally happy and who is nice to be around.
- Someone who takes things in stride, is able to enjoy oneself and is able to adapt to the situation at hand.
- Someone who sees things clearly and accepts what is or cannot be changed and doesn't spend time fighting it.
- Someone who continually explores new areas of life, and who can accept others who are different as unique.
- Someone who has enough faith in themselves to see them through a crisis.
- Someone who describes a pessimist as a person with potential.

Roses have both beautiful petals and piercing thorns. Where do you choose to place your attention?

6. Grandmother McNulty

I HAVE A TRADITION WHEN I BEGIN MY FIRST CLASS of the semester or a weekend workshop, where fostering a sense of camaraderie is paramount to the success of the class. The tradition is in the form of an icebreaker, a question that invites students to do a little soul searching. Then, one by one, we share the answers and reveal a little bit about ourselves to initiate the connection process. One question I often ask is this: What person outside of your parents and siblings has been the greatest influence in your life?

One reason for asking this question deals with the self-esteem. In all my years of teaching stress management, I have come to learn that high self-esteem is the foundation upon which all other stress coping skills and relaxation techniques rest. While there are many theories of self-esteem, one that I have been attracted to is the idea that self-worth is comprised of four aspects: Uniqueness, empowerment, social support, and role models.

This particular icebreaker honors the concept of role models. What I typically find is that the basis of each person's answer ties directly to the notion of love. Indeed, love is the greatest and most lasting influence in every person's life.

Although I have been influenced by a great many people, from schoolteachers and college professors to humanitarians, one person who comes to mind every time is my maternal grandmother. The youngest of nine children, she was the sole surviving member of her family's generation. From as long as I can remember, there was a sense of dignity about her. I grew up hearing countless stories of her colorful past, thinking how great it was to be related to her. Her father was a secretary to President McKinley, and stories abound of her playing as a young girl at the White House, even sitting on the President's lap. She told me that she was asked out to a movie on her first date. When she and her escort walked out of the theater, news broke that the Titanic was sinking. In high school I learned that her uncle was killed at the Battle of Little Big Horn with General Custer (talk about stress!). She was born before women had the right to vote, but when that amendment passed, she never missed an election.

My grandmother lived in an age when national celebrations included ticker-tape parades for celebrities like Charles Lindbergh—

167

which she saw from the grandstand—and national mournings, like those of Presidents McKinley and Kennedy. I once asked her why she didn't like to fly and she told me that when she was quite young, she saw the Wright Brothers ride their plane over the Potomac River. "I wasn't impressed then, and I'm not impressed now," she told me with a slight smirk.

These and other historical moments were fascinating, but it was her compassion and grace in everyday life that made the deepest impression on me, for she had seen much change (from the Wright brothers to the first space shuttle) and weathered great difficulty in her life. Yet through it all, she held her head high, and always kept her heart open to those around her.

One day, I arrived at her apartment to find the door ajar. She was crying and badly shaken. As she turned to greet me, I saw blood dripping from her forehead. I then learned that she had just returned home from a quick trip to the grocery store, in anticipation of my visit. Halfway between the store and her apartment, she was robbed and thrown to the ground by two teenagers. A trip to the hospital revealed a concussion and two broken ribs. That evening, my grandmother put it all in perspective.

"I'll be OK," she reassured me. "I have been through a lot worse. I don't know what makes people do that. They must need the money quite badly." Harboring no grudge, she steered the conversation toward me and my first year at college. Getting up to make some tea, she smiled. "They might have stolen some money, but they did leave the groceries. Can I fix you some dessert?"

I was not only greatly influenced by her, I was greatly inspired by her as well.

In the words of Alex Haley, " Nobody can do for little children what grandparents do. Grandparents sort of sprinkle stardust over the lives of little children. "

7. That Special Something...

I DO SEVERAL EXERCISES ON THE TOPIC OF SELF-ESTEEM in stress management workshops, because when self-esteem is high, problems, big or small, tend to roll off your back, whereas when self-esteem is low you become a magnetic bulls eye for the negative impact of daily stressors. One particular exercise regards the aspect of uniqueness, an essential component of high self-esteem.

We each have a gift or unique quality that makes us special. Moments of stress, where the ego is caught in a downward spiral of self-defeating thoughts, can disempower our unique attributes. At worst, we lose track of our particular gifts and feel we aren't worthy of anything.

That's why I love this exercise, which requires each person to list five attributes that make him or her special. Typically when I first give this assignment, I am greeted with long stares and oppressive silence. The silence continues as people stall to come up with even one item on their list.

As a rule, people focus on their weaknesses, not their strengths. Ironically, those things that we see as our imperfections are often viewed by others as rare jewels. To illustrate the point and get people thinking, I tell workshop participants this story:

I am in Lake Placid, for the Biathlon world championships. As one of two sport psychologists, I have been working diligently with the six-member Olympic team to refine their mental training skills for the big event. Three years of relaxation techniques, positive affirmations, visualizations, mental rehearsal, goal setting, and team dynamics have been set in motion for this one day of competition.

On this particular day, the weather was ideal for racing. Cool but not freezing, sunny, but not windy. The athletes were primed for the "home court" advantage. I walked off the field, heading toward the lodge to warm up by the wood stove and fetch a cup of hot chocolate. Inside the lodge, several athletes were waxing their skis and a few officials were attending to some last minute details. Standing by the fire, I was approached by Chip, a seasoned veteran of the U.S. Olympic team. Chip's imposing height was disarmed by his smile, a feature commonly found on his face.

"Great day for a race, huh, Chip?" I inquired.

"I guess," he answered. Then he paused and looked down at the ground. "You know I've been bothered by something and I've been wanting to talk to you. Is this a good time?" he asked.

"Sure," I answered, thinking he might want to review some mental training tips.

"You know, I just get the impression that women don't think I'm attractive. I have these real thin lips and when I smile I've got these huge dimples."

My first impulse was to laugh out loud, thinking you've got to be kidding, you've got a world champion race in a half an hour and you're thinking of this? My next thought was, I have failed in my mission to help the team win a medal. But rather than react, I responded with this comment: "Chip, listen, let's talk about this later. I promise! Right now I want you to focus on the race. Get psyched, rehearse your technique in your mind, OK?" I gripped his shoulder and gave a good squeeze, then patted him on the back as he turned for the door. "Good luck," I yelled.

Moments later, just as I drank the last drop of cocoa, a young attractive woman approached me.

"Hi," she said, "was that Chip, the Olympian you were just talking to?"

I wasn't sure I wanted to admit it, but I nodded my head yes.

"Oh," she continued, "he is so cute, so handsome. He has the thinnest lips and I just love it when he smiles, cause he has the cutest dimples," Rolling her eyes back, she sighed.

I stared at her, nearly in shock.

"Quick," I yelled, "go tell him!"

Leo Buscaglia, author of a great many books on love, often spoke on the nature of self-love. Until we learn to accept ourselves with all our pluses and minuses he explained, we cannot love ourselves unconditionally. Buscaglia referred to uniqueness as the X-factor.

So what are your unique attributes? Your special qualities? Your X-factor? This is where your strength lies. If you are having a hard time coming up with any, try focusing on your points of weakness, and ask some trusted friends what traits they admire in you (you'll be surprised!).

Within everyone is a rare precious gem.
When we scrape off the ego's dirt and grime, we shine.

8. Friends in Need

IMAGINE LIVING A LIFE IN TOTAL ISOLATION. It's not possible. By nature, human beings are social animals, and although it's nice to have a moment or two to yourself—complete independence, after a while gets old, and lonely. Undeniably, we are all connected. In the words of John Dunne, "No man is an island," nor should we try to be.

Studies show that under increasing personal and professional demands, prolonged periods of isolation lower our sense of self-esteem and increase our stress exponentially. Common sense would indicate and research bears out that keeping the company of friends tends to take the edge off a bad day, a bad week, or, for that matter, a bad life. Medical science hasn't figured out exactly how this works. Some credit the endorphin response, while newer research suggests it has something to do with the human energy field. Regardless, it appears that sharing our problems with friends and being in the physical presence of those who support us (even if they don't always agree with us) dissipates the negative effects of stress. In academic circles this is known as the buffer principle. To the average person on the street, it is known as a friend in need. Just like the tablets one takes to relieve (buffer) the build up of acid in one's gastro-intestinal tract, friends neutralize the toxic effect of stress. Misery loves company — for company, it seems, dilutes misery to tolerable levels.

Perhaps the most amazing evidence of the buffer theory was shown by Dr. David Spiegel, a faculty member of Stanford University's School of Medicine. Chagrined by the claims of Dr. Bernie Siegel's work with cancer patients, and often confused for him due to the similarity of last names, Spiegel set out to prove Siegel wrong. His hypothesis: support groups did not prolong the life of patients with metastatic breast cancer. To Spiegel's surprise, however, he found that those woman who participated regularly in a patient support group lived, on average, five years longer than those who did not.

Statistics and number crunching may satisfy the clinical bean counters, but stories are the proof of the pudding.

Michelle is the director of Prestige Plus, a seniors program at Longmont United Hospital in Boulder County, Colorado. Originally created as an off-site health care program, it has become the local support group for over 2000 area seniors. Much of Michelle's job is to organize various health screenings for her membership, although lately, due to their interest in alternative medicine, Michelle has integrated massage therapy, acupuncture, reflexology, and herbal remedies into her services. Occasionally, when a member goes into the hospital, Michelle will make a visit to see how they are doing.

"One day, I went to see Alice who was dying of cancer. Many times these people have no families, or they live too far away to visit. For some members, I am their family. I sat there with her for a while visiting, and then she turned to me and said, 'Michelle, I'd like to be held. Would you hug me? When you have cancer, no one wants to touch you. But we need touch like everyone else.' "

Michelle didn't skip a beat. She climbed up into the hospital bed and gave Alice a long, loving embrace. Then the tears rolled down Michelle's face.

"I thought I was doing her a favor, but the truth is, I needed the hug as much as she did," she said.

It wasn't just a hug that surprised Ian O'Gorman, but he was amazed nonetheless. Ian was diagnosed with cancer around his tenth birthday. He was warned that the chemotherapy treatment might make his hair fall out, and it did. To avoid the embarrassment of looking like a Cabbage Patch kid, he decided to have his head shaved. When he was well enough to attend school, he walked into his classroom to see his teacher and all his buddies with their heads shaved too!

Sometimes the littlest gesture of friendship can have an extraordinary impact, as evidenced in a letter I received a while ago.

Dear Luke,

You probably don't remember me, so let me give you a hint. I was the guy with ALS (Lou Gehrig's Disease) that approached you in Houston while you were giving a presentation some time ago. Thank you for your kindness and generosity of mailing me a book. I apologize for not writing to you sooner to thank you. Shortly after I received your gift, my brother was killed in an accident and this is just one of the few problems I am trying to deal with along with my illness. Right now I am focusing on my wife and three kids, and keeping life as normal as possible for them. Man, I tell you, I know you have heard the saying, when it rains, it pours. Well

I can tell you I don't think there is any facet of my life that is not being tested right now.

I want you to know that in times like these, it's those things, like what you did, that keeps a person with hope and the ability to face another day.
Sincerely,
Randy

Friends in need are friends indeed.
Be a good friend to someone in need.
You will be paid back immeasurably.

9. Christmas Lights

JOANNE WANTED TO BE A MOTHER from the moment she got her first doll at Christmas when she was five years old. But it would be many decades later, including eight years of marriage, when she finally got the news from her physician, that indeed, she was pregnant. Joanne was elated! She wasted no time getting ready for THE day. Anyone who knows Joanne, will tell you that assertiveness is one of her strengths; it's how she exhibits empowerment. From Lamaze classes and parenting seminars to relaxation tapes, she did everything in her power to give this baby the warmest welcome on the planet earth.

Sometime toward the end of her sixth month, the course of events changed slightly. One night after fixing supper, she went upstairs to the bathroom before heading to bed. Looking down on the bathroom floor, Joanne saw blood everywhere. "Call the doctor," she screamed to her husband. What seemed like moments later, with her husband driving at light speed toward the hospital, Joanne felt a kick, enough to know that her little miracle was still alive.

"As they whisked me up to Labor and Delivery, the bleeding had stopped and I thought somewhat naively that everything was fine," Joanne explained. "As it turned out, I was in labor. They gave me medications to try and stop the contractions and I used what I had learned about relaxation and went to sleep just after one o'clock," she said.

The next morning the hemorrhaging began again and this time the decision was made for her to have a cesarean immediately. Joanne awoke in the recovery room to learn that her baby daughter was in critical, but stable condition. Wednesday, December 8, 1976 the world welcomed Michelle Annelee Hill.

Because Joanne's hemorrhaging was so bad, she was confined to bed for three days, unable to see the baby she longed to hold. Taking a deep breath, she affirmed to herself that when the time was right, she would be reunited with her child. Meanwhile, a team of physicians broke the news to her and her husband that the baby's chance of survival was less that 50 percent. Again Joanne affirmed her belief and placed the outcome in God's hands. On Friday evening, December 10th, Joanne made it to the intensive care nursery to see Michelle for the first time. A collapsed lung kept the "preemie" on a respirator.

Joanne could only stroke her with a few fingers, yet the contact was energizing, and the love from her heart was immense. She smiled constantly with confidence at her daughter.

"I had Catholic friends lighting candles, Buddhist friends singing chants, and every nurse in intensive care pulling for her. I knew she was going to make it. I nicknamed her SAM for 'small adorable miracle.' Miracles do happen and Michelle certainly was a miracle by everyone's estimation." Drawing on faith, hope, and love, Joanne prayed like she never had before. This is one way she empowers herself.

Empowerment is the last of the four pillars of high self-esteem. Many people confuse empowerment for control, yet they are not the same. Control involves ego. It employs manipulation and often deceit. Control is fear acted out. On the other hand, empowerment is the realization of personal strength and the cultivation of inner resources. Whereas control is akin to giving your power away, by thinking you can control others (the illusion of control), empowerment is reclaiming your personal sovereignty even when what's ahead appears to be a dead end. Empowerment is knowing you have a can-do attitude and letting that positive energy flow. In her situation, there was absolutely nothing, no final outcomes that Joanne could control. Yet empowerment was her ace in the hole, and she played this card every day.

As days passed into weeks, SAM got off all machines, but she was still too little to leave the hospital. More than anything, Joanne wanted to have her baby home for Christmas. The team of physicians assured her that the baby, born so premature, must stay in intensive care for several more weeks. Honoring their expertise, she affirmed her desire to be together as one family.

On Christmas Eve, Joanne made her daily visit to the hospital to see her daughter, secretly hoping that Michelle would go home with her. It appeared, however, that Michelle's first "real" Christmas would have to wait.

"There was only one nurse in the unit due to a low census," Joanne explained. "She saw me holding back the tears and tried to comfort me."

"What do you mean, no Christmas!" the nurse exclaimed. "You must be kidding. Joanne, we have Christmas in this room every day," said the nurse. "Just look around the room, look at all these babies.

Isn't Christmas about little babies? Isn't Christmas about God's love? Isn't Christmas about miracles? Some of these babies have no medical reason to be alive right now, save a miracle. Christmas—why we have it every day in this room." At this point she hit the light switch for a moment and the room succumbed to darkness, save for hundreds of red and green lights from all the monitors. Christmas lights.

As it turned out, another miracle happened on Christmas day. Joanne and her husband received a phone call from the hospital. Little Michelle was strong enough to leave. They could come and take her home. So they drove to the hospital, picked up Michelle, and then home they went.

That evening, at her sister's house, with the living room lights off, Joanne sat in a chair in front of the fire holding her small little miracle. She glanced over at the tiny lights on the Christmas tree.

"Tears of joy welled up in my eyes," she said, "as I realized what Christmas lights really are."

Empowerment isn't a gift, it is a birthright. Yet like a plant, it must be nurtured and cultivated to grow. The source of power comes from within, yet it manifests as assertiveness through our thoughts and actions. When you think of someone who appears to have little or no stress, you are viewing empowerment.

10. The Burlington Book Club

BURLINGTON, VERMONT, IS A SMALL CITY that sits on the pristine shores of Lake Champlain. This lake is over 130 miles long, starting deep in New York State and emptying into Canada's St. Lawrence Seaway. Perhaps because of its length, and the boundary between Vermont and New York, Lake Champlain is affectionately called the west coast of New England. Due to what the Weather Channel calls the "lake effect," Burlington has a lot of cloudy days. You can go the whole month of February and never see the sun. So what do people do in a town like Burlington on cold rainy days or snowy evenings? They read lots of books.

Not long after I moved to Burlington, Vermont, in 1987 to work with the Olympic Biathlon team, I met Laurie through a mutual friend. Laurie is a vivacious character who knows practically everybody in the state of Vermont, most likely all of New England, and quite possibly the entire world. It is not an understatement to say she is extremely well connected, and she knows the importance of making and keeping good friends. She didn't actually coin the term "support group," but she might as well have. She definitely appreciates the value of connectedness.

When you move to a new area, feelings of loneliness and isolation are not uncommon. New friendships, and old acquaintances, if you are lucky enough to have them, are crucial to one's health. Because health is so inextricably linked to self-esteem and self-esteem enhanced by social support, support groups—be they book clubs, single parent clubs, Alcoholics Anonymous groups, or summer softball teams—constitute one cornerstone of any successful stress management program.

The Burlington Book Club was one of many of Laurie's ideas to foster a sense of camaraderie among friends. It wasn't long after I met her that I was invited to join. And it wasn't much longer before I realized that reading wasn't really a criteria for maintaining club membership.

My invitation to join the club was extended over lunch one day on the shores of Lake Champlain. As we walked inside the restaurant, a waiter came right over to us, kissed Laurie on the cheek, made a comment about the cloudy weather, then showed us to our table. As we sat down, the owners came over and greeted Laurie, each with a hug.

"Everyone is so friendly here," Laurie said (I was to realize over the course of many months that it was she who had cast a huge net of friendship over the region). Once we had ordered, the book club became the focus of our conversation.

"We meet the first Tuesday of each month. I'm not sure what the book selection is this month. I am so far behind in my reading, but it doesn't matter. Just come. Oh, yeah. It's a potluck, so bring something to eat. It doesn't matter. Anything will be OK."

Curious about the club's format and history, and wanting to make a decent appearance, I followed up with some questions. "Laurie, thanks," I said, "Now what types of books do you guys normally read? novels, science fiction, autobiographies?"

"Well, it varies, really. Someone makes a suggestion and, oh, you'll see. It's pretty casual," she explained. Then she paused for a moment, looked out the window at a sailboat, waived at the crew, then brought her attention back to the conversation.

"Everyone has become so busy that we have gotten in the habit of picking books that have been made into movies. That way, if you don't have time to read, you can rent the video. I do this all the time. Let's see, I think next month's book is *Out of Africa*, or is it *Dancing With Wolves?* I forget. It doesn't really matter.

"This is a very stress-free book club, right up your alley," she continued. "There is no obligation to actually read books. It's just an excuse to get together and visit. Sometimes no one has read the book we selected and we end up talking the whole night about politics, cross-country skiing, or Hawaii, or something."

Our attention was redirected to a couple walking into the restaurant. They immediately came over to our table and greeted Laurie.

"Do you know everyone," I asked, smiling, as the couple walked away.

"No, this is a small town, it just seems that way. You'll make lots of friends too. Just wait and see. Now, can you make next Tuesday night? It's a lot of fun."

Indeed, the Burlington Book Club lived up to its reputation. It fostered a sense of friendship, which is what good support groups do.

It didn't take long to realize that although, books were the primary vehicle to get everyone together, it was a sense of belonging, a sense of connectedness that was the real driving force which kept it going.

Good friendships are paramount to high self-esteem and good health. A sense of belonging is an essential coping technique for stress. If you don't have a strong support group, start a book club, (or a CD club) as a catalyst for connectedness.

11. Welcome To the Half-Century Club

I WAS IN COLLEGE WHEN MY MOM TURNED FIFTY. The year was 1975 and to be honest, she wasn't too excited about the prospect of what she perceived as "getting old." Back then, as perhaps now, there was a certain stigma associated with turning fifty. It was old, with a capitol O. Being the naïve young sophomore that I was; I was a bit clueless to this extent of this social stigma. I saw turning fifty not only as a milestone, but a merit badge of sorts. I mean if truth were told, several decades earlier many people never reached the age of fifty. The average life expectancy at the turn of the twentieth century was fifty, give or take a few years. A whole host of infectious diseases, from the Spanish flue and German measles to Rubella and Tuberculosis leveled the playing field quite easily. Throw in a few world wars and gee, turning 50 was really something to be proud of, or so you would think. My Mom was unimpressed with the birthday card I sent her with the inscription, "Welcome to the half century club!" I don't think she talked to me for a month after that episode. Sadly, she didn't live much beyond 50 either, but that's another story.

I never gave much thought to turning 50 myself. I do remember being in high school when a bunch of us began to calculate just how old we would all be in the year 2000, a year that seemed as distant as the fartherst galaxy. While we stared at the number 44, none of us could imagine being that old. Heck, for many of us, our parents weren't even that old. Those of us who had grandparents still living could project what the aging process could or might do to our parents, but as far as we were concerned, we were immortal, invincible and basically age-proof. We only had one thing on our minds, turning 16 so we could get our driver's licenses. That was all that mattered.

On August 29, 2006 I turned 50. To be honest, it wasn't a milestone, nor was it a right of passage. Rather it seemed like just another day, pretty much like those celebrated in the past several decades. With the exception that my hair has turned gray (those few follicles that have chosen to remain attached to my scalp), my beard has turned gray (actually white) and a few more smile lines, I'm doing pretty good. All those decades of swimming, running, organic foods, yoga, T'ai Chi and herbal supplements have paid off. I don't need glasses, hearing aids (or even Viagra). But I know that I am the exception to the paranoia of aging in our country. Fifty is the new thirty and people are doing whatever it takes to hide their true age.

In fact, have you noticed how stressed people are about aging? Facelifts, tummy tucks, collagen cream, Botox, liposuction, manicures, and that's just the men. It has become a crime to get old these days. Whatever happened to honoring the sage, age before beauty, and respect your elders? Sometimes I feel like we have entered the set of the movie *Logan's Run* where no one is supposed to live past the age of thirty.

Being the introvert that I am, I decided to leave the country on "holiday" rather than have my friends roast me with a party and silly gag gifts. When I turned thirty I took a trip to New Zealand and Australia to celebrate that milestone. It was the experience of a lifetime. With a lifetime goal of traveling to all seven continents (I am happy to say that I only have three more to go), I planned to travel to Africa on my fortieth birthday. Sadly, a failed attempt at marriage ruined that plan. When I turned forty-five, I jumped off a mountain in Aspen, Colorado to go paragliding. Let me tell you, that surge of energy lasted several years hence. For many reasons I turned to Canada as a safe haven for my fiftieth birthday. Vancouver Island and Whistler exceeded all expectations.

As luck would have it, my friends threw a surprise birthday party for me when I returned home from being "out and about." Turning 50 is a right of passage, I was told, and no one should do this alone. In hindsight, they are right!

I read somewhere that the Australian aborigines don't celebrate their birthdays. Instead, they celebrate their achievements and accomplishments. I like that idea. After all you get to a certain point when you don't need any more gifts or knick-knacks. You just need good friends to tell you they love you. I arrived home to a flurry of voice mail messages, emails and birthday cards (not to mention my AARP card), many of which welcomed me to the half century club (wink). I guess what goes around comes around. Unlike my mom, who shunned this honor, I am delighted to become a member. And I hope when you get to the threshold of this exciting decade you will remember, if not to celebrate your achievements, to honor your friends and give thanks for the pleasure of this wonderful human experience.

We are all just visitors to this time and place.
We are just passing through.
Our purpose is to observe, to learn, to grow, to love,
then we return home.

—Ancient Aboriginal proverb

12. One Person Can Make A Difference

A PEBBLE THROWN IN A STILL POND will not make a huge wave, but it will make a ripple, which then reverberates outward till it reaches the edge of each shore. Like pebbles, we too, have such an effect. With six billion people on the planet, it may seem as if each life is infinitesimal in its meaning, yet each person is essential to the whole and holds the potential for greatness. Significant and lasting changes don't require huge committees or mythical heroes. All that's required is love.

In the summer of 1998, at the Institute of Noetic Sciences Conference in Kansas City, I stood upon the metaphorical shores of humanity and was touched by the ripple of one such pebble.

Balbir Mathur was raised in Allahabad, India as one of five children. The son of an army officer, Balbir came to the United States in 1958 to study business at Wichita State University—with only six dollars in his pocket. He must have learned his academic lessons well, for within a short time he became a successful business executive, traveling to all corners of the earth.

It was on one such trip flying over the Mediterranean, gazing at a view of the island of Cyprus, that Balbir had what he calls a "mystical experience." What began as a conversation with God became a life long mission.

"Someone—in a voice I do not understand, nor can fully describe—asked me what I saw as I looked down. High above the earth I saw extremes and opposites: light and dark, hope and despair, wealth and poverty. It was after this moment that I began to have a pain in my finger. Soon the pain invaded my whole body. Unable to walk, I eventually became bedridden."

For two years, Balbir was immobilized with pain. All he could do was rest and eat. A suggestion by his sister prompted him to fast for several days. Denying himself the only pleasure he could enjoy, he began to fast from both food and water. On the fifth day a miracle occurred. Balbir experienced a vision of trees. At that moment, he knelt and dedicated his life to alleviate world hunger. He arose out of bed and went for a five-mile walk, as if he had never been sick. He knew he was healed.

But life did not become easier for Balbir. He lost all interest in his business. Family savings disappeared. There was no income. "I was in an awkward place," Balbir explained. "I had left one shore, but had not yet arrived at another." Guided by unseen forces, Balbir raised his sails to catch the winds of grace. Once again they led him across the Atlantic.

Within a month's time, Balbir took a trip to Zimbabwe as a delegate to an African-American Conference. It was there the mystical voice returned to whisper in his ear a name that would repeat itself for three days, "Johnny Appleseed." Balbir got the message. He canceled the remainder of his itinerary and returned to his mother's home in India to formulate his plan. He would plant one hundred trees from the seeds of a lemon tree in his mother's yard. Why a lemon tree? As it turns out, Balbir had made a secret promise to the tree as a child, that one day he would plant one hundred trees from its seeds. The time had come to honor the promise. With the blessing of a local healer, Balbir distributed the lemon saplings. Those who took a sapling, promised in turn, to plant eighteen more trees each to keep the legacy strong. Back in the States, his mission really took root when a group of 8th graders in Wichita, Kansas, upon hearing his story, raised money for 103 fruit trees in India.

Today Balbir, with his wife, Treva, head a volunteer organization out of Wichita called Trees for Life, a self-help movement involving millions of people. Through their efforts, trees have been planted in Balbir's native India, Guatemala, and Brazil, supplying nutrient-rich fruit to community villages.

A week after first observing Balbir accept the Temple Award for Creative Altruism, the winds of grace brought him to Boulder, Colorado, where we met for lunch. It was there that Balbir shared more of himself with me.

"I must say this experience was long in the making. A series of events took place that led up to it. At each step I merely agreed to move forward. I was terrified, but I said yes anyway. And yes, life became very tough after that. It tested every single fiber within me. My family and all my relationships were put to an extreme test. This is very important for people to understand. Otherwise they may think that visions solve all problems. In our culture, we seek fast results. The reality is just the reverse. Visions simply open the door to new horizons, and one cannot escape paying the full price.

"This is really a story of transformation. Perhaps the only reason I allow this intimate aspect of my life to be shared is because it is not just my story. In one way, it is the story of each and every one of us. Perhaps those who read it may get the courage to say yes when their time comes," Balbir said. There he repeated the closing comments he shared upon receiving his award: "I do not wish to change God's world, that would be arrogant. What I do is an act of worship. How does one quantify worship? We really do not plant trees, we plant love, one tree at a time."

One person can make a difference. The deed need not be monumental in scope, nor brilliant in fashion. As we assist those in need, we too share in the harvest of celebration.

STRESSED is DESSERTS Spelled Backward

Going With The Flow

THERE IS AN OLD PROVERB WHICH STATES 'you cannot push water up hill.' As simple as this message is, how often do we question this wisdom and often try to fight the currents of life's river only to end up exhausted?

If each human journey is a passage on the river of life, then it is fair to say that hope and confidence are the oars that we paddle with to navigate the shoals of stress. Sometimes the rapids are exhilarating, occasionally harrowing. Sometimes the placid waters are a welcome respite, other times they don't quite hit our threshold. Regardless, each and every time, we must remember to go with the flow and expect the best outcome. The following stories offer insights into the process releasing expectations and taming the ego, in short, moving like water.

1. Surf's Up, Dude

IT'S HARD NOT TO NOTICE PEOPLE SURFING along the shores of any of the Hawaiian Islands. People will stop their cars along the road and get out and watch practically anybody on a board. I know, because for many years I was one of those people who got out and watched, living vicariously in an aquatic world where many never venture to go. Long boards, shorts boards and everything in between dot each coastline practically every day of the year. Surfers all over the world know that winter time on the north shore of any of the Hawaiian Islands produces the best waves, some as high as four-story buildings. For this reason, this is the time when you will see the best surfing. And the best hotdogs out there doing their stuff. They make it look so easy.

Surfing, it is said, was first a sport of the Hawaiian Kings and until the 1950s there were few people who engaged in this activity. What started in Hawaii soon washed up on the shores of California beaches and then everybody who was cool or wanted to be cool was "hanging ten." As the story goes, surfing became mainstream when a young teenager named Gidget immortalized the sport. What Gidget started the Beach Boys continued with their steady stream of hits including Surfing Safari and Catch a Wave. Over the next several decades, sportswear companies could barely make the boards fast enough as demand exceeded supply and the several islands that make up the newly acquired state of Hawaii were forever changed.

Growing up in New England, surfing was always something other people did: the golden boys of southern California with chiseled looks and bleach blond hair (actually the ones who look like Laird Hamilton, today's surfing poster boy). For one thing, the water temperatures in New England were frigid in the summer and that's with a wet suit. Secondly and perhaps most importantly, there's not much good surf rolling in toward the shores of Connecticut, Massachusetts, and Maine, unless you're on the cusp of a hurricane, and even then the undertow will practically kill you. If you really want to learn to surf, go west, young man. So I did.

My first trip to Hawaii was in the summer 1994 and I had just turned thirty-nine, a little late in the game to take up surfing, or so I thought. So I parked my rental car off each road I came to and watched the surfers on the north shore of Maui, Kauai and Oahu. As much as I enjoyed watching these beach bums, surfing isn't really a spectator sport. As one surfer told me as he walked back to his car and threw his board on the top, "Dude, you just get out there and go for it. The waves are radical."

Surfing is as much a part of the Hawaiian tradition as the hula dance, luaus and flowered leis, so perhaps it was only a matter of time before I ventured into the deep blue with a long board and tried my hand at catching a wave and sitting on top of the world. It would be another decade before the opportunity would make itself known.

In the fall of 2005, I was invited to Hawaii once again to give a daylong workshop to a group of Home Care nurses in Honolulu. This, I decided, was the year to learn to surf. This was the year to take the plunge, and become a "surfer-dude" once and for all. The day of my group lesson, a storm kicked up the surf several feet (in fact, local news reports stated that this was one of the biggest surfs on the north shore — in decades.) My instructor was undaunted. Off we went to a "safe" bay in Hale'iwa, (near the Jamison by the Sea restaurant, for those who are familiar with this area) and for the next two hours, we "hung ten." Sometimes five but mostly 10. To say that I got the lion's share of attention during this lesson was no exaggeration. The other two people didn't seem that into it. One gal was so paranoid about sharks, that she parked herself prone on the board till it was time to head back in (I learned a secret about sharks. The sea turtles won't hang around when there are sharks present and on this day there were sea turtles galore). My other classmate was about 13 years old and at that awkward stage in life where the arms and legs are too gangly to be of any coordinated use in sports. He was never able to stay on his board longer than two seconds max.

I am happy to say that I got up on the board each of the 15 attempts… and managed to have many great runs. I figure I must have done well because my instructor called me "dude" at least 10 times, (come to think of it, he seemed to call everyone dude, oh well!) To say that I am now hooked on surfing is no exaggeration. Gidget and the Beach Boys were right. Surfing is The Best!

After the lesson was over, exhilarated, I headed back to the hotel, grabbed my camera and drove back to the beach and spent the next few hours photographing the REAL surfer dudes at the infamous pipeline; poetry in motion. To say that this experience was an unadulterated rush of excitement was no understatement!!!!!

So what did I learn from my surfing experience? To be honest, the topics of surfing and stress management have a lot in common (and I am not saying this for tax write-off purposes). The concepts and ideas that I have been sharing over the decades as I speak about balance, self-reliance, and muscles of the soul (faith, courage, humor, optimism and joy!) are the hallmark of this Hawaiian water sport. Surfing, I discovered, is a great metaphor for coping with stress: Quite literally, it is going with the flow. So hang 10, dudes and dudesses. When the going gets rough, start paddling toward shore, keep your balance, stay focused, and by all means, enjoy the ride!

In the words of one of many surfing dudes who I am sure speaks for all: "I've spent most of my entire life surfing, the rest I've wasted."

2. No Time for a Flat Tire

OH, IF ONLY IT WERE A PERFECT WORLD. But then again, a perfect world would be boring and perhaps quite predictable. So often we wish we could control everything in our lives, yet the simple truth is that we can't. Relinquishing the illusion of control goes a long way toward eliminating stress in our lives and empowering us to take what action we can. It is a lesson we must remind ourselves of daily. In hindsight, it is often said, everything is perfect, most likely because the past cannot be changed or controlled. It can only be appreciated. Take a flat tire — please!

If you were going to drive from Denver to Vail, there is really only one way to go, Interstate 70. Often called the ski resort highway, I-70 is one of the most scenic interstates in the country. It is the same road that Bill and his wife, Margerie, took to Vail one summer afternoon. Bill was to be the keynote speaker at a sales conference, and even though he and his wife had been to Vail before, this time seemed special. There was magic in the air. As they exited off the highway and headed into Vail Village, Bill leaned over and gave his wife a kiss at the stop sign, and whispered the words "I love you."

After they checked in and freshened up, the couple took a walk outside to admire the alpine view. More than once, Bill stopped along the banks of a nearby stream and after taking deep breaths of the fresh mountain air, told Margerie how great it was to be alive.

The conference started early the next morning and Bill's presentation was extremely well received, so much so that the question and answer period was extended, making Bill late for his departure back to the airport. During the last break, Margerie checked out, put their luggage in the rental car and waited in the parking lot for her husband, the car motor running.

Due to the time crunch, the ride back to Denver, which normally takes about two hours, became a marathon of sorts. The two were scheduled to fly back to the East Coast in time for another conference the following day. If things went according to plan, it would work out, but there wasn't much room to play with in the schedule. So when a loud rumbling noise started to come from the left rear of the car, Bill got worried. He knew immediately what it was. A flat. Pulling the car over, the thought occurred to him that this would be a ten-minute stop. They could still make it. It wasn't until he got all the luggage out of the trunk that he found out that the spare tire was also flat. At this point, there was no way they were going to make their flight out of Denver. Margerie said she could see steam coming out of Bill's ears. Raising his hand to the sky, Bill gave God the finger.

Within twenty minutes, a truck pulled up and offered to take the couple to the nearest garage. An hour later, Bill and Margerie pulled out of the gas station and headed to the airport in the hopes of catching the next available flight.

It was at this point, that his wife decided to turn the radio on and listen to the news. What they heard made them pull over to the side of the road once again. A jet bound for Chicago from Denver had crashed in a cornfield in Iowa. The radio announcer repeated the airline flight number. Bill's wife pulled the tickets out of the envelope and gasped. "That was our flight," she said.

Bill stared out past the windshield for a moment and then quickly turned around to give Margerie a hug. Then he opened the door and stepped outside and looked up. The initial curse he had silently flung at the God who flattened car tire(s) now became a prayer of gratitude.

We are instruments in the symphony of life,
and God is the composer/conductor.
Now and then we may play a solo and march to a different beat, but
there is an inherent tempo and rhythm to all of life
that we must honor.

3. Dinner in a Noisy Restaurant

By all accounts, embarrassment is a significant stressor. After all, who wants to be the focus of attention, the point of endless ridicule. No one! Yet sometimes it is just unavoidable, particularly in our youth. The three most embarrassing moments in a child's life, all of which might take place in school, are the following: 1) walking around with your fly open (for guys!), 2) vomiting in front of your friends, and 3) dropping your tray in the school cafeteria. The first may elicit a few giggles, the last typically elicits a round of applause from all those who witnessed the event, as your face mirrors the color of a cooked lobster.

The ambiance of The Grill, a popular Denver eatery, looks nothing like a grade school cafeteria, but it does share a few things in common, most notably the applause when something hits the floor.

I learned this not long ago while eating lunch at The Grill. As I dove my fork into a pile of bow tie pasta, I looked up to see a waiter across the room bump into a customer and lose his grip on some dishes he had just cleared. *Boom! Bam! Crash!*

Now, typically when this happens in a restaurant, a hush can be heard as the last pieces of glass hit the floor. Perhaps even a few gasps. Never applause. But not at this restaurant. Within seconds, the entire staff of food servers broke out in a round of cheers and applause. I was astonished. This happened again a few minutes later, and I could have sworn that this time it was intentional.

As my waiter came by with my dessert, I inquired about the unique response to dropping dishes. He replied, "You see, the philosophy here is to have a good time. Waiting on tables can be very stressful, especially when it's really busy. So, with the encouragement of the management, as a means to reduce our stress, every now and then someone drops a plate or cup. It's a signal to others on the staff to lighten up. Of course when it's an accident, it's even better. Overall, it's a great stress reliever. Here, check this out," as I watched astounded, he tossed a plate on the floor. A thunderous round of applause soon followed. My server took a Broadway bow. All I could do was laugh.

A toast: To life! (now sip and throw the glass behind your back, just don't hit anybody. Then wait for the applause!)

4. Relieving Road Rage

WHEN I GET IN MY CAR, ONE OF THE FIRST THINGS I DO is shove a CD in the CD player and turn up the music. I have several favorite tapes, one is a mix I made I call "Passport to Ecstasy," which are songs from around the globe: Canada, Europe, Africa, Asia, Hawaii, Brazil, and Jamaica. Driving to the airport, this tape gets me in the mood for travel. It's an hour drive from my house to Denver's new airport, and that's during non- rush-hour times. In highway traffic, it can be as long as 90 minutes; the music calms my nerves. Sometimes I see people putting on make-up or shaving, or eating something while talking on the cell phone, and I wonder why there aren't more accidents on our nation's highways. I hear that cars of the future will have fax machines and microwave ovens in the dashboard. My favorite bumper sticker these days is, "Hang up and drive."

Psychological studies show that if you put a small number of rats in a cage, more than likely they will get along. But if the space for each rat decreases as more rats are forced to cohabitate, tension begins to mount. Each rat defends his or her own physical space; the over-crowded conditions lead to frustration and soon fighting occurs. The end result is that some rats die off. Perhaps it comes as no surprise that in many ways, rats and humans are very much alike. Lately, the rat race is becoming more like a rat fight in an over-crowded cage, particularly when people get behind the steering wheels of their cars.

Today, road rage has become the rage on the nation's highways. What was once known as something that could only happen in California, such as drive-by shootings, has now spread eastward—clear to the Atlantic seaboard.

Even Colorado, a state known for its laid-back citizens and polite drivers is no longer immune to the problems of road rage. With over two million people driving to and from work in the Denver Metro area, frustrations hit an all time record in the summer of 1997. A task force was created to examine the situation. A recommendation was made to place more police on the roads, hoping to minimize raging tempers. It was rumored that people were getting tickets for flipping the bird, and cutting off motorists without the proper use of a signal. Governor Roy Romer came up with his own idea as well. In an effort to bring peace to the mountain state, Romer suggested to Colorado drivers that rather than raising the middle finger as a non-verbal gesture of hostility, they raise two fingers, and give the peace symbol instead. It really does work!

In a moment of frustration remember,
two fingers are better than one!

5. The Reluctant Nurse

BEFORE WESTERN MEDICINE BECAME OBSESSED with diagnostic technology, the foundation of nursing consisted of tender loving care. The advances of modern medicine have been nothing less than phenomenal, yet this aspect of holistic caring has often been neglected, much to the detriment of patient care in general. Given the chance, nurses from Maine to California will tell you they spend more time monitoring screens and filling out forms than attending to the specific needs of their patients.

At the same time as advances in technology raced into the hospitals, an interest in the ageless wisdom of healing began, that which accesses and influences the human energy field. Energy medicine suggests that human beings are comprised of layers of energy, the most dense layer being the physical body. By and large, these layers of energy are undetected by the human eye, but there are those throughout the ages who claim to see these layers of the human energy field, which they describe as layers of consciousness. Physicists call this phenomenon the human energy field. Shamans, healers, and sages refer to them as auras. These same wisdom keepers tell us that love is the greatest healing energy, bringing harmony and balance to the layers of energy, the emotional, mental, and spiritual layers in the human energy field.

In the early seventies, two nurses, Dora Kuntz and Dolores Krieger, synthesized several esoteric aspects of energy healing into a systematic style that they called Therapeutic Touch (TT). For over twenty-five years, the technique of TT has been taught all over the country to nurses as a complementary form of healing in hospital settings. Moreover, although the exact dynamics are not understood by western thought, there have been several clinical studies that document the effectiveness of TT as a therapeutic healing modality. The premise of TT is the healing power of love.

When new ideas (or in this case, old concepts that have been revisited) emerge, they can be perceived to be very threatening to those who, at best, are very attached to their old ways of thinking. Such was the case with the head nurse at a midwest hospital. When she learned that several of her staff were enrolled to take a course in Therapeutic Touch, she was outraged. "That stuff is quackery! Hocus pocus! Nonsense," she yelled! A woman quite attached to her ego, she forbid any of her staff to attend the workshop for fear of reprisal. The staff went anyway. When the group of nurses came back to work the next day, they saw a sign posted on the entrance to the hospital: "There will be no healing in this hospital."

The biggest roadblock on the journey of life is our own ego.
When we encounter a roadblock on our own life journey,
may we first turn within to begin to dismantle it.

6. The Priest and the Snake

MOST OF US KNOW THAT STRESS PRODUCES the fight or flight response. What we tend to forget is that anger is the fight emotion of the fight or flight response (fear being the flight emotion). That's why anger had not received adequate press over the years. It is normal and even healthy to feel brief moments of anger—it's a natural reaction to stress. It is said the average American gets angry at least fifteen times a day. If that number seems high to you, you're not alone. Many people simply ignore these feelings. Perhaps because of the extreme violence associated with anger, we are taught by our parents and teachers not to feel or express our anger. The result, however, can be quite damaging, as the body becomes the battlefield for the war games of the mind. Suppressed anger can result in several physical problems, from migraine headaches and ulcers to TMJ and hypertension.

Current studies on anger reveal that most people don't express anger very well. Actually we do it rather poorly. We either stuff our frustration, or explode with vengeance. In the end, we either abuse ourselves, or manipulate others, neither of which is healthy or productive. Venting anger is thought to be good as long as you vent to the person who angers you; otherwise venting simply validates your anger and the process repeats itself. Exercise, diplomatic communication, and refinement of expectations (every episode of anger is the result of unmet expectations) are three good ways to creatively release anger feelings. But first and foremost, we have to learn to recognize our anger feelings, then honestly validate them.

As a child, I was taught not to show anger. Irish temper not withstanding, I was raised to keep a happy disposition. Later I learned just how toxic to the body this could be, and I began to learn to feel and creatively express my anger. Sometimes, when the moment calls for it, all one needs to do is simply say, "I'm angry." Then let it go. In fact, saying these words helps to let it go. Here is one of my favorite stories about the benefits of anger:

In a remote village at the foot of the Himalayas, where the pine trees of the foothills meet the palms of the rain forest, there was a monk who studied to become a priest. Upon ordination, he was given a plot of land by his elders and with money borrowed from his father, he built a glorious temple. Finely crafted and ornately decorated, the temple took him five years to complete. Because he was so well liked, friends would donate proceeds from their crops, but surprisingly none would assist him in the completion of the temple.

On the day of completion, he hiked the four-mile path to town and posted a proclamation announcing the opening of his temple. So fine was its design and construction, he thought people would come from far and wide to worship there.

Days and weeks past and yet no one came to the temple. Baffled, the priest hiked down the hill to town to inquire why no one would come to worship there. He was told that many people ventured the four-mile hike, but about a mile before the temple, they were chased away by a huge vicious python snake. The villagers were quite scared. It was rumored that the snake had eaten at least four people that year.

Upon hearing this, the priest said he would have a word with the snake, which he did as he headed back home.

"Snake!" he yelled. "You are intimidating the village people who wish to come to my temple. Why do you do this?"

The enormous reptile slithered from behind a large tree and replied, "The village people make too much noise. They disturb my sleep. They irritate me to no end. In my frustration, I scare them away, so I may have some peace."

"Then I will talk with the village people and ask them to be quiet and leave you alone. If they proceed quietly, will you allow them safe passage?" the priest asked.

The snake agreed. So the priest posted a new proclamation announcing his temple with the request to silently pass through the forest.

When the village folk came to the temple to worship, they were awestruck with its craftsmanship. Its beauty was equal to that of the Taj Mahal. Word spread far and wide and soon people came from far away lands to worship there.

So it was time to express his gratitude to the mighty python. The priest walked down the four-mile path to offer his thanks. It wasn't long before he found the snake on the side of the path pulverized, nearly beaten to death.

"Snake! What has happened to you?" the priest asked.

"You told me to let the people pass and that I did. In return, one day they came with clubs and repeatedly hit me."

"Snake, I asked you not to strike and bite. I never said you couldn't hiss."

When you get angry, count to ten, say you're angry, and then let it go.

7. Embracing The Shadow

THE NEXT TIME YOU COME TO COLORADO, plan a visit in the fall, right around the autumnal equinox. It is at this time of year when the aspens begin to turn yellow, setting the mountains ablaze in gold. It is also at this time when the elk start their mating season, a ritual which is fascinating to watch as the bulls strut around the female cows looking for a date. They emit a peculiar noise from their vocal cords that is known in the Rocky Mountain region as "bugling."

Recently, a good friend of mine, Darren, called me up announcing plans to move to Colorado. As part of the long-standing spirit of hospitality in the West, I offered him a place to stay while he came out to scout jobs and apartments. Darren is quite the handsome guy, with a smile that oscillates between naiveté and danger. He stands six foot, two inches tall and has the kind of body you see on the cover of men's magazines. Women swoon over him. It's no secret that Darren has a great many likable qualities. I'm particularly fond of his sense of humor. He's also the best storyteller east of the Mississippi. On the day he arrived, the aspens had just started to turn. He took one look at the mountains and told me he was ready to make Colorado his new home. That afternoon, in an attempt to satisfy our cravings to be outdoors, we took a drive up to Rocky Mountain National Park for a hike. Before we even got to the trailhead, we heard scores of bull elk bugling. We climbed up on some rocks for a better view, and like the other tourists there for the same reason, we became engrossed in this intriguing mating behavior.

It might have been the bulk elk prancing around the meadow that became the catalyst for Darren's lead in the conversation, or it might have just been his mood that particular afternoon, but he cocked his head toward me and said bluntly, "I've started going to therapy."

I turned to look him in the eyes, wondering what he might say next.

"I've come to learn that I have a sexual addiction," he explained. "I have a history of infidelity when I'm in a relationship. I finally admitted to myself I need help. So I began counseling sessions with a therapist back east. He's really good."

The conversation was broken by a disturbance among the herd of twenty elk below. Another bull, about 100 yards away was calling to the cows in an attempt to lure them to his harem. One cow got up to check him out. The bull in her group followed. She was quickly re-directed back to the meadow where she eventually sat down.

With peace re-established among the herd, Darren continued. "As a child all the way through high school, I was really a fat kid. Then one year, I got really sick and lost a lot of weight, about forty pounds. When I came back to school I was getting all this attention from the girls. Being a nice guy, I simply tried to be attentive in return. Between hormones, social pressures, and some unresolved family issues, sex became a way to ease my emotions. What started in high school got worse as I got older. In college I had girlfriends, but I could just look at a woman at any party and draw her in. I wasn't devious, although you could certainly call my behavior self-centered."

"So I'm at this wedding a few months ago with my current girlfriend, and during the reception, I meet this woman, a friend of the groom, and we start kissing—right in front of my girlfriend. It was then I thought to myself. This is sick! I really need some help."

I motioned to the trail and we got up off the rock and began our hike toward the lake. I was quite impressed with Darren's openness. Here was a friend I had known for ten years. Although our conversations covered a great many topics over the decade, this was a new level in the depths of personal sharing. I thanked him for revealing this to me.

Darren commented on how hard it was to admit to himself those attributes that are less than flattering. In turn, I commented that he had begun a long, but fruitful process of "embracing the shadow," an expression used in Jungian psychology in which we acknowledge the dark side of our persona, the underbelly of the ego. By coming to terms with these insecurities and related behaviors, we embrace, rather than ignore, these aspects. In doing so, we learn to modify our behavior, or as they say in the Eastern cultures, "domesticate the ego," deflating it to a more manageable, less stress-producing size.

"Sexual addiction is a very common addiction, perhaps too common," Darren explained, "and like other addictions, the fix is short-lived, until the next one comes along. Before I went to therapy,

I thought counseling was for weak sissies. I don't anymore. I think therapy would help a great many people. There are a lot of people like me out there. I know you use a lot of stories in your talks. If you think this will help anyone, you have my permission to use this one too."

The conversation turned once again to the shadow. "My therapist recommended a really good book. It's called, *Out Of The Shadow*. I've also started keeping a journal where I write down my moods. It really helps. Now that we've completely covered the topic of infidelity, my therapist wants to explore the topic of abandonment and of course anger some more. Layer by layer we're uncovering some really important issues."

We walked in silence for several steps. Each of us pondering the challenge that personal growth demands. Darren, who was ahead of me, reached the lake first. He took a seat on a rock at the water's edge. I stood behind the rock looking up at the sky. Distant thunder broke the silence. Moments later, two ducks flew overhead to circle the body of water, descending slowly for their landing. We talked some more about the growing pains of life and concluded that hard as they are, the end result is worth it. With another clap of thunder, Darren stood up and we decided to head back toward the parking lot.

As we approached the car, the calls of two bull elk reverberated in stereo. Darren smiled at me. "I've decided when I move to Colorado next month, I am not getting involved in a relationship. I've got some more work to do on myself first. And I'm going to try a committed relationship with nature," he said.

All of us have a shadow, a dark side where our less-than-favorable attributes appear. It could be said that it is the shadow of the ego that we must come to terms with, to acknowledge, to understand and to reconcile behaviors associated with the dark side. These can range from judgments and prejudices to full blown addictions. Like an orphaned child, the shadow begs to be embraced. In doing so, we begin to stop the cycle of one or more unhealthy stress-prone behaviors.

8. Downsize This!

A WORD THAT TODAY IS USED SYNONYMOUSLY WITH STRESS is change. As a rule, people don't like change. Change tends to disrupt our comfort zones, that area of security created by our thoughts, ideas, perceptions, possessions, and even our locale. As the expression goes, 'the only person who likes change is a wet baby.'

As we spin into the twenty-first century, change is not only present, it is here with a vengeance. Sociologists tell us that while change has always been a factor in human evolution, the rate of change we are experiencing today is unparalleled to any other time in history. And people are finding this rate of change quite stressful.

A common reaction to unsuspecting change is anger. Feelings of anger can manifest from impatience to all-out rage. Like an airborne virus, there is much anger in the air today. As a consultant who goes to corporations to conduct stress management seminars, I often come in contact with a great many angry employees — employees who will soon be restructured out of a job. And because everything connects, the reverberations of changes in the corporate landscape ripple out to reach every community, and every family.

It is fair to say that every sensation of anger is the result of an unmet expectation. By and large, most unmet expectations these days deal with job security or lack thereof. A critical aspect of the American dream is based on job security—the ability to make house payments, finance a child's tuition, or vacation once a year on remote exotic islands of the Caribbean. Moreover, the Puritan ethic still dominates the American psyche, where people typically see their self-worth in the form of a paycheck.

Due to the dynamics of the current corporate landscape, change, in the form of downsizing and rightsizing is an annoying common occurrence. As such, a life-long career with one company is quite rare and job security is a thing of the past. While anger is an appropriate response to losing your job, it's important not to get stuck in it. Rather, we must grieve and move on.

Like me, Todd got his aerobic exercise by swimming. I would see him in the pool when I would workout in the early mornings. Our conversations would range from the water temperature to the global economy and most everything in between. An engineer with a technology company, Todd, a young married man with two children, was well situated on the corporate ladder of success.

One day I changed my exercise routine and headed to the pool at mid-morning. As I walked onto the deck, the pool was empty, save for one man ready to enter the water in lane five. I walked over and greeted Todd with a handshake.

"On vacation this week?" I asked.

"Yeah, a permanent vacation, you could say," he replied. "I got laid off from work yesterday. Corporate restructuring! Can you believe it?"

"Wow!" I said with a sigh. "Sorry to hear that."

"Me too," said Todd in a huff. "Excuse me, but I have to work off some frustrations." Adjusting his goggles one last time, he dove into the water.

A week later, I saw Todd at the pool again. Standing chest deep in water, we talked about his situation once more. He was still angry, but more mellow than our last exchange. He indicated that his severance package was good enough to last a few months and he was taking time to think over his life and spend more time with his children.

It was more than a month later before I saw Todd at the pool, again at mid-morning. This time his eyes were bright with excitement and no trace of resentment was in his voice.

"Howdy Todd. What's up?" I said.

"Things are pretty good. I have started my own consulting company. I'm really enjoying it."

"Hey, that's wonderful!" I replied.

"You know, I never would have thought I could have said this, but losing my job was the best thing that ever could have happened to me. For ten years I felt like I was selling my soul to the company, only to get kicked in the ass. Now, I am my own boss. I call the shots. I can truly say I know what it means to feel empowered."

For those people who work through the grieving process of loss, Todd's comments are not uncommon. In times of stress, it is easy to fall into the role of the victim. But to stay there very long is neither healthy to body nor soul. Every unmet expectation is a death and dying process. And every death, big or small, requires grieving.

The personal answer to career changes isn't always self-employment. But the answer is always found within.

Security is not found in a job, a spouse, or home. Like the Kingdom of God, security is found within, and when we realize this we can be secure anywhere.

9. Aloha! (A Post Card from Hawaii)

PERHAPS BECAUSE THERE IS NO OCEAN ANYWHERE NEAR the Colorado Rockies, I have an affinity for all things aquatic. Ok, I'll be honest, all things aquatic in Hawaii. I am sitting by the shores of the southern Pacific Ocean on the big Island of Hawaii, and it is a side of heaven I cannot glimpse from my daily vantage point looking at Rocky Mountain National Park every morning from my backyard patio. Call me spoiled, but I walk in two worlds. Azure blue waters lap the shore as I write these words. A cool ocean breeze seduces the senses and this is only equaled by the fragrances of plumeria, a heavenly scented flower in shades of yellow, pink or white that smells nothing less than divine. If it sounds like I am in love, you're right. I am in love with life. Hawaii has cast its spell on me. Yet I am not alone. Everyone walks around with smiles on their faces. And it's no wonder that this place is crawling with newlyweds.

I have just finished facilitating the Spirit of the Hawaiian Landscape workshop and it is no exaggeration to say that it was an extraordinary event. The town of Palhala (the southern, undisturbed by resorts, part of the isle) where the workshop was held is the closest town to the island's only black sand beach, a location where the sea turtles love to congregate. We saw many. They are huge, perhaps 3-4 feet long. They are adorable, too.

Days before the workshop began, I was busy at work (smile) building my stock of island photographs in the hopes to have one or more images grace a future book cover.

Of all my Big Island adventures, the highlights include a 3.5-mile trek across hardened black lava at sunset (and back in the dark) to take a peek at Pele, the Hawaiian Goddess of Creation. A previous visit to honor Pele ten years ago met with disappointment — no one was allowed anywhere near the red lava. This time I was more fortunate. I took several photos that night. The best images came when it was completely dark. Perhaps equally amazing (and not captured on film, oops — digital flashcard) was the star-filled heaven replete with the star-studded Milky Way that nearly everyone except me, mistook for a long cloudbank. There were no clouds in the sky that night, save the steam from the volcano.

Not to be outdone by the active volcano was another evening snorkeling at sea with giant Manta Rays. On this particular night, there were about six Manta Rays swimming with us in an event that can only best be described as an underwater ballet. These magnificent creatures, with up to fourteen-foot wingspans, would perform these graceful somersaults in an effort to scoop the plankton drawn to us by our flashlights. Completely harmless (no stingers or teeth) these behemoths sailed around us like eagles hovering over the earth on a warm thermal. Amazing! Unbelievable! I even tried to capture the moment with my underwater camera.

What would an essay about Hawaiian healing be without a little insight to the Polynesian culture that imbued such a rich tradition of sacredness toward the land? Here are a few of the glimmers of wisdom shared by the Kahunas during the workshop. Enjoy.

- Hawaii translates as: Ha- *the Breath of Life* Wai- *the Water of life* i- *divinity*

- Aloha translates to mean: *Alo* (in the presence of) *Ha* (breath of life)

- Spiritual Energy is called *Mana.*

- The first medicine is Forgiveness
  If a grudge is held, it will become your burden (kaumaha) and your illness

- In the Hawaiian culture the mind and body are never separate from spirit.

- Native Hawaiians believe that nature is one of our greatest healers.

- A great many diseases are believed to be the result of obsession and acquisition.

- Hawaiians believe if you really wish to pursue something with the right intention, Ke Akua (God) will bless you.

- Before the missionaries came, Hawaiian's melodic language was only spoken, not written.
  All words have mana (spiritual energy). Words can heal or destroy. Use all your words wisely.

- The Hula is a Hawaiian visual expression of praise.
- Family ('ohana) is not just blood relatives but all close friends are considered family.

  'Ohana means a sense of belonging, a sense of direction and a sense of self.

  'Ohana is always there for times of need and celebration.

- Hawaiian Hospitality (ho'okipa) is the way of life. You never turn anyone away. You always share what you have. One never hides or hoards anything.
- Hawaiians know that man is not superior to nature. We are all stewards of the land and ocean. Aloha is to share, to give and receive.

The word aloha has many meanings, from hello and welcome to I love you. The Hawaiian culture is the epitome of going with the flow. In this crazy 24/7 world of cell phones, urban sprawl, laptops, terrorism, iPods, corporate mergers, text messaging, and global warming, we should take a lesson from our Hawaiian brothers and sisters and honor the aloha spirit everyday.

On the last day of my island trip a storm began to move in and torrents of rain came down everywhere. I sat at the Kona airport, soaking wet. Suddenly, where there was nothing but a grey sky, there appeared the most beautiful double rainbow to the east. Hawaii, it is said, is the land of rainbows.

The Hawaiians have an expression to suit every occasion including my last experience, an expression that we would all do well to remember: No rain, no rainbows.

STRESSED is DESSERTS Spelled Backward

Holy Moments
Divine Inspirations

A HOLY MOMENT IS A PERSONAL EXPERIENCE where we are embraced by the arms of God. Psychologist Abraham Maslow called these 'peak experiences,' a period when, through some situation or circumstance, we unexpectedly encounter the divine—however we conceive this to be. With the understanding that we are always in the presence of the divine, a holy moment is a conscious recognition of this divine presence, a gentle awakening of sorts. Examples of holy moments include mystical dreams, synchronistic events, magical happenings, or a flash of brilliance, to name just a few. These moments may be extremely brief, but they typically end the same way; each time we kiss the face of God.

Holy moments are mystical and exhilarating. By all accounts, a holy moment is *the* most pleasant human experience. Some people even call it a 'spiritual orgasm.' Anyone can have a holy moment, and Maslow argued that we should strive to have as many as humanly possible. We may never fully understand it, but this should not deny our appreciation of the mystery.

Distress may grab the headlines each night, but there are two sides of the stress coin; distress and *eustress*, the good kind of stress. If we are honest with our memories, then we know that life's balance sheet is pretty well even with both. A beautiful sunset, a warm furry puppy, or the reunion of good friends are indeed special events that simply remind us to live in the present moment. Like a pearl in an oyster, holy moments can appear in the ugliest situations, and every stressor is an opportunity for spiritual growth. As Maslow explained, you don't have to climb a mountain to have a peak experience. Holy moments can happen anywhere, at any time.

1. The Day of The Dolphin

ON A 1989 TRIP TO FLORIDA WHERE MY FATHER HAD RETIRED, I discovered he had contracted cancer. It was rather unsettling, but he assured me that with chemotherapy it would all be under control. After visiting a few days, he suggested I take the car and drive up to Disney World's Epcot Center, which I had not visited before. He declined to come, saying that he had been so many times, he preferred to sit this one out. Reluctantly, I packed a small suitcase, took the car keys, and headed north toward Orlando.

At the time of my visit, there was a lull in the tourist season. I arrived at the gates to Epcot early and never once saw an unbearable crowd. Perhaps it was the circumstance of my Florida visit, but Epcot did nothing for me. Where others were amazed and amused, I was bored and discontent—too much plastic, too many mechanical devices, and too many recordings telling me to keep "your hands inside the rails." I had planned to spend three whole days at Disney World, but after the first few hours, all I wanted to do was leave. By day's end, I wound up at the aquarium watching the fish. A fellow tourist from Nebraska, much more enthralled than I, turned to me and said, "Isn't this place great?" The disappointment on my face spoke volumes. I explained my dismay and my new acquaintance came up with a plan.

"You should go to Sea World," he said. "You can't beat nature and there is plenty of it there."

I thanked him and considered the possibility as I walked toward my car in the massive parking lot.

Taking his hint, the next morning I woke early and drove over to Sea World. As I waited for the gates to open, I was relieved to see few tourists clamoring to get in. I flashed my ticket to the man at the turnstiles and walked slowly into the grounds, map outstretched, trying to get my bearings on the theme park grounds. I stopped at a small tank and pulled out the day's list of events so I could coordinate my visit. A large part of me still wanted to leave Orlando, and a bigger part of me was concerned about my dad.

I faced the tank and looked up from the schedule for a moment. The deep pool before me was filled with a rich blue water, but not one sign of marine life. Every round corner was empty. I returned to the map again, but I became distracted moments later by a noisy splash.

There in front of me was a dolphin, nearly out of the water, eye to eye with me, moving its tail back and forth to hold his position. I dropped the map and schedule on the pool edge. Then I smiled.

I don't know why, but suddenly, I felt compelled to put my arms around the dolphin and give it a hug. The embrace seemed to last for minutes, although I know it was less. Then, as if to say good-bye, the dolphin slowly sank back into the water, gave a few clicks, and was gone.

I was pleasantly stunned. I even wondered if I imagined the whole thing, but my shirt was soaked—this was no hallucination. Some lady quickly approached, said hello and asked why the dolphin came to me. I had no idea what to tell her. I was as surprised as she was, perhaps even more so.

I stood at the tank for another twenty minutes hoping to see the dolphin and thank it, but the tank was empty once again. I was speechless and filled with joy.

To catch a falling star, you have to stand underneath it.

2. A Fish Called Allison

At the mid-point of every semester in my stress management class, after I have introduced and the students have practiced a host of coping techniques, I teach something called 'confrontation of a stressor.' In this exercise, I explain to my students that the concepts of stress management are only concepts if they are not practiced outside the classroom. To really make these concepts concrete, one must employ them in times of stress. So I ask them to make a list of their top ten stressors and pick one of the top three and come to terms with it, to face it and resolve it—like a fight with a roommate, issues with parents, or money problems. In doing so, I ask that they not come away the victim. Rather, everyone is instructed to walk away the victor, even if there are some cuts and scrapes along the way. I explain that avoidance is the number one coping technique for stress, but typically, avoidance does nothing to resolve stress. Rather, it is the perfect recipe for perpetuating stress. Confrontation of a stressor is an exercise in resolving stressors, no matter how big or small.

I give each student two weeks to work on this assignment. In turn, they are asked to write about their experience and describe what they learned from it. When I get done explaining the assignment, I get looks from students as if to say, "You've got to be kidding!" On that day, they walk out the classroom door to scores of problems begging to be resolved. Before you give it a try, which I sincerely hope you will, I'd like to tell you a story.

In the spring of 1991, I had a student named Allison Fisher. Allison was bright, energetic, and beaming with success. A radio and television major, Allison was a graduating senior and looking forward to a promising broadcasting career. In an earlier class assignment in Art Therapy, Allison drew herself as a fish. The picture was quite revealing, even to a novice in art therapy. The fish was an orange color, a goldfish; the color orange signified change. The green plant near the fish symbolized groundedness and stability. If a fish could show confidence, this fish did—an underlying sense of accomplishment through a great many achievements and accolades that Allison shared as she explained her illustration.

Two weeks after I announced this particular assignment, students filed into class to see a lit candle in the center of the room and the lights dimmed. I invited everyone to sit in a circle around the candle and then asked if they would be willing to share their experiences with confronting their stressor. In a typical fashion, I explained that we are all teachers and we can learn from each other. I asked that no one pass judgment if a particular student's choice in dealing with a stressor differed from their own. They all agreed.

First I shared my experience. Then I asked for a volunteer. Allison spoke next.

"My stressor is breast cancer, it runs in my family," she explained. "My mother has had it, my aunt, and my grandmother too. For a great many years, I have been scared of breast cancer, even though I know that I, too, am at risk. So upon hearing this assignment, I decided it was time to go for a mammogram. I was extremely nervous, but, last week I made an appointment with my physician."

The class was silent, all eyes fixed on Allison. With an air of confidence, she concluded her story with a nervous smile, "The test was negative. What did I learn from this experience? I learned that by running away from my fear I was really running toward it. Making us do this assignment was hard, but I now know that I can face anything," she said. Little did we know how prophetic these words would be for her.

One by one, each student shared his or her story. One student coming to terms with a promiscuous past took an AIDS test. Another student renewed her relationship with her estranged father. Another student quit her job to focus on school work. Yet another confided about a recent abortion. By the end of the hour, the students had formed a powerful support group. Much healing took place that afternoon.

Five years later, I was visiting a colleague who happened to mention a friend of hers who had survived breast cancer. "A classic case of heredity," Karen said. "Her grandmother, her mother, and now her." Then came more bad news. Her friend, now living in L.A. with a job in broadcast media, had been diagnosed with breast cancer once again.

"Are you speaking of Allison?" I inquired.

"Why yes, do you know her?" Karen said.

"Yes, she was a student of mine," I said, shocked and saddened at the news. I thought back to the illustration of the goldfish and something told me it was going to be all right.

Later that summer, I found myself in L.A. as part of my book tour and arranged to meet Allison for lunch where we shared snippets of our lives after each of us left The American University.

It was Allison who brought up the subject of cancer. She shared with me her healing journey, her dissatisfaction with some of her physicians, her disdain for the health care system ('a sick care system,' she called it), and her introduction to various forms of complimentary medicine—herbs, T'ai chi, homeopathy, and acupuncture.

The focus of the conversation shifted to an award she won as a promising black leader in broadcast journalism. Allison was beaming. "I want to be involved with quality programming on television. There is so much junk out there," she explained with a glowing vitality. I thought to myself, if there is anyone who can do it, it's Allison. I later learned that Allison played no small part in social activism, assuming the role of a Big Sister, and volunteered countless hours of community service to help the city's underserved population.

On a recent trip to L.A., for my last book signing, I saw Allison again. She had unsettling news. The cancer was back, this time in her lungs. She was going to take time off from her graduate studies and focus all her energies on healing.

I thought that night, as I gave my last book presentation, about the nature of healing and wholeness. As I have taught my students, healing is the integration, balance, and harmony of mind, body, spirit, and emotions. Healing differs from curing in that it's not simply removing symptoms of disease and illness. Healing is coming to a sense of peace about who we are and why we are here, no matter the course of our illness. Allison is at that place of peace. In the words of Carl Gustav Jung, we come into the world to bring light into the darkness and Allison has done just that!

When you were born, you cried and your family rejoiced. Live your life so that when you die, you rejoice and your family cries.

P.S. Allison Fisher crossed the threshold of heaven on March 9, 1998.

3. Tell Me About Your Saints!

I AM CONVINCED THAT THERE ARE MANY SAINTS WALKING AMONG US. More often than not, they are unrecognized by the general public and definitely not canonized by any church. These people are the real unsung heroes of humanity, and it is only with hindsight that we may ever know their true identity, for they don't seek the public eye and their names are never mentioned in the headline news. But they are the teachers of compassion in action.

It is not uncommon in the course of a workshop for people to ask me why such chaos has entered their lives—illness, death of a loved one, bankruptcy. So many of us face such difficult circumstances. Is it fate? Maybe karma? Who knows? We many never understand why catastrophic events befall us. Rather than shake our fists at the sky, it might be best to take a deep breath and count our blessings. Perhaps instead of seeing ourselves as victims we should look upon ourselves as teachers. Indeed, it is a courageous soul who braves the harsh emotional elements of planet earth for the responsibility of daily life is a heavy load. This is a story I have shared to comfort those who seek to remove the yoke of victimhood.

Several years ago, I had an enlightening conversation with an acquaintance over a pita sandwich on this very topic. Originally from Asia, Ranjan was in the United States for graduate studies. It was a common interest in tennis that brought us together, but being rather new to the Western world with an insatiable appetite for Western culture, Ranjan soon turned the conversation to other topics.

On this day, after swallowing a bite of his sandwich, he took a sip of iced tea and said, "Tell me about your saints."

After mentally switching gears, I looked up with a smile and replied, "If you knew my behavior as a child, you'd realize I am the last person to answer this question." Not satisfied with my reply he repeated his question, "Tell me about your saints."

Trying to sound as intelligent as I could with what I felt was an inadequate background in matters of theology, yet keeping my tongue partially in my cheek, I proceeded to explain the nature of sainthood in the Christian Church.

"Well, as I understand it, a saint's life begins like anyone else's, really. But within a few years, perhaps a few decades, things go downhill. Usually there is some transformational life crisis they experience, but just when all seems lost, there is some divine intervention, an epiphany, and this individual's life is transformed to do good deeds for humanity.

"Oh," I added, "there is one more thing. They have to perform a few miracles before they die. But it doesn't end there. To qualify as a real saint, anyone up for nomination has to do a miracle or two after they die as well, otherwise, they are out of contention.

"The whole process is quite complicated. It's kind of like getting nominated for an Academy Award, and sometimes just as political," I said with a faint smile.

I paused, and glanced up at my friend to observe his reaction.

He looked attentive and intrigued. "I see," he said.

After a few more bites on our sandwiches, with an air of curiosity, I started up the conversation again. Naively I asked, "Are there saints in your culture?"

"Yes," he replied, "but not quite as you have described."

What he said next brought comfort to my mind, and continues to do so each time I reflect on it. His words made more clear an understanding of the mysteries of life—those moments of mayhem or misfortune may be intended for a higher purpose, to help others. While the burden is indeed heavy, there is no room for victimhood.

"In our culture," he continued, "we believe each person lives many lives. When one reaches a point where one has balanced all his or her karma, they come to a place we call *nirvana*, what you might call heaven. Yet there are those souls who, given the chance to move to a higher level of consciousness hesitate. For as great as the pleasures as this new journey holds, a few souls look back with regret because the peace of heaven is a shallow victory when not shared by those they loved on earth. So, in an effort to help elevate the souls of their loved ones, they brave the dense earthly existence once more. In most every case they take on a hardship, a disease, some catastrophe or burden for the sole purpose to provide an opportunity for love to manifest from the hearts of those they touch. These are the one's we call *saints.* "

Each burden we carry is opportunity for spiritual growth, not only for ourselves but for those we come in contact with as well. Carry your burden gracefully. Likewise, be mindful of those you walk past or meet, for there are saints among us everywhere.

4. Cell Memory and Body Wisdom

AFTER PRESENTING A SEMINAR TO A GROUP OF EDUCATORS in Des Moines, Iowa, I was approached by a young woman named Sheila. She was quite moved by something I had said. In my talk I had explained that every cell pulsates with energy directly connected to our emotions through substances called neuropeptides. Citing the work of my colleague, Candace Pert, who is credited with discovering this mind-body link, I then went on to discuss the concept of cell memory and body wisdom, particularly new discoveries with organ transplant recipients. Apparently not only cell tissue is exchanged during an organ transplant. Part of the donor's human spirit, contained in each cell, goes along for the ride (to learn more about this, read *The Heart's Code* by Paul Pearsall or *A Change of Heart* by Sylvia Claire). I cited some remarkable examples of cell consciousness, and it was this that inspired Shelia to share her story with me.

A nurse for the Des Moines County School district, Sheila was moved by an article she saw in the paper one day about bone marrow transplants. Feeling blessed by her physical health, Sheila heard a calling to investigate what this was all about. So in April of 1997, she signed up for a test to see if she was eligible to make a donation—the gift of renewed life.

For Sheila, making a donation was more than an altruistic act. In her heart she felt a drive to help someone else in his or her healing process. She explained to me that although she had been through the typical experiences that test our patience, she was now on an even keel. She was happy and felt the need to share it. At age twenty-five, it wasn't curiosity that lured Sheila to be tested, it was compassion.

"They do a blood test to see if there is a possible match through tissue type. As I was tested, I was told that there is a 1 in 2 million chance of having a match. As I walked to my car, I kind of forgot about it. But then a week later, I received a phone call to confirm the test—there was a match. I was so excited."

The match was an eight-year-old girl with leukemia. Sheila was scheduled for a bone marrow extraction and then waited to hear about the results. "When you donate bone marrow, you're not allowed direct person contact with the recipient for a whole year. I sent her cards and a cute little teddy bear. But I felt a bond with this little girl like you wouldn't believe. It went far beyond thinking about her and correspondence. I could feel myself as a part of her, and perhaps equally strange, I could feel her in me."

Sheila described this bond as being so strong that she could practically feel her bone marrow cells in the little girl's body. Things changed dramatically on July 29th, for on this day, Sheila learned that Laurie Minor, the eight-year-old girl whom Sheila had bonded with in spirit and body cells, had died.

"It was all so devastating. Never once did I think that it wouldn't work," Sheila explained. But something happened that Sheila finds difficult to put into words. As she described it, "Just as I became a part of her, she became a part of me. It's as if I can now feel her presence. I know she's with me."

Within a few months, the girl's mother contacted her. "I think our meeting was healing for all of us. I saw some photographs and videotapes of Laurie. Let me tell you this kid was full of life. She may not be here on earth, but her vitality is still very present," Sheila said.

Sheila's life has been changed from the experience. When not performing her role as a school nurse, she is actively involved in fund-raising activities, primarily for bone marrow transplants.

"Through Laurie's parents, I met Dan Burl, the executive director of STRIDE, an organization that puts on charity events for leukemia patients. Dan Burl, it turns out, ran a marathon to raise money for Laurie's medical expenses. Next year I am going to run a marathon in Disney World to raise money," Sheila explained. "I have over $2000 so far and a new purpose in my life." And the spirit of Laurie Minor lives on.

Life is a balance of giving and receiving. There is pleasure and pain in both. The physiology and spirituality of stress, both good and bad, reside in every cell. As the advances of technology increase our ability to prolong life, so too, do the mysteries of life unfold. Gifts of the heart need not be big, only sincere to make a big difference in the world.

5. Holiday Stress Survival

REMEMBER THE DAYS WHEN THE WINTER HOLIDAY SEASON used to be fun? There was plenty of excitement, if not magic in the air. People would say, "How are you?" and really mean it. Don't laugh, but it wasn't that long ago that people took vacation time the last two weeks of December — just to relax and be with the family. The Christmas holiday season was a time of family get-togethers, great food and engaging conversations. Oh, those were the good old days.

Today the holidays have become hijacked by corporate America as an excuse to push consumerism to the nth degree. For most, the season is anything but jolly. Tensions are high and people are stressed to the max. Kids and adults are drowning in presents, adults are afflicted with an extra serving of guilt about not doing enough or buying enough for the kids. In addition to Chanukah and Christmas, we have Kwanzaa, the Winter Solstice celebrations and perhaps some new holidays, all with pending commercial implications. Ugh! Traffic jams, credit card debt, rude shoppers, batteries not included, last minute Christmas shopping and unmet expectations have made the holiday season a mockery of itself. As Linus said to Charlie Brown, "Whatever happened to peace on Earth, goodwill toward men?" What is supposed to be a joyous time of merriment has become a black hole in the winter calendar, sucking people in as they disappear in the fog of pre and post seasonal, shopping-induced depression. Are these the good old days our children will remember?

Have no fear, my friends, there is a way out of this mess. It takes a little bit of courage, some discipline and an ounce or two of creativity, all of which is at your disposal right now. You just have to want it. As Mitch Album described in his book, *Tuesdays With Morrie*, we don't have to participate in the American culture. We can rebel. We can be a culture of one. We can start our own culture. And that is exactly what Molly did. She started her own holiday culture. Her family has thanked her many times over for pulling them out of the black hole and into the light, which after all is what the season is all about.

Fed up with what she felt was the manipulation of the holiday season, Molly decided to reinvent the holiday. First she made up a list of new holiday rules and then asked her family, and her husband's family to honor them. She confided in me that at first it was hard because friends and extended family just didn't get it. But over time, with an air of assertiveness, the culture of Molly's family changed. Here are her winter holiday rules.

- Each person shall pick the name of a family member with whom to exchange gifts. One gift per person. No exceptions.
- Each person must make the gift, not buy something. (The purpose of this rule was to encourage the creative process within the family).
- Exchange of gifts will follow the Christmas Eve dinner.
- All family members will eat together at all morning and evening meals.
- No television watching allowed from December 20 through January 1 (listening to music or playing group games is highly encouraged).
- All family members will offer to serve one hour in the local soup kitchen on Christmas day, offering a helping hand to those who are in greater need than oneself.
- Get outside into nature: take a walk, snowshoe, anything but get some fresh air and enjoy part of the day outside!

Molly noticed that Christmas actually became a more joyous time in the house. There was less stress and quarreling among the kids and the interactions began to nurture healthier relationships among all family members. If you think Molly's holiday culture is something you would like to join, step right up. You can, however, make your own holiday culture. Here are some ideas:

Tips for getting through the holidays with a smile on your face:

1. Consider having family members pick a name from a hat for gift giving. Not only does it keep the focus on family relationships it also keeps the bottom line in focus.
2. For a joyous time in the calendar year, many people are quick tempered and short fused. Learn to fine-tune your expectations for the holiday season.

3. Best to keep the sweets to a minimum. Refined sugar tends to suppress the immune system, making one more susceptible to colds and flus. Sweets aren't the only thing that can topple your immune system; fats and alcohol are also known to have an adverse effect as well. As the rule goes, keep everything in moderation.

4. Consider some interactive games with family members such as a game of charades. Try something other than sitting around the television. In fact, consider unplugging the television! Make the holiday season worth remembering.

5. Home made gift certificates are always a good idea (e.g., mow the lawn, a night by the fireplace, etc.)

6. Consider opening gifts on Christmas Eve, after dinner, leaving Christmas day set a side for family, food and giving thanks.

7. Get outside on Christmas morning. Take a walk in the nearest park or beachfront. Enjoy the solitude of a quiet morning to yourself. Go hiking, skating, snowshoeing, skiing or boarding, but get outside and enjoy nature.

8. Consider watching *"It's a Wonderful Life"* as a family then when the movie is over, talk about the movie's theme with your spouse, children or parents.

9. Consider being thankful for all the things you have rather than the things you don't have.

May we bring light into this world to make it a safer and happier place for everyone. God bless us all, everyone.

6. A Cosmic Joke

JUST AS STRESS AND SPIRITUALITY ARE PARTNERS in the dance of life, so too are fate and free will. But if there is an overriding game plan to our lives, and I believe there is, then certain forces will prevail to right us on our track, should we stray too far from the divine game plan. Synchronistic moments are more than an acknowledgment and appreciation of our divine connectedness. Quite possibly, they are signs of the cosmic correction factor when free will has taken a turn that is not in our best interest.

Katy is a dear friend of mine. We attended college together at the University of Maine. Fifteen years later, I was living in Washington D.C. She had just changed jobs in Boston, and she had some time off before she started at a new advertising firm. She called one evening to chitchat and get caught up on things as we typically did once or twice a year. This phone call was different than the others though. She called to tell me she was dating a guy named Stanley and he had just proposed to her; she was now engaged. Although excited for her, something was amiss in her voice. I could tell she was aware of it too.

Later in the conversation she indicated that there was something a little off in the relationship with Stanley, but she couldn't quite put her finger on it. "No relationship is perfect," I commented. As the conversation continued, Katy mentioned that Stanley had left for Europe on business and would be gone two weeks. It had been over five years since Katy and I had visited, so I invited her down to the nation's capitol for the weekend, to get away and gain perspective on things. She agreed. Friday night we fixed dinner and talked for hours. The plan was to go sightseeing on Saturday. Although I had the best intentions to be a good tour guide, I also had exams to grade over the weekend. So excusing myself for a few hours, I dropped Katy off at the nearest metro stop, gave her complete instructions on the Metro rail system (D.C. has a superb subway) and off she went to explore the Smithsonian.

In D.C., clocks are set in a time warp. Everyone is late. On that day, so was I. Consequently, I missed our appointed rendezvous at Metro Center by almost an hour. I ran up to Katy at the platform to apologize, but there was no forgiveness on her face. She was livid! As I tried to explain, she waved her hands. Within seconds I was to learn that I wasn't the focus of her anger. What she proceeded to tell me was beyond belief. More accurately, it was divine intervention through the grace of synchronicity. The morning at the metro stop was not the chance coupling of two random events. But first, let me set the stage.

Each Metro train has about ten cars, with two doors on each side. Trains come and go every few minutes, with hundreds of people entering and exiting the subway cars. To a visitor, it looks like mass confusion. To D.C. residents, it's just organized chaos. The chance of what was to happen that morning at the platform, before I appeared, is a zillion to one. Katy had waited patiently for a train to arrive and take her to the Smithsonian. Lights flashed on the platform indicating a train was approaching. The Metro pulled up and came to a stop. The train doors opened, directly in front of Katy, and out stepped Stanley, holding hands with another woman. Katy was aghast! She just stared at him in disbelief. Their eyes met and locked. In less than a nanosecond, Stanley yelled out to Katy, "What are *you* doing here?" Then, as if the imposition was too much to handle, he turned and quickly walked away, arm in arm with his new woman.

Once Katy calmed down, I said, "Wow! I think God is trying to tell you something here."

We made our exit above ground and headed to the Pavilion for lunch. It didn't take long for her to realize the meaning of the coincidence. Later, over a cup of coffee, she confided that intuitively she felt he was seeing other women, but a part of her (ego, perhaps?) just wasn't ready to admit it, that is until now. In the course of a few hours, grief yielded to humor, as Katy smiled at the cosmic joke played on her.

There are no random events in the universe. A coincidence is God's way of remaining anonymous.

7. For Pete's Sake

OF ALL THE STORIES IN MY BOOK, *Stand Like Mountain, Flow Like Water,* one seems to bring up more questions than the rest. It's the story of Peter, the little boy with bone cancer. People often ask me how he is. Until a few months ago, I could only answer with, "I don't know." But as fate would have it, I ran into Pete once again. Here is the story of Pete, and as Paul Harvey says, "the rest of the story."

I met Peter Knuti on a plane ride from Denver to Los Angeles. Typically I use time in the air to recharge my personal energy, so I don't engage in too many conversations. This trip was different. I struck up a conversation with Peter because for the entire trip, his foot rested on my lap. Peter had the window seat (mine actually), I had the aisle, and his mother sat in between us. The weight of his leg suggested a pretty heavy cast somewhere between his seat and mine.

Peter, I learned, was ten years old, heading out on a trip to Disneyland.

"So," I began the conversation, "Tell me about your leg."

"Well" said Peter, "I was diagnosed with bone cancer a few months ago. I had an operation that is why my leg is in a cast. It's OK! They thought they might have to amputate, but it turns out my leg's fine," Peter explained.

"I was rather upset, as you can imagine," he continued, "but I realized something soon after I learned I had cancer."

"Oh yeah," I said, "what's that?"

"Well, I remembered seeing this TV show. Every kid who has cancer gets to make a wish. You know what my wish was?" he inquired with an optimistic smile.

"No, what was it?" I asked.

"Well I always wanted to swim with dolphins, and you know what? I did! I made my wish and it came true. Last month I swam with some dolphins in Florida."

I sat in my seat, 35,000 feet above the earth smiling at a little boy with blond hair and a great big smile thinking to myself, this kid has so much optimism, he doesn't need a plane to get to L.A. Hearing his story, I thought, with his level of optimism, I'll bet there isn't a cancer cell left in his body.

Peter's mom, Bonnie, jumped into the conversation. "Tell the man about what you're doing now, Peter."

"I've become a spokesperson for the Make-a-Wish Foundation," Peter said with a smile. "I go around and give motivational talks to kids like me who have cancer."

Here's a kid, I thought who has definitely made lemonade from lemons.

The conversation jumped around various topics before the plane landed and soon we were at the baggage claim area before we parted ways.

Before I tell "the rest of the story," a little background information is needed to set the stage. For the past 20 years people unknown to me walk up and ask me for my autograph. As it turns out, they don't want mine, they want the person they think I look like. Since the "JT" album came out in 1975, I have been mistaken for the singer, James Taylor, at least two to three times a week—for over twenty years. I have to admit there is a striking similarity with facial features, even mannerisms and expressions (despite the fact that he is five inches taller than I). I once met his brother, Livingston Taylor, and the first thing he said to me was "God, you look just like my brother."

This particular summer, James Taylor was coming to do a benefit concert for the NPR program, "E-Town." I decided to buy a ticket. I thought on the chance I were to meet him, shake his hand, and get a photo, perhaps I could "break the spell," so to speak.

That night at dinner in a downtown restaurant I got stared at a lot. Three times I was asked, "Are you James Taylor?" The concert wasn't for another two hours and I knew it was going to be a long night. I took my seat inside the theater and waited for the show to start.

After the first set, there was a twenty minute intermission. I decided to head down to the stage and see if I could meet my "double." Stagehands just gave me double takes. People walked by and pointed. I turned my back to the audience and waited.

As I was doing so, I saw from the corner of my eye, a teenager approach me.

"Hey," he said, "Are you..." (All I could think of was, please kid, don't ask me that question.)

Then came the rest of the question..."Brian Luke Seaward?"

I was stunned. Somebody actually knew *me*—a first at any concert. Who was this person, I thought?

"Yes," I answered. "Who are you?"

"I'm Peter Knuti," he said with a huge smile. "The guy with two great legs."

It had been over five years since I had met Peter. Boy, had he grown! He was nearly six feet tall. I barely recognized him. I reached to shake his adult size hand and then proceeded to give him a hug. It was a special reunion.

"So Peter," I said, "how the heck are you?"

Tapping on his left leg, he answered, "Good as new."

I had no doubts. I gave him another big hug and wished him well, knowing quite well he really didn't need it.

A few weeks later I got a letter from him. It read,

Dear Dr. Seaward,

It was so nice to see you again at the James Taylor concert. I was happy to see that you have been living well. I hope this letter finds you in the same condition as when our paths have crossed on the two previous occasions. You seem like a very upbeat positive person, and it has been very pleasant spending time with you.

Lately I have been doing very well and I have simply been having a blast in life.

Hope to see you again soon.

Sincerely,
Peter

Follow Peter's lead and seize the day, no matter your troubles.

8. The Man Who Wouldn't Die

How do you know when your life mission is complete? In the words of Richard Bach, author of the book, *Illusions*, if you're still alive it means there is work remaining to be finished. Such is the case of Seaborn "Beck" Weathers.

By now most everyone has heard of the ill-fated event on Mt. Everest in the summer of 1996, where nine climbers died. Perhaps the most remarkable point of this story is about the one man who was left for dead—twice, but actually lived.

Beck Weathers is a physician from Dallas, Texas. His ascent toward the top of Everest that summer was his first, and like many others in his party, there was the usual apprehension. On that fateful day when his team of climbers was set to reach the summit, a ferocious storm blew in, leaving a handful in his party stranded for hours in sub-freezing temperatures as night set in. Extremely tired, cold, fighting for oxygen, and practically blinded from the inhospitable conditions, Beck's condition, which was poor at the start of this day, like the weather, only got worse that evening. In an attempt to warm his right hand and place it in his jacket, he took off his mittens, only to see the wind carry them off the mountain. Left unshielded, his hands were to become casualties of the harshest of elements.

One team member from the fractured group braved the ferocious elements to find the camp and return with help. When a group of rescuers returned hours later, Beck Weathers was found lying in a snow bank, severely frostbitten and presumed dead. Since there was no way to bring his body back, he was left there, as many corpses are. Early next morning, however, Beck Weathers woke from what fellow teammate Jon Krakauer, author of *Into Thin Air*, described as a 'hypothermic coma.' As if guided by unseen forces, Beck made his way back to camp, missing a precipice that would surely have ended his life. His return to camp amazed everyone, but those who saw him knew his time left on earth was indeed very short.

In an essay for the National Geographic book, *EVEREST: Mountain Without Mercy*, Beck wrote of his first of two episodes at the edge of death, "Sometime the next afternoon, I found myself alone on the ice. I was not terribly uncomfortable, and I was convinced I was dreaming. The hardest part was coming to grips with the fact that my situation was real and serious. I rolled over and looked at my hand, which appeared like an unnatural, plastic twisted gray thing attached to the end of my arm—not at all the hand I knew. I banged it on the ice, and it made a hollow sound, a sickening thunk."

With his right hand, forearm and nose completely frost bitten, he lay in his sleeping bag hovering on the verge of death. Those in camp who could descend to the lower camp, did. Assuming he was too weak to follow, Beck was once again left to die on the mountain. Hours later, however, he shuffled into the lower elevation camp, once again defying the odds and apparently the grip of death as well.

"I had a heck of a lot to live for and wasn't going down easy," said Beck. My family [an image in his mind], standing there before me became an incredible driving force.... When a middle-aged guy like me can survive that, it gives truth to the possibility that this kind of strength resides in each of us."

At this point he got help from others, one of who was David Breashears, a world-renowned climber in a different party, who set out at the same time to make an IMAX film of his expedition to the top of Everest. In a slide presentation made to a Boulder audience a year later, Breashears described his personal experience with this most remarkable man.

"Beck Weathers has an incredible sense of humor, and I am convinced this is what got him through his ordeal. We were tied together with a rope walking down, and he turns to me and says, 'You know I told my wife, Peach, that this trip was going to cost me an arm and a leg. Little did I know.' And then later he breaks into a version of the song, "Chain Gang." I wanted to say, 'Beck, how can you be making jokes about something like this? Stop this.' But Beck told me he had to, it was the only way to survive such a harrowing ordeal." And that he did.

One can only speculate as to why some die while others live in a single moment of tragedy. If we are still alive, then our work here on earth, whatever that might be, is still to be completed.

9. Saint Taylor

I HAVE A NEW HERO. HER NAME IS TAYLOR, Julia Taylor Hyman to be exact. I met Taylor in November of 2005 while conducting a holistic stress management instructor certification workshop at Duke University in November of that year. I am not sure that she would call herself a saint, but in my humble opinion she qualifies. I think most everyone who knows her would definitely say she is a hero.

Taylor called me on the phone one hot August day prior to the workshop to see if there was still room to attend. I assured her there was. She ended the conversation by sharing with me that she would be the one in a wheelchair.

It wasn't hard to spot Taylor on the appointed day. The buzz of her wheelchair was the unofficial announcement of her arrival. After the introductions, I began to delve into the content of the workshop. Once I had completed sharing several teaching tips and giving a little overview of energy medicine and the relationship between stress, disease and the human energy field, we jumped right into a session of art therapy. It was through art therapy that Taylor began to share her own dramatic story.

"My illustration is that of a mermaid,"she said as she held up her stunning picture of a blond haired mermaid. "I was in a bicycle accident nearly a year ago. I have no feelings below my nipples (the point where the mermaids scales ended and the woman's flesh began.) "Before my accident I used to compete in triathlons. I loved to swim. Through the grace of God, I still can. It is my driving ambition to walk again and perhaps even compete in triathlons once more."

We soon learned that Taylor was a nurse and had worked at a University in her town of Moorehead, North Carolina. Teaching was her life and it didn't take long to realize that she knew her purpose in life was to help others and to honor the nursing profession by training new students with a similar passion. Taylor's passion was infectious, as was her smile. Upon the completion of the workshop, Taylor gave me a big hug and told me she would miss me. I insisted that it was I who would miss her.

Over the next several months Taylor and I would share emails, phone calls and cards. I was fascinated with her progress and her commitment and discipline to walk again. In one phone conversation in early spring, she couldn't wait to tell me that she was accepted to the Shepherd Rehab Hospital in Atlanta, Georgia. There she was taught several exercises to help regain her upper body strength, her fine motor skills and the initial steps toward independence. Her husband, Sonny, was by her side every day for the entire two-month duration of her stay. I marveled at Taylor's zest for life and her unyielding devotion to her family, friends, and colleagues, who in turn gave back a devotion of love and support as well.

If there was ever a moment of pity and sorrow in Taylor's voice, she never shared it with me in all the many exchanges we had. If anything, she was the role model for optimism and compassion. For me, Taylor has become the epitome of persistence to achieve a personal goal, and in doing so, show everyone else the way it can be done. This is the work of saints. And it is certainly the work of heroes.

Saints, whether they are Christian, Hindu, Buddhist, or any other denomination, all have a cross to bear. Their hardships, often arduous and humiliating, tend to mirror our own problems, crises and dilemmas. Through divine grace they reveal how they overcame adversity. Like them, we can rise above life's difficulties and reach our highest human potential. Saints become teachers of love and compassion, though to the uneducated mind, they appear like mere mortals clinging to life. I know a saint when I see one. Taylor is still teaching students, though the ones she comes in contact with now are in a different classroom setting — the classroom of life. Love is still the lesson.

A year after I first met Taylor she flew to Colorado to attend my annual mountain retreat. Although she had learned to use a walker, she rested comfortably in her wheelchair, acclimating to the altitude. I joked with her that she was using the chair as a decoy to race against me at the pool. To be honest, I didn't even notice the wheelchair. Her smiled beamed from ear to ear. Yet it was the glow around her that I was aware of, the same glow she had when I first met her, but now it was ten times stronger. I could have sworn that the music in the lobby was playing, "When the saints come marching in."

"Accustom yourself continually to make many acts of love, for they enkindle and melt a hardened heart."

— Saint Theresa

10. Stand Like Mountain, Move Like Water

AFTER GIVING A PRESENTATION ON THE TOPIC OF STRESS and human spirituality at a conference in the summer of 1996, I was approached by a man who introduced himself as a singer/songwriter with songs of a similar message. Sticking his hand out to shake mine, he thanked me for my talk, asked me for a business card, and, waving a quick good-bye, said he would be in touch. I meet several hundred wonderful people this way each year. I have come to appreciate that even if our only encounter begins and ends with a handshake, hug, or smile, it is a special one. With several more conferences and workshops that summer, the musician's handshake accompanied by his leprechaun smile soon faded from memory.

But later that summer, I did hear from him. As I walked back from my mailbox, I curiously opened a package from TuneTown Records. Inside were two CDs from Greg Tamblyn. I recognized the photogenic smile on the album cover. I walked over to the CD player and put the first one in, then smiled, laughed, and pondered for the next fifty minutes of musical interludes and witty lyrics. The second CD had the same effect. Greg's promotion materials revealed that he spent several years as a singer/songwriter in Nashville, followed by a calling to tour on his own. His concert schedule typically includes Unity Churches, mind-body medicine conferences, and exotic beach resorts. In the accompanying letter Greg wrote, "You talk about the topics I sing about. We should write a song together sometime."

About a year later, Greg and I sat in my living room discussing the possibilities of collaborating on a song. I told him of my new project, *Stand Like Mountain, Move Like Water*, a book on the topic of stress and human spirituality (the title was slightly changed at press time). I recall mentioning to him that although the title was a Chinese proverb, in my mind I could definitely hear someone like Mary Chapin Carpenter singing a song with the same title, perhaps with a folk or country flare to it. With an elfish smile, Greg said, "Yeah, and she's the only one who could pull it off, too!"

In the course of the afternoon we discussed several concepts in the soon-to-be published book. Briefly skimming the manuscript, Greg said emphatically, "I love the title."

Over a glass of iced tea, I commented that I saw two possibilities for a song. The first was a story of a person who triumphs over stress. The second was a song about the theme of the book: stress provides the opportunity for spiritual growth. I recall making a comment that the song should have a special essence, underscoring the divine nature of the human condition. Greg agreed. At the end of the day, he waved good-bye with a reassuring nod that a song was indeed, in the works.

There are many lessons I have learned on the nature of stress and human spirituality, but one of the most profound is the idea that although space and time seem to separate things, all things connect. Chief Seattle said it, Einstein said it, and Jung said it, to name a few. Something undetected by the five senses, immeasurable by Western science, yet obvious to the intuitive mind, something mystical, (the poets say love) unites everything together. In the fast-paced lifestyles we live, our myopia often blinds us to this connection. In fact, our rushed and hectic demeanor tends to reinforce the illusion of separation. But every once in a while, we are jolted into remembering.

That's what happened to Greg and me. Months later, in what can only be described as a divine moment of synchronicity, Greg began to write the lyrics to "our" song based on a story he read in the Kansas City Star, about a Chinese woman locked in prison for nearly seven years, falsely accused of being a spy for the British government. The woman's name was Nien Cheng, author of the book, *Life and Death in Shanghai*. Nein is a friend of mine and I shared her story in the first chapter of *Stand Like Mountain*. While Greg was composing the song, I hit the road on a seven-month book tour. During that time, I pretty much forgot about the song project.

I arrived home one day in October to find a package from Greg in the mail. I placed my suitcase by the hall closet, walked over to the stereo, and placed the demo tape in the tape deck. My eyes welled up with tears of joy as I listened. Let me tell you, Mary Chapin Carpenter's got nothing over Greg Tamblyn (and co-songwriter Richard Helm). The CD, *Art from the Heart*, recorded in Nashville, arrived in the mail around the Christmas holidays. However, it wasn't until March 1998 when the magic of the song was truly revealed.

"Greg, I sent a copy of the CD to Nien Cheng. She was very moved," I said in a late night phone call to Kansas City.

"You mean you *know* her?" Greg asked.

"Sure, she's a friend of mind. Didn't I mention to you that I wrote about her in the book?" I replied.

"I had absolutely no idea, I don't think you even told me."

"You mean you wrote this song about her not knowing her story was in the book? I cannot believe it," I said in astonishment.

"Amazing! Simply amazing," Greg replied in disbelief.

We both laughed knowing just how divinely inspired our collaboration really was.

Stand Like Mountain, Move Like Water
(Greg Tamblyn, Richard Helms, & Brian Luke Seaward, TuneTown Records)

At the foot of a mountain, in a bamboo cafe
Sat an old Asian lady with eyes full of grace
I felt myself drawn to her calm quiet way
And as her story started to flow, I was carried away

She told of a night when soldiers appeared
And chained her in darkness for seven long years
There's a wall in her country a thousand miles long
And they wrapped it around her for thinking all wrong

Chorus:

Stand like mountain, move like water
Earth and heaven have this to offer
Strength will flow from life with honor
Stand like mountain, move like water

She knew in her heart that she committed no crime
And a story to tell is what kept her alive
In a cell with no windows she nurtured the seed
That one day light would shine in and people would see

I thought how her life was so different from mine
And the insight that came has remained in my mind
Here is a woman who knows who she is
Through good times and bad, she's the same, the way that she lives

At the foot of a mountain in a bamboo cafe
We bowed to each other and I made my way
And I carry with me like the seeds on the wind
Her spirit and her story to tell, and so it begins

Perhaps there is no such thing as a coincidence, a purely random occurrence of two events. I believe holy moments are the connection points in the web of life. They lend balance to what some might call the unholy moments of life's tensions and frustrations. An ancient proverb states "God is the maestro, and we are divine instruments." May we honor the connection process so that when we meet, we make beautiful music together.

11. Heaven and Hell

IN THE PAST FIFTEEN YEARS, I HAVE READ MANY ACCOUNTS of near-death experiences, but recently, in the course of three days, I met two people who shared their "heading toward the light" adventures. Ironically, both had very similar stories.

"Do you believe in guardian angels?" I was asked point blank by Eric a middle-aged banking executive.

Before I could give an answer, Eric proceeded to tell me why he did. I was to learn there wasn't a doubt in his mind whatsoever!

"I believe we each have a guide who watches over us. I know I do." As he said this, he threw his leg up on the table, rolled up his pant leg, and showed me a scar the size of a half dollar, four inches below his knee. "Ten years ago, I was electrocuted." Pointing to the scar he explained, "That's where it exited. I was dead for over a half an hour—no heart rate, no blood pressure—well beyond brain damage time. The paramedics explained to me later that the hospital was just too far away. I was on my way to the morgue. Imagine their surprise when I came to!"

He stopped to organize his thoughts. For a subject as ineffable as this, he was determined to make it as articulate as he could. "It's true what they say about the light. It's hard to describe. It's like nothing here on earth. The only way to describe it is wonderful. The physician who treated me tried to explain this as some biochemical process going on in my dying brain, but he couldn't explain what else I saw. He also couldn't explain why my internal organs weren't fried. People who are electrocuted look like they have been microwaved inside. The kidneys, liver, and heart get cooked like burnt toast, but not mine!"

Again, Eric paused to formulate his thoughts. "I saw my brother who had died two years previously. I saw this entity which I can only guess was my guardian angel. It might have been God, but I personally don't think we have the mind to comprehend what God really is. I saw my whole life reviewed before my very eyes. Let me tell you this; it wasn't pretty. I think the hell they talk about is the sensation of intense pain you experience when you realize all the hurt you have inflicted on other people. Heaven is the rush of love you feel afterward, as you move closer to the light."

Michael's story was nearly identical. He and a neighbor were clearing some dead branches in his mother's back yard when his chain saw touched a high voltage wire and BOOM! His neighbor was airborne and knocked unconscious. At that same moment, over 2000 houses in the community lost power. Michael took a trip to the next dimension.

"It is so hard to describe, but the most real experience I have ever had. I was moving at warp speed, you know, like the U.S.S. Enterprise on Star Trek. I saw hundreds of faces, not really human faces, more like spiritual entities. Then there was the light."

From her living room window, Michael's mother and sister saw the whole thing. Each gasped in horror. Both women saw Michael's body simply vanish, as if it vaporized. While his body might have disappeared, his soul migrated toward a bright loving light for a very short, but memorable visit.

When he "reappeared," moments later, he was standing, fully conscious, but the soles of both boots were completely blown off his feet. A utility crew arrived shortly thereafter and they couldn't believe Michael was alive, uninjured, with no internal damage!

"Before this event, I knew God was around, but I always thought I was in charge. I'm no longer afraid to ask for help. I know there is a protective force in my life," he said.

"Now let me tell you something. Whatever happened opened something up in my mind. Since that day, my values have changed. I appreciate everything. I don't take anything for granted anymore. I know I am here to experience and share unconditional love, like the kind that I experienced on the other side. In truth, that's what we're all here for, most of us just don't know it. And I might add, the world could use a lot of love right now.

"You know," Mike concluded, "you don't have to experience death to know heaven or hell. They're both right here on earth. Each moment we make a choice in what direction we move toward. I've already made my decision."

The difference between heaven and hell, for some, is a perception. The same can be said about stress. Stress is a perception: where we chose to place our attention, and how we choose to use our intention. To some extent, both heaven and hell are here on earth. Where do you place your attention and intention?

12. To Do the Work of Angels

FEAR OF DEATH IS CONSIDERED BY MANY FOLKS to be the worst fear of all. Second to love, the topic of death has made for the greatest subject matter in the most classic of plays, operas, poems, songs, and books. For many of us, this is as close as they want to get to death. Simply put, death is much too stressful to face head on, either our own mortality or that of someone close to us. Avoidance is a common coping technique, albeit an ineffective one, for death can never be avoided.

The American culture has a way of shielding the process of dying from the collective consciousness. As if the consequences might prove to be too painful, the topic of death and dying, not to mention the exposure to it, are often sanitized to become more palatable. It is quite possible today to go through life and never see a dying loved one or deceased relative, whereas in other cultures and even in this country a century ago to be in the presence of a dying person was not an uncommon occurrence.

The work of people like Elizabeth Kübler-Ross and Steven Levine have brought dignity to the topic of death and dying and have helped minimize the element of fear involved with this stressful event. In Kübler-Ross's words, *"No one should ever have to die alone."* The hospice movement, which she helped pioneer several decades ago, has been remarkable in its efforts to give dignity to chronically ill and dying patients. My first exposure to the mission of hospice workers came in the last few days when my aunt was dying of stomach cancer. It was then I knew unequivocally, that no one should ever die alone. A year later I was to face death again, but this time with more direct contact and closer heartstrings. Although not afraid of death, I realized in hindsight, that this time, I had a special role to play.

My father was a project engineer for a large aerospace company. In 1978 he was transferred to Florida were he worked for several years before he retired to play endless games of golf and take countless deep-sea fishing trips. In the spring of 1993, I was making a career transition from Washington D.C. to Boulder, Colorado. It was at this time, a year after his sister's death with cancer that I learned that, he too, was diagnosed with cancer, again. "Not to worry, " he assured me. "It's nothing. It will be gone in no time." I took his comment at face value. I'm sure there was an element of denial on my part, perhaps his as well.

By the end of August I had a strong premonition that all was not well, despite his comments to the contrary. So I canceled several speaking engagements and quickly made plans for a visit at the end of September. Three days before my departure I received a phone call from my sister, who lived nearby, telling me that indeed, Dad was deathly ill. "Get here as soon as you can. He's on his last leg and asking for you," she cried.

Greeted at the airport by his wife, I was quickly briefed on his condition. With over sixteen tumors, his situation was well beyond chemotherapy and radiation. He had a week at the most, she explained, perhaps only a few days. Through her tears, she tried to warn me how bad he looked. When I walked into his bedroom, the man I knew as my childhood hero was nothing more than a frail, emaciated skeleton. It was quite shocking and despite his wife's warning, I was still caught off guard. Dad offered a weak smile, raised his arm to shake hands, and then closed his eyes in fatigue.

That first night, lying in bed, I reflected on the man I knew as my father. Baseball was his passion. He was even recruited by the Red Sox before WW II, but he had been drafted into the Navy instead. He valued a good education (a Yale graduate), yet advocated travel as life's "real school." He secretly admired Vince Lombardi and always rooted for the Green Bay Packers. I remembered his taste for fine restaurants, excellent wine (perhaps too much wine), the stock market, and Ian Fleming novels. As an aircraft engineer, he somehow made planes fly, but his work with the government never allowed him to talk about his job. He married young. His first wife, a nurse, caught tuberculosis and died. He never talked about her. At the age of twenty-three, he contracted tuberculosis himself and nearly died as well. Three years later he married my mom. She died in 1981. He was stoic, yet had a good sense of humor. Being more of a right-brained person than his left-brain personality, I never really knew what he thought of my work and interest in matters of stress and human spirituality, that is, until this visit. That night I stared at the ceiling for many hours, as he lay in the next room, knowing a chapter was closing on his life and mine.

During my short visit, there was plenty of time to talk, joke around, smile, and reminisce. On what was scheduled to be my last day, my father took a serious turn for the worse. My sister and stepmother absent (in their grief, they explained, they could just not be with him), I sat alone by his side, holding his hand, whispering loving words of kindness and veiled glimpses into his future. Early that morning a knock at the door informed me the hospice nurse arrived for what would be her final visit. Because of a hectic schedule she couldn't stay long, she explained as she made her way to her next appointment. I sat in silence and prayed. As my father's breaths grew extremely shallow to his final inspiration, I held his hand tight and offered my love, and congratulations on his transition.

I would like to say the room grew bright at his passing, but if it did, I didn't notice. There was certainly an air of calmness and a feeling of what I could only call "grace." Within moments of his passing, I was moved to open the windows, perhaps as a symbolic gesture of his soul's freedom. Then I left the room to tell his wife that my dad had died. I offered her a warm embrace.

There is nothing to fear in death. In the words of Elizabeth Kübler-Ross, "I want to assure you that it is a blessing to sit at the bedside of a dying patient. What you learn from dying patients you can pass on to your children and to your neighbors, and maybe our world would become a paradise again. I believe the time to start is now."

13. Man's Best Friend

MAY 1, 2006 WAS ONE OF THE SADDEST DAYS OF MY LIFE. I had my beloved dog put to sleep. I don't think I have cried this hard in decades, perhaps ever. Shasta was in pain, something I should have seen earlier than I did. Funny thing how denial protects our feelings, but often fails to help others.

My canine love affair began on January 1, 1999. I had always wanted a Siberian Husky since I was a little boy. After doing much research on the topic of huskies, I contacted a husky rescue outfit in Fort Collins, Colorado, about an hour north of Boulder where I live. To adopt a rescued dog is no easy feat. You just don't walk in, pick up a dog and drive home. These people interview you. Perhaps cross-examine you is a better description. If you pass this first test, then they come to your home to check your living conditions. They check up and follow through with character references and make sure you have the income to properly care for a dog. After passing all tests, I drove up to Fort Collins to meet Shasta. It was love at first sight. I'll never forget the 10-minute kiss pooch smooch he gave me, perhaps a greeting; perhaps a thank-you for saving him from all the alpha dogs in the same pen that he spent the last month surviving. Shasta was anything but an alpha dog. As many people confided in upon meeting Shasta, he was an old soul with a young spirit.

When I drove to Fort Collins to pick up the dog, I asked his spirit what he wanted to be called. The name "Shasta" hit me like a bat over the head. Not a name I would have picked for a dog, I decided to mull it over before I met this new canine roommate. When I asked Ingrid, the lady who ran the husky rescue operation, about a new name, she advised me not to change it. As it turns out, when the dog arrived at her facility it was call *Zodiac*, a name she disliked intensely, so she changed it to Cody. You should know that living in Colorado nine dogs out of ten are named *Cody*. I decided to trust my intuition and stick with *Shasta*. To be honest, this dog would have answered to anything, but the name Shasta fit like a glove.

I never learned much about Shasta's first three years or his previous owner, although I heard of possible physical abuse. I can say he was well trained and extremely well behaved. The first night in my new house, he jumped up on my bed and staked his claim next to me, snuggled up by the down pillows. That night and many that followed he cried and yelped in his sleep. Nightmares, I suppose. I would comfort him with something close to a massage. As weeks turned into months we bonded in a way that only dog lovers understand. Inside the house, he was nearly human. Outside the house, he was all dog!

I'll never forget the first time he found a skunk under a bush while out for a walk. Ugh. Phew! Or the first time he rolled in horse droppings in a National Forest area, all the while smiling with predatory prowess. Coincidently, this was the same day he was groomed at Petsmart that morning. His first surgery in 2002 revealed an aggressive malignant tumor. Thankfully, the vet removed it all, saving his life. Another malignant tumor appeared a few years later, but was removed successfully once again. Shasta, it should be known ate only the best food. Organic dog cereal. All natural treats, no junk foods. And at least once a week, Alaskan salmon and/or buffalo. So it was a mystery (to me and my vet) how so many bone spurs grew on his vertebra, fusing his spine together, that ultimately pinched his spine into dysfunction. It was this condition that tormented him with undeniable pain and led to his ultimate demise.

Shasta (who graces the cover of this book) was not only a pet. He was a roommate, a confidant, an icebreaker with strangers and above all, my best friend. He never drooled. He never even barked. Rather, he communicated with body language; a glance, a dance, or a multitude of ear positions conveying everything from a sense of curiosity to complete boredom. Perhaps what I will miss most will be the "jump for joy" (a 360 spin in the air) when I got out of the car from each road trip. That welcome home routine, complete with a canine kiss, will always be cherished.

Shasta was a special guest at all my Colorado workshops, too. Under the guise of pet therapy, he made the rounds to all the participants making sure everyone returned home with at least one, if not several dog hairs on their cloths. Perhaps it's no surprise that he often received more fan mail than I (an author, no less) after each workshop or book signing, including a plethora of dog treats.

Speaking of dog hair, the first time I had him groomed, the gal at Petsmart asked me if I wished to save his fur. Only in Boulder, I thought. When I inquired why, she mentioned that some people like to make sweaters from their dog's fur. Now, you might think this crazy, but I love sweaters, and so I said "Yes." In about a year's time, I had enough of Shasta's undercoat to make not one, but two sweaters (and several pillows). I found a gal who could not only spin the fur into yarn, but knit a sweater as well. I even asked to have a little blue woven in to symbolize his blue eye. I get a lot of jokes from friends about the sweater. Mostly people ask if I smell like a dog when it gets wet (the answer is No). I joke back and confide that every now and then however, I do have the urge to water a tree.

A friend of mine, renowned British actor Michael York, once posed with Shasta for a picture that soon found it's way into the fifth edition of my textbook, *Managing Stress.* Michael always referred to Shasta as his "canine co-star." I e-mailed Michael a few days after Shasta was put down to tell him of the news. He too, was filled with remorse. The next day, I received a fax. It was from Michael. He had shared with his neighbor, comedian Steve Martin, the plight of my dog. Steve, who had just written an essay about his dog, Roger, for an upcoming book, offered Michael the essay and asked to pass it along to me as a means of comfort. Can you imagine coming home to a fax from Steve Martin? It surely helped.

The words "dog" and "unconditional love" are often heard together in the same breath, but you should know that dogs have more than one emotion. Shasta could get angry. He could pout and at times he definitely showed fear, hiding behind my legs in times of panic. I don't know if dogs embody unconditional love, although I would like to think so. This I do know. We, as pet owners (in Boulder we are called "pet guardians"), offer unconditional love to our pets. This may be our salvation. Pet owners, as a rule, tend to be healthier than non pet owners. I can only imagine it has to do with our capacity to express and receive love, something that should be done every day.

I recall wiping the tears from my eyes, as Shasta was about to leave this earthly world, that one of the people in the vet's office told me that she never saw her husband cry till he had to put his dog to sleep. Since the day that Shasta died, I have heard this same story from several women and men. The strongest man will be reduced to tears when his dog dies. I now know why dogs are man's best friend. It has to do with love and love is expressed in many ways.

In addition to providing countless holy moments, Shasta was also a great teacher. What did I learn from this canine yogi? Among the many things including patience, humor, joy, tolerance, forgiveness and compassion, I learned that one's grieving is only as deep as one's capacity to love. Good-bye Shasta Bear. You will be greatly missed.

Dog spelled backward is still man's best friend.

14. From Hope to Faith in Thirty Years

AS A CONSULTANT FOR A MIDWESTERN HOSPITAL, I was invited to spend a weekend in Arizona to plan a retreat for the hospital's board of directors. The theme of the retreat was integrating complementary medicine (the new name for alternative medicine) into the existing practice of Western medicine. Rather than stay in a hotel, we were invited to stay as guests of one of the retreat planning committee members. Hotels being stuffy, we readily agreed. The drive from Phoenix to Sedona was about two and a half hours. When we arrived at the house, we found a note on the door and a key under the mat. Our host Carolyn, who worked in an area hospital, would return in a few hours and so we began to make ourselves at home.

Upon entering her house, I could not help but notice a rather large montage of photographs on the wall heading from the living room down the hall to the bedrooms. The montage depicted the family history of Carolyn, her husband and their children, from black and white photos when Carolyn and her husband married to color photographs of her two children. Her son, I could tell, was about twenty-five years old, blonde hair and blue eyes, in the armed services, and had recently married—in a full military wedding. Her daughter, dark hair and dark eyes, seemed a year or two older, and as far as I could tell, not married.

Once Carolyn arrived home, introductions were made and we soon elected to eat out at a local restaurant where we discussed the health care crisis for four hours. Over steaming hot plates of pasta, we took turns describing our various experiences in the health care profession. I explained that my reason for the trip was to participate in a planning session, specifically to organize a retreat for hospital board members to learn about the concept of wellness and complementary medicine. As a nurse, Carolyn expressed a very strong interest in our efforts. She had firsthand experience with the limitations of Western medicine.

That night as I headed to the bathroom to brush my teeth, I again passed by the wall of family photographs. Carolyn met me in the hall and through the photographs introduced her family to me: her husband, Tony, and her two grown children, Jerry and Lori. During the night, asleep on the living room couch, I had a dream. In the dream I walked into the kitchen to get a glass of water. Standing by the refrigerator was a tall man, about thirty-two years old with long brown hair, brown eyes, and a ruggedly handsome face. He introduced himself to me as Larry and said he was Carolyn's son. He asked me to give her a message, "that he was all right, everything was all right—not to worry." I agreed to relay the message.

The next morning, I awoke to hear Carolyn making breakfast. I got up and walked into the kitchen, at which point I suddenly remembered the dream, which I then shared with her. I added, "It's funny, he doesn't look anything like his photograph on the wall." Carolyn's eyes grew wide. She took a deep breath and then gave me a broad smile. "There is no way you could have ever known this. Larry was my first son. He died of Sudden Infant Death Syndrome at the age of six months. He did have dark hair and brown eyes and he would be about thirty years old, had he lived. His birthday was last week and I was wondering about him." Then she added, "I guess I had shut myself off from him, and now he communicated through you to speak to me."

I sat down and drew a big sigh, rubbing the goose bumps on my arms. "Oh, there's one more thing he asked me to mention. He said he loves you very much and that love never dies. We come in and out of this earthly existence, but love never dies.

For the rest of my visit I noticed a slight but welcome change in Carolyn. She walked with confidence. I have seen this before in others. Hope realized will do that.

If the wind in your sails can only bring you to the shores of hope, hoist your anchor and go. But keep your eyes set on the horizon of faith. It's there and in time it will appear.

P.S. In early summer 1997, Carolyn's husband, Tony, died quite suddenly of pancreatic cancer. It was a tragic loss for Carolyn, as well as her two children. Shortly thereafter, a wonderful ceremony was held to honor the man she loved. As Tony's ashes were scattered to the four winds, Carolyn turned to her daughter, Lori, and thinking of the dream I shared with her about her first son, Larry, she then looked up to the sky and yelled, *"Damn it , Tony, don't wait 30 years to tell me you're alright Give me a sign right now."* Within moments the most gorgeous rainbow appeared on the horizon. They all just looked at each other and smiled.

Stressed is Desserts Spelled Backwards

Mountains, molehills and days from hell,
A world with too much change,
But I will make it, I know I will,
All it takes is a seed of faith.
How does that expression go?
Stressed is desserts spelled backwards.

Cancer, loss, and the fear of death,
Those dark nights of the soul,
But the alchemy of love is pure,
Lead always turns to gold,
This much I know this is true,
Stressed is desserts spelled backwards.

Blessings, gifts and silver clouds,
And lemonade galore,
Its humor, hope, faith, and love,
That gets us through the storm,
Looking back, it's very clear,
Stressed is desserts spelled backwards.

— Brian Luke Seaward

The Winds of Grace

Disturbing are the winds of change,
As they produce growing pains.
Oh God, I seek a safe port
To harbor my fears and worries.
Grant me the courage
To endure the winds of change.

Comforting are the winds of grace,
As they instill a sense of faith.
Oh God, fill my sails with love
On this journey of self-exploration.
Grant me the insight
To enjoy the winds of grace.

Blessed are the winds of grace,
As they invigorate my human spirit.
Oh God, I seek to know my purpose
In the community we know as "one people."
Grant me the strength to do my work.
The winds of change are the winds of grace.

— Brian Luke Seaward
© Inspiration Unlimited

Resource Guide

Organizations:

Boulder Institute for Nature and the Human Spirit
Elizabeth Roberts
2434 Mapleton Avenue
Boulder, CO 80304
(303) 216-2293

International Society for the Study of Subtle Energy and Energy Medicine
ISSSEEM
Golden, CO
(303) 425-4625
www.issseem.org

Trees For Life
Balbir Mathur
3006 W. St. Louis
Witchita, KS 67203-5129
(316) 945-0629
www.treesforlife.org

The Humor Project
Joel Goodman
480 Broadway, Suite 210
Sarasota Springs, NY
(518) 587-8770
www.humorproject.com

Institute of Noetic Sciences (IONS)
101 San Antonio Road
Petaluma, CA 94592
(707) 779-8238
www.noetic.org

National Wellness Institute
National Wellness Conference
P. O. Box 827
Stevens Point, Wisconsin 54481-0827
(800) 243-8694
www.nationalwellness.org

Bio-Relax
Mietek & Margaret Wirkus
WYNGATE MEDICAL PARK
5654 Shields Drive at Old Georgetown Road (Rd. 187)
Bethesda, MD 20817
(301- 652 1691)

Tune Town Records	**Inspiration Unlimited**
Greg Tamblyn	Brian Luke Seaward, Ph.D.
P.O. Box 45258	P.O. Box
Kansas City, MO 64111	Boulder, CO 80306
(816) 757-7250	(303) 678-9962
www.gregtamblyn.com	www.brianlukeseaward.net

Books of Interest:

Carnes, P. *Out of the Shadows*, Hazelden Publishing. 1992.

Del Calzo, N., *The Triumphant Spirit.* Triumphant Spirit Publishing, Denver, CO. 1997.

Dossey, L., *Healing Words*, Harper SanFrancisco. 1994.

Epstein, G., *Healing Visualizations.* Bantam Books. 1989.

Gerber, R., *Vibrational Medicine*, (3rd Ed) Bear & Co, Santa Fe. 2003.

Klein, A., *The Healing Power of Humor*, Tarcher Books, New York. 1989.

Kübler-Ross, E., *Death Does Not Exist*, Celestial Arts Press, Berkeley. 1991

Lerner, H., *The Dance of Anger*, Perennial Press, New York. 1985.

Norris, P, and Porter, G., *Why Me? Harnessing the Healing Power of the Human Spirit*, Stillpoint Press. 1985.

Roberts, E., Amidon, E., *Earth Prayers*, Harper Collins, 1991.

Roberts, E., Amidon, E., *Prayers For 1000 Years*, Harper Collins. 1999.

Seaward, B.L. *Stand Like Mountain, Flow Like Water: Reflections on Stress and Human Spirituality*, (10th Anniversary Edition) Health Communications, Inc. Deerfield Beach, FL. 2007

Seaward, B.L., *Achieving the Mind-Body-Spirit Connection*. Jones and Bartlett Publishers. Sudbury, MA 2006.

Scaward, B.L., *The Art of Calm: Relaxation Through the Five Senses*. Health Communications, Inc. Deerfield Beach, FL. 1997

Silvia, C., *A Change of Heart*, Little Brown, New York. 1997.

Guided Visualization CD's By Brian Luke Seaward

A Change of Heart: Four Guided Visualizations & Meditation (Inspiration Unlimited) 2003

Sweet Surrender: Four Guided Visualizations & Meditations (Inspiration Unlimited) 2003

A Wing & A Prayer: Four Guided Visualizations & Meditations (Inspiration Unlimited) 2004

Instrumental Music

One Quiet Night: A compilation CD of relaxation music (Eversound Music)

Stand Like Mountain, Flow Like Water: A compilation CD of relaxation music (Eversound Music)

Words of Gratitude

As a child, my mother would read to me stories, fairy tales, fables and real life adventures—always with a message or moral at the end. I am ever so grateful to her and her spirit which lives on in this tradition. My deepest and most sincere thanks go to my agent, Tom Grady who, quite literally, is a prayer answered. Next, I wish to thank the staff of Conari Press: particularly Mary Jane Ryan who is a master at nurturing creative writing talents; thanks for giving this book a great home! Second edition thanks to Carlene Sippola at Whole Person Books who was so gracious to give "Desserts" a second home. Here's a big bear hug, Carlene! Once again, I wish to express my humble gratitude to my personal assistant, Marlene Yates, who is always an inspiration. Special thanks also to all of those people and friends whose stories appear within these pages who gave me some great feedback along the way, as well as the great many friends who supported my budding career as an author—you know who you are! And thank you, the readers who support my work as well.

My humble gratitude and best wishes go to Joan Lunden for a wonderful foreword. Joan, the next lunch is on me! I am deeply indebted to your kindness. A gracious thank you goes to my colleagues Deepak Chopra, Naomi Judd, Richard Carlson and Dave Scott for their words of praise on the book's back cover. Most of all, I would like to thank all those people who shared their stories with me and invited me to be a part of their lives; Andreí Z., Dan P., Sandi L., John P., Peter K., Donna S., Robert S., Andrew A., Naomi J., Rabia R., Pat N., Pedro E., Betty S., JP, Gail W., Joanne H.,., Balbir M., Darren D. Carolyn Z., Barbara A. Fran S., Katy T., Pete K., Sheila S., Greg T., Eric S. and Michael P. Thanks as well to Peter Alexander who granted permission to me to adapt the Hogan Prayer story from his collection of *Spiritual Archives*. Last but not least, I offer my humble gratitude to the Source of all creation, who blesses my life in every way. Thanks for the gentle winds of grace.

Bon Appetite!

About the Author

BRIAN LUKE SEAWARD, PH.D. IS CONSIDERED A PIONEER in the field of health psychology and he is internationally recognized for his contributions in the area of holistic stress management, human spirituality and mind-body-spirit healing. The wisdom of Dr. Seaward can be found in PBS specials, national magazines, medical seminars, boardroom meetings, church sermons, and college graduation speeches all over the world. It's been said several times that Brian Luke Seaward looks like James Taylor, dresses like Indiana Jones, and writes like Mark Twain. He is the author of several popular books, including *Stand Like Mountain, Flow Like Water, The Art of Calm, Health of the Human Spirit, Hot Stones & Funny Bones* and *Quiet Mind, Fearless Heart*. His relaxation CDs include *A Change of Heart, Sweet Surrender* and *A Wing & A Prayer*. Highly respected throughout the international community as an accomplished teacher, consultant, lecturer, author and mentor, when not instructing, writing or consulting, he relaxes back home in the Colorado Rocky Mountains. He can be reached at www.brianlukeseaward.net.

STRESSED is DESSERTS Spelled Backward

9 781570 252181